UNI WISSEN

A Crash Course in English Grammar

John F. Davis

Ernst Klett Verlag
Stuttgart · Düsseldorf · Leipzig

Die Deutsche Bibliothek – CIP-Titelaufnahme

Ein Titeldatensatz für diese Publikation ist bei der Deutschen Bibliothek erhältlich.

1. Auflage A 1 5 4 3 2 1 | 2004 2003 2002 2001 2000

Internetadresse | http://www.klett-verlag.de
Bildnachweis | © Barton Stabler/Artville.

Redaktion | Margit Künzel
Umschlaggestaltung und Layout | Christine Schneyer
Satz | Hahn Medien GmbH, Kornwestheim
Druck | Gutmann+Co., Talheim. Printed in Germany.
ISBN 3-12-939589-X

Gedruckt auf Papier, das aus chlorfrei gebleichtem Zellstoff hergestellt wurde.

Contents

Preface

Although this book is rather more detailed than a normal crash course would be and although it contains no exercises for readers to test their knowledge with, it is hoped that the title is justified. The author has aimed to provide the reader in a very short space with the essentials of English grammar and with a thorough grounding in grammatical analysis. Most competent English Grammars contain between 300 and 500 pages, the largest between 1000 and 2000. An attempt has been made here to compress into about 160 pages the basic features of English grammar and at the same time to introduce and explain the grammatical terminology necessary for the analysis and description of a modern language. This has been done by starting on the lowest level with the word and by systematically working upwards through the further levels of phrase, clause and sentence. The elements contained in each level are described grammatically and numerous examples illustrate them in context.

It is hoped that the book will thus more adequately meet the needs of beginning students and others who have an uncertain knowledge of grammar and who need a short book to remedy this gap. It should also prove useful to non-native teachers of English who require a brief but detailed survey of the language to brush up their grammar for pedagogical purposes. For all types of readers it should serve as a stepping stone to the larger and more detailed works on the grammar of English.

John F. Davis
im September 2000

1 CHAPTER Traditional Grammar

Introduction

The aim of this book is to introduce its readers to the fundamental concepts and mechanisms of traditional grammar and to explain and illustrate the various levels at which the grammatical analysis of English sentences can be made. This will involve a discussion of the form (structure), function and position of the elements of which sentences are composed. When necessary, comparisons will be made with German and occasionally with other languages wherever they provide clearer examples of the point being discussed.

1 Background

1 General Remarks

Language and Rules

For many people, the word grammar suggests a dry, uninteresting subject that is associated with pedantic teachers and boring lessons in school. However, this need not be the case. If we look more closely at the object of which grammar is the study, namely language, we discover that this is one of the most fascinating creations of the human mind. At the moment there are about six thousand different languages spoken in the world, each with its own unique store of words, its own method of shaping these words, its own rules for combining them into sentences and even for building sentences into larger units which linguists call texts. Although most of these languages have never been written down, each native speaker of any one of them has unconsciously mastered all the rules necessary for comprehensible communication with other speakers of the language. Without knowing it, each speaker is an expert in the grammar of his own language, able to manipulate skilfully a large number of rules, even though he cannot explain what he is doing. Grammar is the study of the facts and rules of a language, how words are formed and then structured into higher units so that speakers can communicate with one another about the environment in which they live.

2 Historical Background

The Ancient Greeks

In the western world there is a very long tradition of interest among speakers in grammatical aspects of the language which they use, as we can see from the written records of various languages. For example, the ancient Greeks from at least the fifth century BC onwards made observations on the grammar of words in their own language. These comments were not always written down, but several are reported in the works of others. To modern readers they may not always seem very scholarly, but they show that the structure and form of the language we use must have a hidden fascination for the human mind. The earliest explicit description of the grammar of Greek was made by the Alexandrian scholar Dionysios Thrax (c. 100 BC), and remained a standard work for more than 1000 years. It is to him that we owe many of the grammatical concepts which are still used by western grammarians today. Although he paid little attention to syntax, i.e. how words are strung together to produce sentences, in his concise grammar of Greek he distinguishes eight classes of words (nouns, participles, verbs, conjunctions, prepositions, articles, pronouns, adverbs), which with minor modifications are still used by grammarians for the description of modern languages.

The Romans

If we trace the history of grammatical knowledge from Ancient Greece down to the present, we find that the next step occurred when the Romans took over the grammatical analysis of the Greeks and used it for the description of Latin. The Greek terms were given Latin equivalents, but very few other changes were made. The term *article* was not required, for example, as Latin did not possess this class of word. The Latin grammars of Donatus (4th century A.D.) and Priscian (6th century A.D.) remained the standard works for the teaching of Latin down to the Middle Ages and continued to have a strong influence on grammatical thought throughout the Renaissance period, when golden-age Greek and Latin were considered to be the finest products of the human mind.

18th Century Onwards

It was not until the discovery in the 18th century of the close relationship between many European languages and Sanskrit, the ancient language of the Indian Vedic scriptures, that western scholars began to turn their attention to the grammar of languages other than Latin and Greek. For most Indo-European languages, the Graeco-Latin pattern of analysis fits reasonably well, but when 19th century and modern grammarians began to analyse languages outside the Indo-European family they sometimes encountered unfamiliar phenomena which posed serious problems for the Graeco-Latin model. How do you cope with a language like Eskimo, for example, in which nouns are regularly incorporated into verbs (rather like *baby* in the English construction *to baby-sit*) and in which one single word may correspond to a whole sentence of many words in English or German? Even within Indo-European languages certain facts challenge the traditional analysis: for example, whereas in Greek the article is a separate word before the noun (*'o anēr* the man), in Swedish the article is an ending on the noun (*mannen* the man). Similarly, whereas Latin has a complicated system of suffixes on the verb to indicate person, tense and mood, English has separate words for these concepts (*laudo* I praise, *laudor* I am praised, *laudat* he praises, *laudatur* he is praised, *laudabo* I will praise, *laudabor* I will be praised, *laudabit* he will praise, *laudabitur* he will be praised).

2 Nowadays

1 What is Traditional Grammar?

Definition

In this book we shall use the term **traditional grammar** to refer to the method of describing English (and other languages) which is based on this long tradition of grammatical analysis dating back to the ancient Greeks and which still uses many of the technical terms which they invented. Although, as we saw above, the ancient grammarians were mainly concerned with words and sentences and devoted little attention to syntax, we shall extend this framework to include phrases, clauses and texts and shall have to give careful consideration to syntax. For this purpose we shall occasionally have to borrow notions from some of the new approaches to grammar which have been developed during the course of the present century. We may note that although these new frameworks (structural, transformational, functional, etc.) may be very different, they all rely very heavily on the work of traditional grammarians for their basic technical terms.

2 Various Levels of Analysis

Form and Function

We saw above that the grammar of a language can be analysed at five different levels: **word, phrase, clause, sentence, text.** In all of these we shall frequently observe that the analysis is sometimes based upon the form of the word or construction (i.e. on its morphology, or structure) and sometimes on its function in the utterance. For example, in the sentences *Tomorrow is Ann's birthday* and *Tomorrow Ann's getting married* we cannot tell from the shape of the word *tomorrow* what class of word it belongs to, but we can from its function in each sentence. In the first sentence, *tomorrow* is what the utterance is about, we are making a statement about *tomorrow*, and in this position, in front of the verb *is*, it is the subject of the sentence, a function that shows it to be a noun. In the second sentence, the subject is *Ann*, i.e. *tomorrow* is no longer the topic of interest, we are making a statement about *Ann*, namely that she is getting married. Here *tomorrow* tells us when this will happen, a function which is carried out by an adverb. If we turn now to the sentence *Ann will have no tomorrows*, we no longer need to look at the function to determine what class of word *tomorrow* belongs to, for we can tell more easily from its form that it is a noun: only a noun can take the plural suffix *-s*.

Words

Let us now make a brief survey of the various levels of analysis mentioned above, giving their general characteristics, so that the reader can obtain an overall picture. Then in later chapters of the book we can deal with the individual levels in detail. If we look first at the word level, there are three aspects under which **words** can be considered: their **morphology** (their shape, what elements they consist of), their **position** in a phrase or sentence, and their **classification** (what word class they belong to). For example, the adverb *slowly* clearly consists of an adjective root *slow* and a suffix *-ly*, which converts adjectives into adverbs. On the other hand the word *early* cannot be divided in this way. Furthermore, before we can decide to which class of words *early* belongs, we must see it in position in a phrase or sentence. Consider the following sentences:

1. *The early bird catches the worm.*
2. *Peter arrived early.*

In (1) *early* comes between the article *the* and the noun *bird*, in what we shall classify below as a noun phrase. In this position and with its function of qualifying the noun *bird* (i.e. telling us something about it), it must be an adjective. In (2), on the other hand, *early* does not come in front of a noun in a noun phrase, but is found alone after a verb. Here it qualifies the verb, i.e. it tells us when or maybe how Peter arrived. It has here the typical function of an adverb. In another context, e.g. in the following sentence about potatoes,

3. *We must plant some earlies this year,*

we can tell already from the morphology of the word *earlies* that it cannot be an adjective or an adverb, since neither of these two word classes allows a plural suffix to be added. This is a characteristic only of nouns. We can check this analysis by replacing *earlies* with another noun and seeing whether the result sounds grammatical, e.g.

4. *We must plant some flowers this year.*

Since the noun *flowers* fits just as easily into this slot in the sentence, we can assume that *earlies* must therefore also be a noun. This does not mean, of course, that the function of *earlies* in (3) is irrelevant. To determine the class of the word here, we have merely taken a short cut by looking at the morphology.

Phrases

On the phrase level the situation is a little different and often more complicated. In the simple phrase *the early morning*, we recognize the pattern which we had above in *the early bird*: article, adjective, noun. The **head** of this phrase (the most important word in it, the word around which the other elements are grouped) is the noun *morning*. We can therefore call this kind of phrase a noun phrase. When we add the preposition *in* to the front of it (*in the early morning*) we now have a prepositional phrase. The head, the most important word grammatically, is now the preposition *in*, on which the noun phrase *the early morning* depends.

Complex Phrases

Let us now look at a more complicated phrase: *the day after tomorrow*. It seems to consist of two pieces: the presence of the article *the* before the noun *day* suggests that this piece is a noun phrase, whereas the presence of the preposition *after* in front of *tomorrow* suggests that this piece is a prepositional phrase, provided of course that *tomorrow* is a noun. We can test this by replacing *tomorrow* by another noun or a noun phrase and seeing whether this sounds grammatical, e.g. *the day after Christmas, the day after the accident*. We find that *tomorrow* following *after* functions in the same way as the noun *Christmas* and the noun phrase *the accident*; so this second piece of our complex phrase must be a prepositional phrase. If we now consider the two pieces of our complex phrase together, we see that the head (the most important word in the complex phrase is the noun *day*, representing the thing about which we are talking, and that the prepositional phrase *after tomorrow* gives the hearer more information about the concept for which the word *day* stands, it tells him which particular day the speaker means. This is a function normally carried out by an adjective. We saw this above where the adjective *early* in the phrase *the early bird* tells us which particular bird is meant. Thus, in our complex phrase *the day after tomorrow*, the phrase *after tomorrow* is functionally adjectival, i.e. behaves like an adjective, but is formally a prepositional phrase. At first this may seem bewildering, but we shall see that grammar frequently takes units from a higher level and makes them function at a lower level: just as in our present example a prepositional phrase is made to behave like an adjective, we shall see others below where this function is assumed by a clause (relative clause).

Clauses

On the phrase level we saw that a simple phrase has constituents each consisting of a single word, whereas a complex phrase may have another phrase as one of its constituents. On the clause level we find a similar situation. A simple clause may have constituents which consist of single words or phrases, whereas a complex clause may have another clause as one of its constituents. It is difficult to talk about clauses without having first looked at sentences. Both clauses and sentences usually have the same structure and the same types of constituents. It will make the discussion easier, however, if we restrict the word *clause* to mean a grammatical unit which has the structure of a sentence but which functions as a constituent of another sentence. Traditionally, a clause of this kind is referred to as a **subordinate clause.** To make the distinction between clause and sentence clear, let us compare (5) with (6).

(5) *Jane played football yesterday.*

(6) *Paul said Jane played football yesterday.*

The structure (5) is a sentence. It consists of four functional units each of which is formally also a word. *Jane* functions as the subject of the sentence and is formally a noun; *played* functions as what may be called the verbal constituent (the unit which tells us what action Jane is doing) and is formally a verb; *football* functions as the object of the verb *played* (i.e. it answers the question *played what?*) and is formally a noun; *yesterday* is an adverbial constituent telling us when Jane played and is formally an adverb. If we now turn to the structure (6), we see that it too is a sentence. It has a subject *Paul* (which answers the question who *said?*), a verbal constituent *said* (which tells us what Paul did), and an object *Jane played football yesterday* (which answers the question *said what?*). Notice, however, that the last four words of (6) are here not a sentence, but a clause. Within this clause they have exactly the same functions as they have in (5), but now as a unit they are a constituent of another sentence. In fact as a unit they have the same function in (6) as the noun *football* has in (5): they are, as we saw above, the object of the verb in the verbal constituent, in this case of *said.* Since they behave like a noun, we can refer to them as a noun clause.

Structure

In (5) and (6) we have seen that both a clause and a sentence have the same types of constituent. They typically consist of a subject and a verbal constituent often accompanied by other constituents such as an object or an adverbial constituent. Notice, however, that a sentence can stand alone between two full stops, whereas a clause cannot. Furthermore, clauses may have one feature in their structure which is not found in that of a sentence: they are often introduced by a special word, a conjunction such as *when, before, after, although,* or by more complicated introducers such as the complex conjunctions *so that, in order that, even if.* These conjunctions and others will be treated later in the book, but we shall see an example of a *before*-clause immediately below in our brief discussion of complex clauses.

Complex Clauses

We mentioned earlier that a clause may have another clause as one of its constituents. Before we leave the clause level, let us consider just one example of this, illustrated in the following sentence:

(7) *Paul said that Jane played football before she married.*
The last three words of (7) are an adverbial time clause, introduced by the conjunction *before*. We can see that it is a clause because it has a subject (the pronoun *she*) and a verbal constituent (the verb *married*). We can tell that it is an adverbial clause, because it is the adverbial constituent in the noun clause *that Jane played football before she was married*. It has the same adverbial function here as *yesterday* has in (5) and (6) above. Notice that the noun clause which contains the adverbial clause also has an introducer here (the conjunction *that*), showing that it too is a subordinate (embedded) clause. Noun clauses which are introduced by *that* frequently omit this conjunction in short simple sentences (e.g. in (6) above), but usually retain it in longer complex ones.

Sentences

Much of what we need to say about grammatical analysis on the sentence level has already been said in our discussion of clauses. We observed that both clauses and sentences consist of the same functional units (subjects, verbal constituents, objects, adverbial constituents) but only clauses can be introduced by a subordinating conjunction. We also saw that in some sentences the object or the adverbial constituent may be a clause, i.e. a unit from a higher level than the word. Just to complete the picture, we may take a brief look at a sentence in which some of the other constituents are also more complex. Let us return for a moment to sentence (5) *Jane played football yesterday*. In the following expanded version of it we see that each constituent that was formerly a single word has been replaced by a structure from one of the higher levels:
8. *My cousin Jane had been playing a splendid game of football when my father arrived yesterday.*
Functionally this sentence still consists of the same four elements as in (5): a subject (*my cousin Jane*), a verbal constituent (*had been playing)*, an object (*a splendid game of football*) and an adverbial constituent (*when my father arrived yesterday*). However, each constituent is now more complex. The subject is represented by a noun phrase with *Jane* as its head, and the verbal constituent by a structure consisting of three verbs. The object is even more complex, consisting of a noun phrase with *game* as its head and containing another phrase (the prepositional phrase *of football*) inside it. Finally, the adverbial constituent is a whole clause (an adverbial clause of time, introduced by the conjunction *when* and having a subject *my father*, a verbal constituent *arrived*, and an adverbial constituent *yesterday*).

Sentence Types

In addition to analysing a sentence according to the form and function of its constituents, we can also classify it according to its function in a text. Some of the most common types of sentences are **statements, questions, commands, wishes,** etc. However, even here structure cannot be ignored, for sometimes it is only the order of the constituents that determines which type the sentence belongs to. For example, *I can go* is a statement but *Can I go* is a question. Word order is an important structural factor which we shall have to take into consideration at many points throughout this book.

Texts

Let us conclude this short survey of grammatical levels by going beyond the sentence to the text. Linguistically, a **text** may be defined as a **group of sentences** which are **felt to be connected with each other** and **which together form a united whole.** There are many kinds: conversations, notices, poems, recipes for cooking, instructions on how to use something, a paragraph in a textbook, and so on. Unfortunately, the limits of this book will not allow us to spend any time later on the grammar of texts, but perhaps we can whet the reader's appetite by examining here the following short conversation:

9. *Shall we take Emily to visit Windsor Castle?*
10. *Well, she went to the Royal Apartments yesterday.*
11. *So we don't have to go there today.*

Theoretically, these three sentences could be a random set, totally unrelated, perhaps picked haphazardly out of a book. However, when we read them one after another, we automatically look for clues to see whether they are connected. The first clue we find is the presence of the word *well* at the beginning of (10). In sentence-initial position after a suggestion from another speaker, this adverb (some people prefer to call it a sentence connector) is used to show that the second speaker in principle accepts the proposal made by the first but has certain reservations. Notice that not only the position of the adverb is important but also the semantics, i.e. the meaning which it has in this position. The second clue is the pronoun *she*. In itself the word has very little meaning. We know that it refers to a female person but that is about all. In this case it is the function which is important. The usual function of a pronoun is to refer to an already mentioned noun and to stand in place of that noun, hence the name pro-noun. When we hear the pronoun *she* in (10), we automatically look back to find the nearest noun to which it can refer and we discover *Emily* in (9). The pronoun *she* thus binds sentences (9) and (10) together. The third clue is *so* in sentence (11). It is rather like *well* in (10): its position at the beginning of the sentence tells us that it is an adverb (sentence connector) whose semantics link it with the preceding sentence. The word *so* tells us that the reason for what is said in the rest of (11) can be found in sentence (10). The final clue showing that the three sentences together form a text is the adverb *there*.

In a sense it is also a pro-form like the pronoun: it has little meaning on its own but refers to a place which has already been mentioned. If *there* is given emphatic stress, it links sentence (11) with (10) and refers to *the Royal Apartments*: the speaker is suggesting that they do not have go to the Royal Apartments but they could visit another part of the castle. If *there* is said without stress, it now refers to *Windsor Castle* and links sentence (11) with sentence (9): the speaker is now suggesting that today they should abandon the idea of visiting Windsor Castle altogether. The reader will have already noticed that the analysis of texts involves rather more factors than grammar, for example semantics and especially pragmatics, i.e. what the speaker and the listener know about the world in which they live, e.g. that the name *Emily* refers to a female person and that Windsor Castle contains apartments for the Queen and her family. It is for this reason that we shall have to leave texts out of consideration. The interested reader, however, can find more information in one of the standard textbooks on discourse analysis or text linguistics mentioned on page 175.

3 Conclusion

Criticisms

To conclude this introductory chapter let us look back at some of the criticisms which have been levelled against traditional grammar in the past. We have already mentioned that the early traditional grammarians of the last century often tried to **force the language** which they were describing **into a Greco-Latin mould** although this did not always fit. An even more serious criticism was that right up until the middle of the twentieth century **very little attention was paid to syntax**; traditional grammar was concerned mainly with the classification and morphology of words. Grammarians were interested in the various shapes that different kinds of words could take, but not in how these words could be put together to form sentences. For example, nouns were of interest mainly because of their inflections: if they showed differences of gender and used different suffixes or other mechanisms to form the plural from the singular, they could be put into various classes. Similarly, if the language under discussion used grammatical case, nouns could be classified according to their case suffixes, etc. Thus the grammarian restricted their activity mainly to the word and phrase levels and rarely looked beyond to the clause or sentence level. Fortunately this is no longer the case and the syntax of clauses and sentences now occupies an important place in grammar. Another criticism that was made, especially in the middle years of the twentieth century, is that traditional grammars have **often** been **prescriptive instead of descriptive**, i.e. instead of describing the language that speakers actually use, they often tell people what the grammarians think they ought to be saying. Another criticism linked to this one is that traditional grammar, especially in the nineteenth century and in the early twentieth century, **concentrated entirely upon the written language**, which was the language of education and prestige, and completely disregarded the spoken language. Nowadays, we find that grammarians and dictionary makers try to avoid these pitfalls. Leech 1975 is a grammar which particularly stresses speech and the communicative function of language, and the latest comprehensive grammar (Biber etc. 1999: 'Grammar of Spoken and Written English') puts spoken before written English even in its title. Much has also been done to counter the charge of prescriptiveness. In many modern English dictionaries we now find usage notes, which may often reject the prescriptions of earlier grammarians. For example, the 1986 edition of Collins English dictionary has a note under the entry for the word *preposition* which points out that although the practice of ending a sentence with a preposition (as in *They are the people I hate talking to*) has been much condemned, careful users avoid it only if it would be stylistically clumsy. One final criticism is still valid though one could argue about whether it is really important. Some critics observe that there is **little consistency in the definition of many of the terms used in traditional grammar**. For example, some parts of speech (word classes) are defined on formal grounds: a word is called a preposition because of its usual position (its pre-position) in front of a noun or pronoun. On the other hand, a word is called a conjunction not because of its position but because of its function in joining together (conjoining) sentences or clauses. Other technical terms are defined semantically: a noun is so called because it is the name of something. The English word *noun* has come down to us from Latin where the word *nomen* meant both *name* and *noun*. Despite the heterogeneous nature of these technical terms, they present no real problem for the modern grammarian. They have the advantage of being familiar to most people because of the long tradition behind their use, and where the traditional definitions are inadequate, the modern grammarian can use other features to improve them. For example, in the next chapter we shall see that nouns can be at least partly defined by the kind of neighbours they can have in certain types of phrases.

2 CHAPTER Word Classes

Introduction

In this chapter we shall look in detail at the various kinds of word which can make up phrases, clauses and sentences and show the reader how to recognize them. Traditionally they have been called **parts of speech**, but nowadays they are usually referred to as **word classes** or **word categories**. We saw in the previous chapter that there are nine word classes altogether: **nouns, adjectives, determiners** (including the definite and indefinite articles), **pronouns, prepositions, verbs, adverbs, conjunctions** and **interjections**.

1 Nouns

1 Determination of Nouns

Position

How can we tell that a word is a noun? We observed that traditionally a noun is said to be the name of a thing or person. Usually, there is no problem in recognizing persons, and therefore words like *Ann, Peter, Jane, Paul* or *Smith, Brown, Clinton*, which are names of persons, can easily be classified as nouns. However, many people may feel less sure about words for abstractions like *love, hate, friendship*. They are nouns but are they also the names of things? A better proof would be to find one or more test phrases in which a noun regularly occurs in a certain position with certain classes of words as its neighbours and then to see whether the word in question can take this same position. For example, most nouns occur in the following two patterns (where ART stands for the articles *a, an, the* and ADJ stands for an adjective, and the line shows the position of the noun):

1 ART ADJ ______ 2 *my* ADJ ______

In phrases such as *a fierce dog, an empty pot, the tall cathedral, my best friend*, we can tell that each of the words *dog, pot, cathedral, friend* is a noun because of its position after an adjective preceded by the indefinite or definite article or by the word *my*. Note that any of the nouns we have just listed can be used in both patterns (*a fierce dog, the fierce dog, my fierce dog*). The nouns for abstractions will also fit into both patterns (*an intense love, the strong hate, my long friendship*), though in pattern 1 with the article they may sound better if the phrase is extended (*an intense love of music, the strong hate which he felt*). The important thing, however, is that pattern 1 still remains unchanged even if it is part of a larger pattern. In the case of the nouns which are names of persons, we find that they do not fit at all happily into pattern 1 (?*a wretched Ann*, ?*the poor Peter*) though they do occur in pattern 2 (*my beloved Jane, my dear Smith*). We shall see below, when we come to the classification of nouns, that certain kinds of noun do not normally take an article in front of them because what they refer to is uncountable. Proper nouns, i.e. names which are written with a capital letter, are of this kind: it sounds strange to say *a Peter* or *the Smith* if you are referring to your brother Peter or to your neighbour. This property of being uncountable is what makes the use of proper nouns in pattern 1 feel uncomfortable. Notice, however, that proper nouns, like words for abstractions, can be used with just an adjective in front of them: *happy Ann, little Peter, great love, close friendship*, whereas *fierce dog, empty pot, etc.* do not sound natural here.

Inflection

Another test for a noun is to look at the morphology of the word. Does it take a plural inflection, i.e. can it be made plural by adding the suffix *-s* or *-es*? Can it take a genitive inflection, i.e. does it have genitive forms ending in *-'s* and *-s'*? In other words, does it fit into one or more of the following morphological patterns?

3 ______ *(e)s* (Plural)
4 ______ *'s* (Genitive Singular)
5 ______ *s'* (Genitive Plural)

All the nouns that fit easily into patterns 1 and 2 are usually also at home in pattern 3 (*dogs, dishes, pots, cathedrals, friends*) though some (*dish, pot, cathedral*) may feel a little uneasy in patterns 4 and 5, for reasons which we shall discuss below when we come to the gender scale in our discussion of case in nouns.

2 Classification of Nouns

Common/ Proper

We have just seen that the morphology of nouns as well as the syntactic patterns in which they occur are partly determined by the classes to which the nouns belong. The two largest classes are common nouns and proper nouns. We can define a **proper noun** as the name given to a person or pet animal (*Tom, Helen, Clinton, Yeltsin*, or *Jumbo, Rex*), to a geographical location (town *London*, country *Australia*, river *Rhine*, mountain *Everest*, etc.), to certain institutions (*Congress*) and to certain titles which people use before their names (*Lord, Lady*). As proper nouns refer to persons or things which are unique, they are written with a capital letter in English. All nouns which are not written with a capital and which are not proper nouns are **common nouns**. Instead of referring to an individual person or thing, a common noun refers to a member of a group of persons or things that share the same characteristics. Typical common nouns are *dog, book, water, anger.*

Count/ Uncount

Common nouns can be divided into two subgroups: **count nouns**, i.e. those referring to single things that can be counted, and **uncount** (also called **non-count**) **nouns**, i.e. those referring in a general way to abstractions and shapeless things which cannot be counted. Thus *dog* and *book* referring to individual members of a class of things with recognizable characteristics are countable and can therefore be used with an indefinite article and have a plural form (*a dog, a book, dogs, books*). On the other hand, words like *happiness* and *anger*, which do not refer to individual things but have only general reference, are uncount and therefore cannot take an indefinite article or have a plural form.

Uncount → Count

In some cases, an uncount noun can be made count and then there is slight change of meaning. If the uncount noun refers to something concrete like *sugar, wine,* the count forms of the noun mean *a kind of .... , kinds of ....* Thus when a chemist talks about *a sugar* or *different sugars,* he is referring to one or more varieties of sugar with different chemical formulae, e.g. dextrose, fructose, maltose, etc. However, there seems to be a scale of acceptability for this conversion from uncount to count. Whereas there is no problem for most people with *sugars, wines,* certainly most speakers would reject *breads* and prefer the more explicit phrase *kinds of bread.* (For examples of abstract uncount nouns changing to count, see Concrete/Abstract below). Notice too that proper nouns behave in a similar way. Since they refer to unique entities they are normally uncount, but when used in the plural they too change their meaning and usually refer to something countable connected with the proper noun. For example, the uncount proper noun *Hoover* is the family name of an American manufacturer of vacuum cleaners. In British English his name has been used for this product since 1927 and, as a count noun, is now written with a small letter and can be used with the indefinite article and take a plural (*a hoover, two hoovers*). Another famous example is the uncount proper noun *Bikini.* When written with a capital letter it is the name of an island in the Pacific Ocean on which atomic bomb tests were carried out by the Americans in the 1950s. The name was later used to denote a very brief two-piece swimsuit for women or a very brief close-fitting swimsuit for men, supposedly because of the explosive effect caused at that time on the opposite sex when one of these garments was worn. With this new meaning the word became a count noun, was written with a small letter and could have a plural form (*bikinis*).

Other Differences

Notice that the distinction between count and uncount common nouns is seen not only in the suffixes they can take (their morphology) but also in the kinds of words with which they collocate, i.e. which are their most frequent immediate neighbours. For example, after the determiner *much* we found only uncount nouns (*not much water, much love*) and neither singular nor plural count nouns (**much dog, *much dogs, *much book, *much books*), whereas after the determiner *many* we find only plural count nouns (*not many dogs, many books*) and never uncount nouns (**many water, *many love*). Another characteristic of uncount nouns which is not shared with count nouns is that they can easily be used without an article in front of them (e.g. in sentences like *Water is colourless, Beauty is only skin-deep*). Count nouns are never used in this way in the singular (we cannot say **boy is a small male human being*; the sentence must begin with *a boy* ...), but in the plural they often occur alone without an article: *dogs are animals.*

Language Specific

Though it would seem logical for countable nouns in one language to have countable counterparts in another, this is not so. The feature of countability is language specific. Compare the following English and German nouns, where [U] indicates uncount and [C] count:

English:	[U]	*information, advice, homework, progress, damage, research*
German:	[C]	*Informationen (Auskünfte), Ratschläge, Hausaufgaben, Fortschritte, Schäden, Forschung(en).*

Whereas in German I can comfortably talk about *eine Information* in the singular and *Informationen* in the plural, in English neither **an information* nor *informations* is grammatically correct: I can either use the uncount noun alone and talk about *information* in a general sense or, if I have to be specific, I can add a quantifying word such as *piece* or *item* and say *a piece of information* or *items of information.* This can also be done with *advice, homework, research* in the list above, but not usually with *progress, damage*, where English is satisfied with the uncount general noun. Thus in contrast to the German *viele Fortschritte*, English cannot say *many progresses*, but only *much progress* or *a lot of progress.*

Changes in Meaning

Some English nouns may show rather startling differences in meaning depending on whether they are uncount or count, e.g.
[U] *lace* = a delicate kind of openwork fabric woven with symmetrical patterns and figures (*The sleeves of her dress were decorated with lace*).
[C] *lace* = a string drawn through holes to hold something together (*You must buy two laces for your new shoes*).
Other pairs of nouns may be more subtly differentiated, e.g.

[U] *hair* = the mass of fine threads covering the bodies of some animals and the heads of (most) human beings (*He asked the hairdresser to cut his hair*).
[C] *hair* = one individual thread growing from the body of an animal or human being (*The hairs in his eyebrows needed trimming*).
Some languages can sometimes use both the uncount noun and the plural of the count noun with exactly the same meaning. For example, in German *Sie hat schönes Haar* is synonymous with *Sie hat schöne Haare*. The English equivalents, on the other hand, show the meaning difference which we mentioned above: *She has beautiful hair* can only refer to the hair on her head, whereas *She has beautiful hairs* sounds distinctly odd, as it seems to be referring to a number of hairs which can be seen individually on some other part of her anatomy.

Concrete/ Abstract

Another distinction which is useful in the classification of nouns is between concrete and abstract nouns. If the referent of a noun, i.e. what it refers to, can be physically touched or seen, the noun can be put in the class of **concrete nouns**, e.g. *tree, bridge, water, bread*. If the referent of the noun is an abstraction, something which cannot be touched or seen, then it belongs to the class of **abstract nouns**, e.g. *remark, idea, anger, happiness*. Note that some concrete and some abstract nouns are count and that others are uncount, i.e. the classes concrete/abstract do not coincide with the classes count/uncount:

Concrete:	*tree, bridge*	[C]
	water, bread	[U]
Abstract:	*remark, idea*	[C]
	anger, happiness	[U]

The nouns in the table above are normally only count or only uncount, but there are many abstract uncount nouns (*hope, pain, thought, joy, etc.*) which can be used freely as count nouns but with a slight change of meaning, rather like the concrete nouns which were discussed above under **Uncount → Count** (page 19). However, whereas the count form of the concrete uncount noun had the meaning *a kind of ...*, the count form of the abstract uncount noun has the meaning *an instance of ..., an example of ...* Thus uncount nouns like *hope, pain, thought* have a general meaning, and can be used without an article in front of them: *She never gave up hope, He was always in pain, The accident gave them food for thought*. However, when they refer to specific instances of hope, pain and thought, they can be used as count nouns: *One of her hopes was that she would meet them, He felt a pain in his leg, They did not give the affair a single thought*.

Mass Nouns

There is one other group of uncount nouns which needs special attention. These refer to concrete things which may be solid or liquid but which have no special shape, e.g. *sugar, salad, soap, soup, beer, water.* If it is necessary to talk about quantities of these things, we can put a quantifying expression in front of the uncount noun, e.g. *a lump of sugar, a portion of salad, a bar of soap, a plate of soup, a glass of beer.* When it is quite clear to the listener that one of these quantities is implied, the uncount noun can be made count and we can say (e.g. to a waiter): *Two sugars please* or *We'd like two soups, two salads and two beers.* In a shop we could ask the assistant: *Are those two soaps for sale?* Nouns which can be used uncount with a general sense and can also be used count to indicate a quantity of the uncount noun are called **mass nouns**.

3 Number in Nouns

General Remarks

When we looked in the preceding section at count and uncount nouns we could not avoid talking about the grammatical category of **number**, i.e. whether a noun is **singular** or **plural**. Count/Uncount is not the only aspect of number which is of interest in the noun. We can also examine how nouns form their plurals, whether they occur only in the singular or only in the plural, and whether the verbs they go with have singular agreement or plural agreement. Let us look at each of these briefly.

Plural Formation

For native English words **three methods** are used to make count nouns plural. The **first** and regular way is to add the written suffix *-s* or *-es* to the singular form. Most nouns take the *-s* ending, e.g. *shops, hats, socks,* but if the spelling ends in *ch, s, ss, sh,* or *x* the suffix *-es* is used, e.g. *watches, buses, kisses, dishes, boxes.* Some common count nouns ending in *o* add *-es* for the plural (*tomatoes, potatoes, heroes*), others add just *-s* (*photos, radios*) and some can take both endings (*flamingos, flamingoes; ghettos, ghettoes; mottos, mottoes*). The **second** method is to make no change for the plural, e.g. *one sheep, two sheep, one fish, two fish* (but also *fishes*). This method is often used in hunting contexts when talking about animals and birds, e.g. *They are shooting duck today and rabbit tomorrow.* To hunters this method sounds more professional than the regular plural with the suffix (*ducks, rabbits*). Fish are often talked about in this way too: *Yesterday we caught two pike, In England a lot of cod is eaten but not much herring*. The **third** method is not to add a plural suffix but to change the vowel of the singular, e.g. *foot, feet; man, men; tooth, teeth; mouse, mice.* This is a very old method dating back to Old English and is referred to in linguistics as **umlaut**. It has survived in only a few common words, whose plural forms in Modern English are now considered to be irregular. Note that the umlaut is not always present in the spelling though it can be heard clearly in the pronunciation: woman/women [′wʊmən/′wɪmɪn]. Another Old English mechanism which has survived in only a handful of words is to add the suffix *-en* to the singular noun, e.g. *ox, oxen*. It is sometimes combined with umlaut as in *brethren*, the alternative specialized plural of *brother*, which is normally used only in a religious or archaic context, e.g. for the members of a sect or community (*Plymouth Brethren, the Brethren of the Trinity*). A common word which forms its plural with both the umlaut and the suffix *-en* is the noun child, children. The change of vowel does not appear in the spelling but is there in the pronunciation [tʃaɪld, ′tʃildrən]. This plural form is even more irregular owing to the presence of the *r* before the suffix *-en*.

Foreign Plurals

In addition to using its native methods of plural formation, English sometimes adopts the foreign plurals for nouns borrowed from foreign languages, especially Latin or Greek. Usually the foreign plural is used in technical or formal language, but if the word is used in more colloquial contexts and particularly in American English, it can also have an English plural with *-s, -es*.

-us → -i

Thus Latin borrowings which end in *-us* take the Latin plural *-i* (*fungus, fungi; nucleus, nuclei; radius, radii; stimulus, stimuli*) but less formally we also find *funguses, nucleuses, radiuses, stimuluses*.

-um → -a

Similarly, nouns ending in *-um* have a formal Latin plural with *-a* (*aquarium, aquaria; memorandum, memoranda; millennium, millennia; referendum, referenda*) as well as a less formal plural form with *-s* (*aquariums, memorandums, millenniums, referendums*).

-a → -ae

A few nouns ending in *-a* take the Latin plural *-ae* (*larva, larvae; vertebra, vertebrae*), but here too the regular English plural can be found in American English (*larvas, vertebras*).

-is → -es

Another group of words, which are derived through Latin from Greek, end in *-is* (pronounced [-ɪs]) in the singular and form their plural by replacing this ending with *-es* (pronounced [-i:z]): *analysis, analyses; basis, bases; hypothesis, hypotheses; parenthesis, parentheses; crisis, crises*.

-on → -a

There are some Greek borrowings which have a singular ending *-on* and a plural ending *-a*. Two of these (*criterion, criteria; phenomenon, phenomena*) are so common in the plural that some native English speakers use the plural form incorrectly as the singular and produce ungrammatical constructions like **this criteria*, **another phenomena* instead of *this criterion, another phenomenon*.

Always Singular

Certain nouns occur only in the singular. Some of these always have the definite article in front of them, e.g. *The public was not interested; His name is in the press again; They were on the brink of war*. Some always have the indefinite article, e.g. *The traffic came* to a standstill; *Did you give your face a wash?*. Others have either an article or another determiner like *their* or *this* in front of them, e.g. *She was seen in the vicinity after the crash, There were no banks in their vicinity; The picture was just a jumble of faces, We lost our way in this jumble of streets*. The two noun *news* and *shambles* need particular attention: despite their final *-s* they are never plural. *News* can only be used with the definite article or a singular determiner like *this, that*, e.g. *The news (This news, That news) is bad*, whereas *shambles* usually takes the indefinite article, e.g. *With litter everywhere the room was a shambles*. We can also mention here the group of uncount nouns which look plural but (like other uncount nouns) usually have no article in front of them and usually take a singular verb. Some of these refer to certain kinds of studies or sports and end in *-ics* (*mathematics, physics, economics, politics; athletics, gymnastics*), while others refer to games (*billiards, bowls, darts, dominoes, draughts*) or illnesses (*measles, mumps, shingles*). Examples in context: *Mathematics is the study of numbers, Athletics consists of track and field sports.*

Always Plural

Some nouns are always used in the plural form and never in the singular. To this group of invariable **plural nouns** belong certain concrete nouns like *arms* (= weapons), *clothes, goods* (= merchandise), *surroundings, troops* (= soldiers), *waters* (= the sea near to and belonging to a country, as in the expression *in British waters*) and certain abstract nouns like *thanks, contents, earnings, riches*. These cannot be used as singular words preceded by the indefinite article form, e.g. we cannot say **an arm* (= a weapon), **a clothe, *a good, *a water* (in reference to the sea), **a thank*, etc.

Pair Plurals

One subset of plural nouns, the **pair plurals** (also called **summation plurals**), are the names of items of clothing, tools or instruments which consist of two parts joined together, e.g. *trousers, pants, pyjamas; scissors, pincers, pliers; glasses, spectacles, binoculars*. When we talk about one or more of these items, normally it is only necessary to add the determiner *some* before the noun (*I need some scissors, some new pyjamas*) and the context will make it clear whether we mean just one or more than one. However, if we need to make the number specific, a modifying expression using the word *pair* can be used in front of them, e.g. *a pair of scissors, two new pairs of pyjamas.*

Unmarked Plurals

In contrast to the nouns with only plural forms, there are also some nouns which look singular but always behave as if they were plural: *people, cattle, police*. They always take a plural verb and either have no determiner (article) in front of them or else a plural demonstrative determiner like *these, those*. For example, *People are upset about this decision, These people have done their duty.*

Collective Nouns

singular + plural

Commonly in British English but less so in American, some nouns which refer to a collection or group of people or things can be used with a singular verb when we consider the group as a unit, or with a plural verb when we think of the individuals making up the group. In the latter case the noun does not have a plural ending. Nouns which behave in this way are termed **collective** (or **group**) **nouns**. Examples: *audience, class, committee, family, government, group, staff, team*. Compare *The audience in the cinema was small last night* (i.e. there were not many people there) with *The audience in the cinema were small last night* (i.e. it consisted of small people, children). Notice that when these nouns refer to groups as units, they have singular agreement with the verb and any determiners and pronouns which follow them, e.g. *When this family lost its father, it collapsed completely*, but when they refer to the individuals in the group, the verb and any determiner or pronoun that refers back to them now become plural, e.g. *When the class leave the school their teacher will take them to the museum.*

Collective → Count

Almost all collective nouns can be treated as normal count nouns when they refer to the group as a whole. They can then be made plural by adding *-s* or *-es* and have normal plural agreement, when we talk about more than one group, e.g. *The audiences in the cinemas have now left, Two classes are refusing to go.*

Collective Proper Nouns

Most proper nouns which refer to institutions, companies or teams can be used as collective nouns: *Parliament, Labour (= the Labour Party), the Post Office, the United Nations, the BBC, Manchester United, etc.* Compare *Parliament has been dissolved* (i.e. the whole of Parliament) with *Parliament have decided to lower taxes* (i.e. the individual members of Parliament). Or *The United Nations* (as a unit) *is seeking peace in Kosovo* with *The United Nations have not made up their minds yet* (i.e. the individual nations are undecided). Note that *the United States* as a single country is treated as singular in English: *The United States has recalled its ambassador.*

Measurements

Many nouns which in the plural are used in expressions indicating time, distance, weight or value can often be used with singular agreement when the measurement is considered as a unit:

1. *Three years (←) is a long time to be ill.*
2. *They walked a good ten miles to the nearest house.*
3. *This two pounds has to last me till Friday.*
4. *I want another six kilos of sugar.*

Notice that in (1) the singular form of the verb (*is*) shows us that *Three years* is being treated as a unit and not as a group. In sentence (2) we see a plural noun phrase (*ten miles*) preceded by the indefinite article (which can only be singular) and the adjective *good*. This combination of *a* and *good* (sometimes also *full* instead of *good*) in front of a plural noun phrase of measurement shows that the latter is being considered as a single unit. Similarly in (3) *two pounds* is being looked upon as a single sum of money and therefore takes singular verb agreement (*has*) and is even preceded by a singular demonstrative determiner (*this*). If we replace the singular demonstrative by the plural form (*these*), we are now thinking of the individual pounds and the verb must take plural agreement: *These two pounds have to last me till Friday*. In sentence (4) we find another plural noun phrase (*six kilos*) preceded by the determiner *another*, which always goes with a singular noun. Whereas we can say *another book, another cat*, the phrases **another books*, **another cats* are ungrammatical. In the case of the noun *penny*, English has two plural forms, one for the unit meaning and the other for the individuals in the unit: thus *twenty pence* refers to the sum of money with this particular value, whereas *twenty pennies* refers to twenty individual coins.

Fractions

Special attention must be paid to singular/plural agreement with nouns denoting numerical fractions, i.e. parts of numbers. (See also Verbal Agreement, page 93). With expressions like *two thirds of X, four fifths of Y, a half of Z*, agreement in the verb is always with *X, Y* and *Z* and does not depend on whether the word for the fraction is singular or plural. Compare the following pairs of sentences:

5a. *Two thirds of the wine has been drunk already.*
5b. *Two thirds of the oranges have been sold.*
6a. *Half (of) the butter is rancid.*
6b. *Half (of) the apples are rotten.*

In both (5a) and (5b) the noun *thirds* is in the plural, and since it is grammatically the head of the noun phrase in which it stands, we should expect the verb to agree with it in number in both sentences. However, in (5a) the verb is singular (*has*) because it is in agreement with *wine*, and in (5b) it is plural (*have*) not because it agrees with *thirds* but because it agrees semantically with *oranges*. Similarly, although *half* is singular in both (6a) and (6b), the verb (*is*) agrees with *butter* in (6a) and is therefore singular, whereas in (6b) it must be plural (*are*) agreeing with *apples*.

Others

Other expressions containing a quantifying noun (*a lot of, lots of, plenty of*) also work in this way. It makes no difference whether *lot* is used here in the singular or plural; it is the grammatical number of the noun after *of* which determines whether verb that follows is singular or plural. Compare the following:

7a. *A lot of sugar has been wasted. There is a lot of rubbish on the floor.*
7b. *A lot of papers have arrived. There are a lot of customers here.*

8a. *Lots of money has been spent. There's lots of food to buy.*
8b. *Lots of shops have shut. There are lots of cars on the road*
Similarly:
9. *Plenty of orders were made and plenty of beer was drunk.*

4 Gender in Nouns

General Remarks

Unlike many languages which have **grammatical gender**, i.e. where all nouns are divided into **masculine, feminine** and even **neuter** mostly irrespective of what they refer to, English usually has **natural gender**, i.e. it uses the category masculine/feminine only in connexion with biologically male or female referents (i.e. persons or animals), and all other nouns are neuter.

Gender Marking

English has four methods of marking gender in the noun:
1. A feminine noun can be formed from a masculine one by adding a suffix (usually *-ess*, but sometimes *-ette* or *-ine*): *prince, princess, waiter, waitress, lion, lioness; usher, usherette; hero, heroine.*
2. Male and female animals of certain species may be referred to by completely different words: *stallion* (male horse)/*mare* (female horse), *boar* (male pig)/*sow* (female pig).
3. A special gender word can be used with the noun to indicate a male or a female person, animal or bird: *billy-goat/nanny-goat, bull elephant/cow elephant, cock pheasant/hen pheasant.*
4. The same noun may be used for both males and females: *teacher, professor, painter, musician.*

-ess, -ette, -ine

In method (1) it should be noted that the suffix *-ette* is comparatively rare as a gender marker, and much more commonly used as a diminutive (*statue/statuette*). Furthermore, some feminine nouns with this suffix do not have a corresponding masculine form (*suffragette*). The suffix *-ine* is even rarer and, with the exception of the word *heroine*, is found only in a few historical titles, such as *margrave/margravine, landgrave/landgravine*. The suffix *-ess* is the most widespread but is often dropped in modern English when the noun to which it is attached denotes a common profession. Many speakers feel that here the feminine ending discriminates against women by calling attention to the person's sex where sex ought not to play any role. Thus nouns like *authoress, poetess, paintress* are rare nowadays and usually replaced by *author, poet, painter*, which have no discriminatory overtones. The context makes it clear whether the speaker is referring to a man or a woman.

Special Words

In the examples shown above for method (2), the nouns *stallion* (for a male horse), *boar* (for a male pig) are always masculine and therefore need the masculine pronoun or determiner (*he, him, his*) after them, whereas *mare* (for a female horse), *sow* (for a female pig) are always feminine and need the feminine pronoun or determiner (*she, her*): *That stallion is looking for his mate, and the sow is suckling her piglets.* Notice that for both of these species of animal there is a superordinate noun (*horse, pig*), which is used when we do not know or are not interested in the sex of the animal. A **superordinate** (or **generic**) noun is a less marked (more general) word whose meaning includes that of certain other more marked (more specified) nouns. The more marked nouns are referred to as **hyponyms**. Thus both *stallion* and *mare* are hyponyms of the superordinate *horse*, and similarly *boar* and *sow* are hyponyms of the superordinate *pig*. Since these superordinates are unmarked for gender, they can only take the pronoun or determiner (*it, its*) after them: *The horse tossed its head and stamped its feet and the pig squealed when they caught it.* Although the superordinate *chicken* has two different words as hyponyms for the male and the female of the species (*cock/hen*), in the case of some birds the unmarked superordinate can also be used as the marked hyponym for the female: unmarked *duck:* marked *drake/duck;* unmarked *goose:* marked *gander/goose*. When we talk in general about these birds, the superordinate *duck* or *goose* is sufficient and these nouns are then followed by the unmarked pronoun or determiner (*it, its*), e.g. *As the goose had lost its way, it waddled into the garage.* On the other hand, if it is necessary to differentiate the female from the male, we still have to use the nouns *duck, goose* for the female, but these words are now marked hyponyms and must be followed by the feminine pronoun or determiner (*she, her, hers*), just as *drake* and *gander* must take the masculine ones (*he, him, his*), e.g. *When the dog attacked the goose, she fiercely protected her young but the gander just closed his eyes as if he had seen nothing.* Sometimes, it is the marked noun for the male animal which is the same as the unmarked superordinate, e.g. *dog* is not only the general word for the species but also the marked masculine hyponym contrasting with the feminine word *bitch*. Similarly *fox* is the general word undifferentiated with regard to sex, whereas when contrasted with the feminine hyponym *vixen*, it is now the masculine hyponym referring only to the male animal and must be referred to by the masculine pronoun or determiner (*he, him, his*): *The dog has eaten all his food, but the bitch has left most of hers.*

Ships, Cars, etc.

In colloquial English it is not uncommon for both men and women to use the feminine pronoun *she* to refer to vehicles and machines which they work with every day and towards which they may therefore have affectionate feelings. When talking about their own car, a man or a woman may remark *She runs beautifully*, or in reference to a troublesome computer they may say *She's given* *up the ghost again!* The treatment of ships as feminine can be found even in formal English. Notice that, though most other vehicles and machines do not receive names, ships are often given feminine ones (*the Queen Elisabeth, the Lady Hamilton*), but even those with masculine names *(the Prince of Wales, the Admiral Nelson*) can take the pronoun *she*. It should however be noted that only the unmarked relative pronoun *which* is grammatically correct with reference to ships and that the relative pronoun *who*, which is used only to refer to male and female animals, would be incorrect here. For example: *The 'Victory', which* (not **who) was a British ship, damaged her rigging when she lost her way in the storm.*

Prefixed Gender Word

In the third method of marking for gender illustrated above, a marked noun used as a gender word is added to another noun which is otherwise undifferentiated for sex. Some gender words are restricted to one species, e.g. *billy/nanny* can only be used with *goat*, while others can be used for several species, e.g. *buck/doe* with *deer, hare, rabbit*. For some animals it is also possible to prefix the pronouns *he/she*. Instead of *billy-goat/nanny-goat* we can also say *he-goat/she-goat*, as well as *he-rabbit/she-rabbit* instead of *buck rabbit/doe rabbit*. For all animals and human beings it is of course always possible to use the adjectives *male* and *female* instead of a gender word.

Same Word

In method (4) described above, where the same word can be both masculine and feminine, the noun usually refers to some human occupation or profession: *doctor, lawyer, artist, bishop*. Normally the context tells the listener or reader whether the person being referred to is a woman or a man, but if there are no clues in the utterance, it is usual to assume that the referent is male, e.g. in the sentence *They had to find a new doctor*. In order to prevent any ambiguity, we can sometimes add the word *woman* as a gender word, e.g. *He refused to go to a woman doctor, They needed a woman artist for the job*. Strangely, when a profession is followed mainly by women, the noun *man* cannot be used as a gender word to denote a male person in that profession. Thus if we wish to make clear that *a nurse* or *a secretary* is not a woman, we cannot say **a man nurse* or **a man secretary*, but only *a male nurse, a male secretary*. In older, more refined English the gender word *woman* could often be replaced by *lady* (as in *a lady doctor*), but here too the corresponding masculine word *gentleman* could not be used for a man in a predominantly female profession, i.e. one could not say **a gentleman nurse, *a gentleman secretary*.

Names of Countries

Nouns which are the names of countries may be treated grammatically in three different ways according to their meaning.

1. When the country is considered merely as a geographical unit, it is usually treated as inanimate and must then be referred to by

the non-personal pronoun or determiner *it, its* and the non-personal relative pronoun *which*: e.g. *Italy, which is a warm country, has a number of famous islands on its west coast. It therefore attracts many tourists.*
2. When a country is thought of as a political or economic unit, it is often made feminine and now referred to by the personal pronoun or determiner *she, her, hers* and the personal relative pronoun *who*: e.g. *At this stage in the war, Italy, who had also signed the pact, agreed to allow foreign troops on her territory. Later she regretted this.*
3. When the name of the country stands for an international sports team, the noun is often treated as a collective noun. Since the speaker is thinking of the individual members of this team, the noun now has plural agreement in the verb, takes a plural pronoun or determiner (*they, them, their, theirs*) and the personal relative pronoun *who* is used: e.g. *Italy, who were playing against Germany in the World Cup, have just lost their best goal-keeper. They are now rather depressed.*

5 Case in Nouns

General Remarks

In many languages the relationships between different nouns in a sentence or between nouns and pronouns is shown by the use of case inflections, i.e. case suffixes which can be added to the nouns and pronouns and often to the adjectives and determiners that go with them. Although Old English, like Modern German, had a fairly complicated system of case endings to show these relationships, most of this task has been taken over in Modern English by prepositions. Basically Modern English **nouns** show only **two cases**: a marked **genitive case** with the suffix *-'s* added to the singular noun and *-s'* to the plural noun; and an unmarked **common case** (i.e. a non-genitive case) which carries no suffix and can be used for all other functions including after prepositions. As we shall see when we come later to pronouns and determiners, only the **personal pronouns** in Modern English are more differentiated. They usually have **three** different forms: one for the **nominative** (or subject) case (*I, he, she, we, they*), one for the **oblique** (object) case (*me, him, her, us, them*) and another for the **genitive** (possessive) case (*mine, his, hers, ours, theirs*).

Genitive

Alongside the **inflectional genitive** (also called *-s* genitive, Saxon genitive), Modern English also has a **prepositional genitive** (*of* genitive) at its disposal. Before we look at the factors determining the choice between these two, let us examine the form of the inflectional genitive in more detail. Notice that both the singular and the plural genitive forms of regular nouns are phonetically identical: we cannot tell from the pronunciation whether speakers are referring to only one boy or to more than one when they say either of the phrases *the boy's books* (= *the books of the boy*), *the boys' books* (= *the books of the boys*). It is the context which helps us to decide. This is probably the reason why English prefers a plural noun after a plural genitive in cases like *the boys' heads* (compared with *the boy's head*). The plural *heads* suggests that the genitive noun preceding it is plural, since when we see many heads there must be many boys. Similarly, the singular *head* suggests the singular genitive, since if there is only one head there can be only one boy. Note that English also looks at the world in this way outside the genitive construction and can only say *The men raised their hats as the Queen went by* (we see many hats when there are many men) whereas in a sentence like this in German the singular noun would seem more logical since each man has only hat: *Die Männer lüfteten den Hut, als die Königin vorbeiging.*

Irregular Nouns

Whereas the singular and plural genitive forms of regular nouns sound alike, this is not so with most nouns that have irregular plurals. Where the plural common case form of the noun differs from the singular in pronunciation (*mouse/mice, wolf/wolves*), the difference between the singular and the plural genitive form can, of course, also be heard phonetically, e.g. *the mouse's* ['maʊsɪz] *tail, the mice's* ['maɪsɪz] *tails; the wolf's* ['wʊlfs] *den, the wolves'* ['wʊlvz] *den.* The phonetic difference may not always be apparent from the spelling, e.g. *the house's* ['haʊsɪz] *roof, the houses'* ['haʊzɪz] *roofs; the woman's* ['wʊmənz] *husband, the women's* ['wɪmɪnz] *husbands.*

Zero Genitive

When English forms the genitive of **Greek names** which end in *es* and have three syllables, they are given an apostrophe after the final *s*, but there is no change in the pronunciation, e.g. *Socrates'* ['sɒkrəti:z, usually not 'sɒkrəti:zɪz] *wife; Sophocles'* ['sɒfəkli:z] *tragedies.* Notice that the Latin form of Greek proper nouns is treated in the same way: *Hercules'* ['hɜ:kjuli:z] *deeds.* One way of looking at this phenomenon is to say that theses nouns carry a **zero genitive suffix**. Proper nouns which end in *-s* and have fewer than three syllables are usually given only the apostrophe in the genitive form but are treated phonetically as if *-es* has been added, e.g. *Zeus'* ['zju:sɪz] *love affairs; Paris'* ['pærɪsɪz] *love for Helen.* Strictly speaking we cannot talk of a zero genitive suffix here, since despite the spelling, the regular suffix is present in the pronunciation. When **native English proper nouns** end in *s,* the usual practice in writing the genitive is just to add the apostrophe, although the full regular suffix is pronounced, e.g. *Mr Davis'* ['deɪvɪsɪz] *book.* However, there is a tendency in recent English to replace the simple apostrophe by *'s*, e.g. *Mr Davis's book.* When a proper noun sounds phonetically like a regular plural, e.g. *Burns* [bɜ:nz] it may take either the zero suffix or the regular suffix in the pronunciation. In either case it is usually written with just the apostrophe (seldom with *'s*), e.g. *Robert Burns'* [bɜːnz, ˈbɜːnzɪz] *poems*. Occasionally, in **idiomatic expressions** nouns other than proper nouns may occur with a zero genitive suffix when they end in *s*. For example, the abstract noun in the expression *for goodness' sake* can only be written with the apostrophe and not with *'s*. Furthermore, the genitive form of this noun is phonetically identical with the common case form: with or without the apostrophe *goodness* is pronounced [ˈgʊdnɪs] and never [ˈgʊdnɪsɪz].

Inflectional or Prepositional?

We saw above that English has two methods of forming the genitive: one with the suffix *-'s* or *-s'* and one with the preposition *of*. There are two main factors determining which of these methods will be used with a particular noun. One factor is the position of the noun on the **gender scale** and the other is the speaker's **focus of information**.

Gender Scale

The gender scale is an imaginary scale starting with human beings at the top and descending through the higher animals (i.e. those which most resemble humans or with which humans have closest contact) to the lower animals (i.e. those which are the farthest remote from humans and the least like them) down to inanimate objects at the bottom. In general the inflectional genitive is used with the classes of nouns whose referents are at the top of this scale and have personal gender characteristics, while the *of* genitive is used for those whose referents are at the bottom and are things which have no gender characteristics. A few examples will make this clear: (personal proper noun) *Jane's violin*, (personal common noun) *the sailor's hat*, (collective noun = a group of people) *the committee's decision*, (higher animal) *the cat's whiskers*, (proper noun, name of a country as a political or economic unit, personified as feminine) *France's enemies*, (proper noun, name of institution, used as a collective noun) *UNO's contribution to the peace talks*. Farther down the scale and at the bottom, the prepositional genitive would be normal: (lower animal) *the body of a python*, (lower organism) *the nucleus of the amoeba*, (inanimate concrete noun) *the bottom of the page*, (inanimate, abstract noun) *the outcome of his research*. One notable class of exceptions are temporal nouns, inanimate abstract nouns referring to stretches of time, such as *hour, day, week, month, etc*. These nouns always take the inflectional genitive when preceded by the indefinite article (*an hour's drive, a day's work, a week's wages, a month's holiday*) and cannot be replaced by **the drive of an hour,* the work of a day, *the wages of a week, *the holiday of a month*. However, see page 37 for examples of the *of*-genitive where the head noun is preceded by the indefinite article and the measurement noun by a numeral.

Information Focus

In noun phrases containing a genitive of the kinds we have described above, the focus of attention is normally on the last noun, which therefore receives more prominent stress. This is the noun that the speaker wishes the hearer to focus his attention on. Sometimes the rule regarding the gender scale is broken in order to bring the noun which would normally be first in the genitive phrase into this more prominent position at the end. This is particularly the case when the noun is qualified by a relative clause. Compare:

1. *The fire severely damaged the factory's roof, which later collapsed.*
2. *The fire severely damaged the roof of the factory but spared the roof of the adjacent canteen.*

In (1) the gender scale rule would require the inanimate concrete noun *factory* to take the *of* genitive, but the rule has been broken so that the noun *roof* can come immediately in front of the relative clause which refers to it. It is the roof which has collapsed. If the *of* genitive had been used, the word *factory* would have been nearest to the relative clause and would therefore have received the information focus. In this case the sentence carries a different message. It is now the factory that later collapsed and not just the roof. In sentence (2) the speaker is contrasting the factory with the canteen and now the *of* genitive required by the gender scale is appropriate since it places *factory* in the prominent final position in the genitive phrase.

Newspaper Headlines

To conclude our discussion of the choice between the two methods of forming the English genitive, we should mention that the gender scale rule is often broken in newspaper headlines with the *-s* genitive frequently being used where in normal contexts it would sound unnatural. This is done presumably in order to save space. When the sentence *Chaos has been left in the wake of a hurricane* is transformed into the headline *Chaos left in hurricane's wake*, the inflectional genitive is preferred as it is shorter than the normal *of* genitive.

Group Genitive

One interesting feature of the *-s* genitive is that this suffix can be placed not only at the end of a noun but also after any postmodification which the noun may have (except a relative clause). This postmodification can be an adjective, a prepositional phrase (especially with *of*) or even another noun phrase, which follows the noun and gives more details about it. The following examples of this so-called **group genitive** should make this clear:

1. *James is the Princess Royal's chauffeur and bodyguard.* (The adjective *Royal* postmodifies the noun *Princess*.)
2. *My mother-in-law's Alsatian dog has just had puppies.* (The prepositional phrase *in law* postmodifies the noun *mother* and in this

particular case is given hyphens. Notice that the grammatical plural of *mother-in-law* is *mothers-in-law*.)
3. *The Duke of Wellington's horse bolted and threw its rider.* (The postmodifying prepositional phrase *of Wellington* tells us which duke is being talked about.)
4. *William the Conqueror's death occurred in 1087.* (The proper noun *William* is here postmodified by the noun phrase *the Conqueror*. When two nouns or noun phrases stand side by side in this way and could be given an equal sign, e.g. *William = the Conqueror*, they are said to be in **apposition** to each other and treated as a group noun when the genitive is required. Compare also *my brother John's fiancée*.)
5. *We went to old Mrs What's-her-name's cottage yesterday*. (This splendid group noun, used in colloquial English when we have forgotten a person's name, has an entire question *what's her name* postmodifying the noun (title) *Mrs*.

Readers who enjoy riddles may like to puzzle over the following sentence, which at first sight appears illogical: *The daughter of Pharaoh's son was the son of Pharaoh's daughter*. If the first noun phrase is analysed as containing a group genitive and the second noun phrase as containing a normal *-s* genitive, we are talking about the son in both cases. However, if the first noun phrase is analysed as containing the normal *-s* genitive (*The daughter of Pharaoh's son*) and the second as containing the group genitive (*the son of Pharaoh's daughter*), we are now talking about the daughter in both cases.
Note that group genitives can also be found with pronouns: *someone else's book, anybody else's opinion*.

Co-ordinate Genitive

Rather similar to the situation we saw in example (4) above (with two nouns or noun phrases in apposition treated as a group) are those cases where two nouns or noun phrases are linked together by the co-ordinating conjunction *and*. These too can be considered as a group, but also treated as separate entities. Thus *John and Mary's children* refers to only one family if *John and Mary* is considered as a group noun; but the expression can also be understood as referring to an individual person called *John* in addition to Mary's children. Note, however, if two different families are involved the construction must be *John's and Mary's children*. Though two genitives are involved in the latter construction, this should not be confused with what grammar calls the double genitive construction.

Double Genitive

This term is reserved for a construction which foreign learners may have difficulty with. It consists of an *of*-genitive phrase containing an inflected genitive noun (or pronoun) and the whole phrase postmodifies another noun, e.g. *a friend of Janet's, an acquaintance of the sailor's, an opera of mine*. The double genitive construction can only be used if the head noun (the noun which the whole phrase is about, e.g. *friend, acquaintance, opera* in the examples above) is **indefinite**, i.e. accompanied by a determiner such as *a(n), any, some*. It must not be preceded by the definite article: we cannot say *He is *the friend of Janet's* or *Allow me to introduce *the acquaintance of the sailor's*. Furthermore, the noun in the postmodifying double genitive construction (*Janet, the sailor*) must be **human** and **definite**. Proper nouns like *Janet* automatically fulfil this condition, whereas common nouns denoting humans like *sailor* must be given the definite article *the*. It is therefore ungrammatical to say *an acquaintance of *a sailor's* (where *sailor*, though human, is indefinite). Neither can we say *a window of *the building's* (where the genitive noun *building* is neither human nor definite), nor *a window of *a building's* (where the noun is indefinite but not human). Notice that when animals are treated as human beings, the noun denoting them can also be used in the double genitive construction: *that's a habit of our dog's too*.

Presuppositions

Normally the double genitive construction *an X of Y's* has exactly the same meaning as *one of Y's Xs*. Thus *a friend of Janet's* is semantically equivalent to *one of Janet's friends*, but note that the former focuses attention on *Janet* whereas the latter has end focus on *friends*. Furthermore, the two phrases carry different presuppositions. Whereas *(he is) a friend of Janet's* can be used whether Janet has several friends or only one, *(he is) one of Janet's friends* presupposes that she has more than one. Notice too that the double genitive construction cannot be used if the head noun that it postmodifies is unique, e.g. **a Pastoral Symphony of Beethoven's* would imply that Beethoven had written more than one Pastoral Symphony. Whereas it would be impossible for Beethoven to write another Pastoral Symphony, Janet could have additional friends, even if she has only one at the moment.

Classification of Genitives

Both the inflectional and the prepositional genitive are used for a multitude of purposes. We have only enough space to consider a few of the most interesting ones here. Basically there are two major classes of genitive constructions depending on the relationship between the head noun of the phrase and the genitive noun postmodifying it. In one class of genitive the relationship is **functional**, i.e. it reflects the functions which certain components have with respect to one another within a sentence: in the other class the relationship is **semantic** and much more open to dispute. Let us look first at the functional relationships.

Subjective Genitive

The relationship between some genitive nouns and the other noun that accompanies them in the phrase is the same as that of the subject noun phrase and the verb in a sentence. For example, the genitive noun phrase *his father's belief* is functionally equivalent to the sentence *his father believes*. In the sentence the noun phrase *his father* is the subject of the verb *believes*. Therefore the genitive in the equivalent noun phrase can be called a **subjective genitive**. Another example of the same type but this time with a prepositional genitive in the genitive phrase, would be *the fall of the dollar*, which could be replaced by the sentence *the dollar fell*, where the noun *dollar* is the subject of the verb *fell*.

Objective Genitive

If we compare these two examples with *Napoleon's defeat by the English*, we see a different functional relationship reflected in the genitive. At first sight, we might think that the equivalent sentence should be *Napoleon was defeated by the English*. However, this sentence is passive, whereas those for the subjective genitives above are active. Since we cannot usefully compare a passive sentence with an active one, the passive must be converted into the equivalent active: *the English defeated Napoleon*. Here the noun *Napoleon* is the object of the verb *defeated*. Since the relationship between *Napoleon* and the noun *defeat* in the genitive phrase is the same as that between *Napoleon* and the verb *defeated* in the equivalent sentence, we can refer to this type of genitive as an **objective genitive**. In many cases the active equivalent sentence has to be given a general subject such as *they*. For example, the sentence corresponding to *the President's election* would have to be *they elected the President*. In this active sentence the noun *President* is the object of the verb *elected* and therefore the corresponding genitive phrase is an example of an objective genitive. Like the subjective genitive, the objective type is not limited to phrases with an inflected genitive noun but can also be found with the *of* genitive: *the use of iron* (= *they use iron*).

Appositional Genitive

Another type of genitive which could be classified as functional is the **appositional genitive**. This construction always contains the preposition *of* between a noun phrase and another noun which are in apposition to each other, i.e. which could have an equal sign between them, e.g. *the city of London* (*the city* = *London*), *the borough of Eton* (*the borough* = *Eton*), *the county of Kent* (*the county* = *Kent*). Note that the noun phrase before the *of*-genitive is always introduced by the definite article *the*.

Possessive Genitive

We mentioned above that the class of genitives which can be labelled as semantic is very large and subject to dispute. For example, the phrase *Jenny's picture* can have many meanings depending on the context: a picture somebody has painted of Jenny, a picture Jenny herself has painted, a picture somebody has promised to give Jenny, a picture in a window which Jenny liked, etc. It would be difficult to give each of these a name, but some can be easily recognized. One of these is the **possessive genitive**. Underlying the phrases *Cyril's sister, the orbit of Mars* are the sentences *Cyril has a sister, Mars has an orbit*. Notice too that the semantic classification can overlap with the functional. For example, *his father's belief*, which we analysed above as a subjective genitive on functional grounds, could also be considered as a possessive genitive since it has an underlying sentence *his father has a belief.*

Maßeinheit

Measure Genitive

Another semantic type of genitive which can easily be recognized is the **genitive of measure**, which can be constructed with either the preposition *of* or with the *-s* inflection. Examples: *a three days' journey / a journey of three days, a five minutes' walk / a walk of five minutes, a two months' holiday / a holiday of two months.* The inflectional *-s* is neither written nor pronounced here but indicated merely by the apostrophe. Also considered as genitives of measure by some people are phrases such as *the height of the tower, the depth of the river, the length of the speech*, which can usually only be constructed with *of.*

6 Gerunds

Characteristics

Before leaving our brief survey of the word class nouns, we must look for a moment at gerunds, which occupy an intermediate position between nouns and verbs. A **gerund** is the *-ing* form of a verb which behaves in some ways like a noun and in others like a verb. Consider the following pairs of sentences:

1a. *The breaking of a promise happens every day.*
1b. *His never breaking a promise pleased everyone.*
2a. *Her sudden closing of the shop had not been expected.*
2b. *Her suddenly closing the shop surprised everybody.*

In all these sentences the gerunds *breaking, closing* are premodified by the definite article or by another determiner (*his, her*), which is characteristic of nouns. In sentences (1a) and (2a) we see two other noun-like characteristics: the gerund is followed by an *of*-genitive in each case, and in (2a) it is preceded by an adjective (*sudden*). In sentences (1b) and (2b), however, the gerund clearly shows more verb-like characteristics: it takes a direct object without a preposition (*a promise, the shop*) and is modified by an adverb (*never, suddenly*) and not an adjective. The gerund in (2a) with premodifying adjective and followed by an *of*-genitive has the same meaning as the gerund in (2b) with a direct object and adverbial modification, but stylistically (2a) is a little more formal.

After Preps	Like nouns, gerunds can also follow prepositions, e.g. *On seeing him they wept with joy. I'm looking forward to meeting them. Why do you insist on keeping those letters?*

2 Adjectives

General Remarks

As a word class, adjectives are not nearly as complicated as nouns. Adjectives can be defined as words which are used to specify the qualities or attributes of a noun or pronoun. They are found either in the noun phrase containing that noun or after verbs like *be*, *seem*. Words such as *big*, *round*, *hopeful*, *complicated*, *wrong* give us more information about the noun or pronoun they modify in noun phrases like *a big smile, the round table, her hopeful attitude* or in sentences like *Jim's answer seems complicated, Something is wrong*. Like nouns, adjectives can usually be recognized by their inflections and their positions. Instead of dealing with these separately, as we did for nouns, it will be more convenient to examine them in connexion with some of the other more important characteristics of adjectives, namely their **gradability**, whether they are **attributive or predicative**, and their **order in the noun phrase**.

1 Gradability

Gradable

Most English adjectives are **gradable**, i.e. the quality or attribute which they specify can be thought of as ranging along a **scale**. Thus we can refer to different degrees of it. In consequence, a gradable adjective can be used in the **comparative** and **superlative** and also be **premodified by a degree adverb**, i.e. by an adverb which specifies the degree to which the quality or attribute is present. Thus we can talk of *a small elephant*, *a smaller elephant*, *the smallest elephant* and *a very small elephant*. There is a scale of smallness along which each elephant can be placed. Note that the scale differs depending on the noun that the adjective modifies: a small elephant is considerably larger than a small rat. The speaker adjusts the scale for each adjective according to his knowledge of the world: he must know the size of a normal elephant or a normal rat in order to be able to refer to a particular specimen as small.

Comparison

The comparison of gradable adjectives is of two kinds:

1. **Synthetic**: the adjective takes the inflectional suffixes *-er* for the comparative and *-est* for the superlative, e.g. (*hot*) *hotter*, *hottest*; (*happy*) *happier*, *happiest*.
2. **Analytic**: the adjective forms the comparative with *more* and the superlative with *most*, e.g. *more expensive*, *most entertaining*.

Synthetic

Synthetic comparison is used with all gradable adjectives of **one syllable**: *big/bigger/biggest, slim/slimmer/slimmest, tall/taller/tallest, weak/weaker/weakest, deaf/deafer/deafest*. In the spelling, a single final consonant after a single written vowel is doubled, as in the first two examples in the last sentence. A final semivowel (*w, y*) is not doubled: *low/lower, gay/gayer*. Also after two written vowels (*weak*) or two written consonants (*thick*) no doubling takes place (*weaker, weakest, thicker, thickest*). Most gradable adjectives of **two syllables** which **end in the semivowel** *y* (*happy, friendly*) or which **have final stress** (*polite, sincere*) also form their comparative and superlative synthetically: in the spelling, the former change the semivowel into *i* before adding the suffixes *-er, -est* (*happier, happiest; friendlier, friendliest*), whereas the latter, since they already end in *e*, merely add *-r, -st* (*politer, politest; sincerer, sincerest*).

Analytic

Analytic comparison is used with all gradable adjectives of **three or** more syllables (*more difficult, more preferable, more sceptical, most democratic, most expensive*) and with most gradable **two-syllable** adjectives which have initial stress and **end in a consonant** (*more cautious, more painful, most selfish, most horrid, most random*). Also with participles when these are used adjectivally: *more criticized, most interesting*.

With Degree Adverbs

Instead of the comparative or the superlative degree of the quality denoted by the adjective, we may also wish to express just a high or medium or small degree. For this purpose one of the following degree adverbs can be used with the adjective: (**high degree**) *very, extremely, incredibly*; (**medium degree**) *rather, quite, fairly*; (**small degree**) *slightly*. The adverbs expressing a high degree are often referred to as **intensifiers**. In colloquial speech several other intensifiers are found, such as *terribly, awfully, frightfully*, and often *pretty* is used as a medium degree adverb: *a terribly interesting film, a pretty stupid idea*. Note too that whereas *quite* is often used in American English as an intensifier, in British English it is a medium degree adverb. Thus the sentence *the child is quite intelligent* said by an enthusiastic American might be understood by a British speaker to mean that the child is of only moderate intelligence.

Limit Adjectives

Some adjectives like *perfect, unique, impossible, worthless, priceless, superb, marvellous* have meanings which are at the limit of a scale. They indicate the highest or absolute degree on that scale. Such **limit adjectives** are strictly speaking not gradable, as they cannot be made comparative or superlative, nor can they be used with an intensifier. However, they can usually take an adverb such as *absolutely, totally, utterly, completely*, which confirms the absolute degree that they express, e.g. *the scene was absolutely perfect; a com-*

pletely worthless painting, and some of them can also be modified by an adverb such as *almost, nearly, practically*, which indicates closeness to this absolute degree, e.g. *an almost impossible solution; this remedy is practically unique in modern medicine*.

Non-gradable

Non-gradable adjectives have meanings which cannot be placed on a scale. They are **classifying** rather than qualitative: they assign the noun which they modify to a particular class. A noun either belongs to that class or it does not. There are no degrees of belonging. An adjective of this kind is the word *female*. Something is either *female* or it is not. Other non-gradable adjectives are *electric, foreign, southern, wooden, woollen, wrong, single, married, daily, monthly, French, German*. Logically non-gradable adjectives have no comparative or superlative forms and cannot be used with degree adjectives. However, sometimes it is possible to give a normally non-gradable adjective a meaning which is scalar. Adjectives of nationality can be used in this way. If I am thinking of the class of people who are Frenchmen or Germans by nationality, then the adjectives *French, German* are non-gradable, but if I am more interested in the qualities or characteristics which Frenchmen or Germans possess, then I can think of a person as having more or fewer of these. In the latter case the same adjectives are now gradable and it is perfectly grammatical to say *Marie is more French than her sister* or *Heinz is very German*.

2 Attributive/Predicative

Attributive

Another important characteristic of adjectives is whether they can be attributive, predicative, or both. An adjective is **attributive** when it is part of the **premodification** of a noun, i.e. when it is found in front of the head noun in a noun phrase. There may or may not be a determiner (article or similar word) in front of the adjective, depending on whether the noun is countable or not. Let us consider again the noun phrases *a big smile, the round table, her hopeful attitude*, which we saw at the very beginning of our discussion of adjectives. The noun in each (*smile, table, attitude*) is premodified by a determiner (*a, the, her*) followed by an adjective (*big, round, hopeful*). Whether the adjective within the noun phrase is itself premodified by an adverb of degree, as in *a <u>very big</u> smile, the <u>extremely small</u> table, her <u>more hopeful</u> attitude*, or whether the adjective is preceded by a determiner or not, as in *our happy memories, good food, cheap wine*, makes no difference. In all these noun phrases the adjective is being used attributively. In a small number of fixed expressions or titles (generally borrowed from Old French) such as *a court <u>martial</u>, a notary <u>public</u>, the Princess <u>Royal</u>,* *the Postmaster General*, the adjective **follows the head noun** but is still part of the noun phrase. Adjectives in this position (**postmodifying** the head noun) are also attributive. Notice that they are usually non-gradable.

Predicative

A **predicative** adjective is one which is found **after a linking** (or **copular**) **verb**, i.e. after *be, become* or verbs of visual perception like *look, seem, appear*, which could be replaced by *be* without much loss of meaning: *the child was (became, looked, seemed, appeared) depressed*. Other verbs of sensory perception also function as linking verbs and can then be followed by a predicative adjective: *the cake tasted sweet, the music sounds pleasant, the cloth felt rough*. Here too the perception verb (*tasted, sounds, felt*) could be replaced by one of the forms of *be* (*was, is*). Note that the predicative adjective is **not part of a noun phrase** but does refer back to the noun in front of the linking verb (*child, cake, music, cloth* in our examples above).

Both

Most adjectives can be used in **both attributive and predicative** position. For example, in the preceding paragraph we can replace all the sentences which have predicative adjectives by corresponding noun phrases with attributive adjectives: *a depressed child, sweet cake, pleasant music, rough cloth.*

Only Attributive

There are, however, a number of adjectives which can be used **only attributively**. Some of these are *chief, main, principal; mere, sheer, utter; lone; inner, outer, upper; hourly, daily, monthly; elder, former, latter.* For example, although we can say *the chief reason, utter nonsense, a lone fox, an upper room, my elder brother*, it is ungrammatical to say **the reason is chief, *(the) nonsense is utter, *the fox is lone, *the room is upper, *my brother is elder.* It will be noticed that many of these only-attributive adjectives are **limit adjectives**, adjectives whose meanings are at the extreme end of a scale. Also belonging to this only-attributive class are many of the **non-gradable classifying adjectives**, which are therefore acceptable in noun phrases such as *the atomic bomb, the bridal suite, a neighbouring country, an indoor swimming-pool* but not in sentences like **The bomb was atomic, *The suite was bridal, *The country was neighbouring, *The swimming-pool was indoor.*

Only Predicative

Some adjectives are found **only in predicative position**. A fairly large group of adjectives which begin with *a-* and which are often derived from verbs fall into this class, e.g. *afraid, alike, alive, alone, ashamed, asleep, awake, ablaze, afloat, aghast*. Many of these have attributive counterparts: *the pilot felt afraid, a frightened pilot; the fish was alive, a live fish; the child is asleep, a sleeping child; her mother was aghast, her horrified mother.* Among those only-predicative adjectives which do not begin with *a-* are the common words *ill,* *well, glad, sure (= convinced), content, ready.* Some of these too have attributive equivalents: *her uncle became ill, her sick uncle; the child looked well, a healthy child; the men were sure of it, the convinced men; the cat seemed content, a contented cat.*

Meaning Change

Some adjectives may have one meaning when they are attributive and another when they are predicative. For example, attributively *old* can mean 'long-standing' as in the phrase *an old friend*, but predicatively as in the sentence *his friend is old* it always means 'advanced in years'. Similarly, in *the late King* the adjective means 'who has recently died', whereas in *the King was late* it means 'not on time'. Some adjectives in attributive position have a meaning which reflects the feelings of the speaker towards the person or thing denoted by the head noun whereas in predicative position they have a neutral meaning. Compare *a close friend* (= a person with whom one has close ties of friendship) with *my friend was close* (= near to me in space); or *this poor child* (= a child whom I pity) with *the child was poor* (= had little money); or *my dear daughter* (= much loved) with *the book was dear* (= expensive).

3 Adjective Complements

Types

When used predicatively, some adjectives are not complete unless they are followed by a phrase introduced by a special preposition, whereas others require a *to* + infinitive phrase or a *that*-clause after them. These phrases or clauses which complete the sense of the adjective are referred to as the adjective's **complement**. Sometimes the complement may be omitted, but it can almost always be restored by the listener. For example, if we say that something is *close*, we can usually tell from the context whether this means *close to us, close to you, close to the railway station, etc.* Notice that most adjectives with a complement can also be used attributively but must then be placed after the noun, i.e. in postmodifying position. For example, in the noun phrase *the large building close to the church*, the adjective *close* with its prepositional complement (*to the church*) postmodifies the head noun *building*.

+ Prep

The most common prepositions introducing adjective complements are *to* and *of*. Some of those **followed by *to*** are *accustomed, averse, close, conducive, devoted, prone, resigned, resistant, similar.* Examples: *They are accustomed to hard work. This pattern is similar to that one.* Among the adjectives **followed by** *of* we find: *characteristic, typical, afraid, frightened, aware, capable, devoid, fond, full, glad, proud, indicative, reminiscent.* Examples: *This style is characteristic of Ernest Hemingway. That book is completely devoid of interest. Her smile is reminiscent of da Vinci's La Gioconda.* Some adjectives are **followed by other prepositions** (sometimes there is a choice between two): *based on, compatible with, connected with/to, dependent on/upon, different from/to, filled with, intent upon, lacking in, parallel with/to, rooted in*. Examples: *This theory is based on Einstein's. The pipe was connected with/to the engine. Emma's views were different from/to her cousin's.* Note that in careful English *different* is usually followed by *from*, but in colloquial speech we often hear *to* and in American English also *than*.

***to* + Infinitive**

Many adjectives can complete their meaning by adding an infinitive preceded by *to*. Among the **commonest** are *able, unable, fit, inclined, liable, likely, prepared, willing, unwilling*. Examples: *The sailors were able to rescue all the passengers. He is not fit to be a governor. They were unwilling to accept the money.* In addition to these, some of the adjectives which we listed above as needing the preposition *of* can also have a *to* + infinitive complement: *They were frightened to look. He seemed afraid to reply. We were glad to go. I was proud to meet her.* Care must be taken with adjectives followed by the preposition *to*, as these require a gerund after the preposition and not an infinitive: *They were accustomed to paying for themselves* (not **to pay*). *The child was close to revealing the secret* (not **to reveal*). *Jack was prone to telling lies* (not **to tell*).

***that* + Clause**

Those adjectives which show what a person thinks or feels can often have a complement that is a clause introduced by the conjunction *that*. Among these are: *aware, unaware, certain, uncertain, sure, unsure, afraid, angry, glad, happy, pleased, proud, sorry, surprised, worried*. Note that the conjunction is necessary in formal English but often omitted in less formal contexts. Examples: *The judges were unaware that he was foreign. The swimmer was proud that she had won the race. The parents were worried that their child might be handicapped. I'm sure I have a cold.*

4 Order of Adjectives

Gradable

When adjectives premodify a noun in a noun phrase it is usual for those which indicate qualities to come before those which assign the noun to a particular class, i.e. gradable adjectives precede non-gradable ones. The normal order of gradable adjectives depends on their meaning: an adjective denoting **a pleasant** or **unpleasant quality** (Q) precedes an adjective of **size** (Si). Then come adjectives of **age** (A), **temperature** (T) and **shape** (Sh), in that order. Up to three gradable premodifying adjectives are acceptable, e.g. *a funny*(Q) *little*(Si) *old*(A) *man, a tiny*(Si) *young*(A) *round-faced*(Sh) *child, a small*(Si) *old*(A) *rectangular*(Sh) *building, a large*(Si) *hot*(T) *thick*(Sh) *steak*, but normally two sound more natural, e.g. *a comfortable*(Q) *little*(Si) *house, a huge*(Si) *fat*(Sh) *pig, an ancient*(A) *frozen*(T) *leaf.* It must be emphasized that this is the normal order, but deviations are possible if the speaker wishes to emphasize one particular characteristic in preference to another. If I have been talking about *hot steaks* already, I can go on to differentiate *thick hot steaks* from *thin hot steaks.*

Non-Gradable

Non-gradable adjectives also normally occur in a specific order in premodifying position: colour (C), origin (O), material (M), purpose (P), e.g. *a green*(C) *Chinese*(O) *cooking*(P) *pot, a red*(C) *silk*(M) *tie, some French*(O) *woollen*(M) *pullovers.*

Both

When both gradable and non-gradable adjectives premodify a noun, the gradable ones usually occur first in the order we have described and are then followed by any gradable adjectives in their own specific order. Examples: *a beautiful*(Q) *small*(Si) *round* (Sh) *Egyptian*(O) *table, a fine*(Q) *old*(A) *Persian*(O) *earthen*(M) *pot.*

Modifying Nouns

The positions which we described as (M) for material and (P) for purpose are frequently occupied by a noun. Nouns in this position are referred to as **modifying nouns** and have adjectival function. For example, instead of *an earthen pot* we could have *a steel pot* or *an iron pot*, where in each case a noun replaces the adjective in describing the material of which the pot is made. Instead of *a carving knife* (= a knife with which we can carve) we could have *a cake knife* (= a knife used for cake). In the case of these *-ing* forms, e.g. in *a cooking pot* or *a carving knife*, we could argue about whether they are verbal participles used as an adjective or whether they are gerunds (noun forms of the verb): not only does a pot cook, but it is also a pot for cooking. Similarly, a knife not only carves but is also a knife for carving. The analysis as a gerund seems to be strengthened by such examples as *a writing table, a walking stick*, where the table is for writing but itself does not write and the stick is for walking but itself does not walk. The reason for the difficulty in the analysis is, as we saw above, that a noun that premodifies another noun is in fact behaving like an adjective. It is also not like a normal noun in other ways: for example, in *a currant bun* the modifying noun *currant* cannot be plural, though a bun of this kind certainly must contain more than one currant (compare also: *a cherry pie, a fig tart, a dog show*). Another oddity of the same kind occurs with pair plural nouns such as *trousers, pyjamas* when they are used as modifying nouns: they lose their final *-s* in this position: *a trouser leg, a pyjama jacket.*

3 Determiners

Note

Determiners and pronouns belong each to a separate word class, but the same word can often be found in both classes. We shall deal with the determiners alone in this subchapter, and then in the subchapter on pronouns we can make comparisons between the two classes.

1 General Remarks

Definition

A **determiner** is a word used in front of a noun to identify it or to limit its meaning in some way, e.g. by making it specific, non-specific, by quantifying it, etc. For example, *horses* refers in general to that species of animal, but *the horses* limits them to a group of specific horses, *several horses* picks out a certain number of them, whereas *his horses* identifies the group as belonging to a certain person. If any adjectives premodify the noun, the determiner always precedes them: *the helpless small child, several large oval windows.*

Table

Since determiners belong to a closed set, the simplest way of presenting them is by listing them, as in the following table:

Predeterminer	Central Determiner	Postdeterminer
a. *all, half, both*	a. Articles: *the, a(n)*	a. Cardinal Numerals: *one, two, three . . .*
b. *double, twice, treble*	b. Demonstratives: *this, these, that, those*	b. Ordinal Numbers: *first, second, third . . .*
c. *what! such*	c. Possesives: *my, your, his, her, its, our, their*	c. General Ordinals: *next, last, other, (another = an + other) . . .*
	d. Quantifiers: *some, any, no* *each* *less, fewer* *much* *enough, several* *either, neither*	d. Quantifiers: *little, few* *every* *least, fewest* *many, more, most*
	e. Wh-Determiners: *what, which, whose* *whatever, whichever*	

Characteristics

Determiners such as the articles, the demonstrative and possessive determiners are classified as **central determiners** because they can be preceded and followed by certain other determiners. Those coming before the central determiners are referred to as **predeterminers**, those that come after as **postdeterminers**. A typical noun phrase with all these three types of determiner is the one you have just read: *all*(preD) *these*(CD) *three*(postD) *types*. Note that the predeterminers cannot combine with every central determiner, nor can the central determiners be followed by every postdeterminer. It will be easiest to illustrate these combinations if we look at each group in the table above separately.

2 Predeterminers

all, half, both

When the head noun is countable and plural, each of the **predeterminers** *all, half* and *both* can regularly precede the definite article or one of the demonstrative or possessive central determiners (*all/half/both the stories, all/half/both these rumours, all/half/both my brothers*). Only *half* can be used with the indefinite article (*half a minute*). Both *all* and *half* can also occur with the definite article or a singular demonstrative determiner or a possessive determiner in front of a non-count noun (*all/half the cheese, all/half that energy, all/half my salary*. The predeterminer *both* cannot be used in this way as it never appears before a non-count noun. Note that when *all* and *both* are used immediately in front of a plural count noun without an article intervening, as in *all birds have wings, both musicians are dead*, they must be classified as **central determiners** as they stand in place of the article here.

double, twice, treble

The predeterminers *double, twice, treble* cannot be used before the indefinite article but do occur in front of the definite article, all the demonstrative and all the possessive determiners, e.g. *He is paid double the wage I get. He gets double my pay. This portion is twice the size of that one. In that bank you pay twice our fees for the same service. You can win treble that amount here. He has just lost treble our wages on one horse.*

what! such

As a **predeterminer** *what!* is found only in exclamations and then always in front of the indefinite article, e.g. *what an idiot! what a good idea!* The **predeterminer** *such* can also occur before *a(n)* in exclamations (*such a nice person! such an ugly remark!*), but is found in this combination elsewhere too (*They made such a noise that she left at once. I need a cigarette, do you have such a thing?*). Both *what!* and *such* can appear before a plural count noun without an article (*what pretty eyes! such large feet! In such cases we always charge a fee*). Since in this position they replace the article, they can be considered here as **central determiners**. In formal English *such* is often used in this way as a central determiner when it means *of this kind*, e.g. *such crimes will be severely punished*. Both *what!* and *such* are also central determiners when they appear directly before a non-count noun (i.e. with no article intervening), e.g. *what impertinence! such elegance! Such people should be ashamed*. Sometimes when *such* means *of this kind*, it is preceded by one of the quantifying central determiners, e.g. *some such idea, any such thought, no such thing,* or by a postdeterminer which is a general ordinal, e.g. *other such suggestions, another such insult*. When used in these positions, it must be classified as a **postdeterminer**.

3 Central Determiners

Articles

Of the central determiners the definite article *the* and the indefinite article *a(n)* are the most common. Normally *the* can be used in front of any common noun, but it is sometimes found before a proper noun when this is postmodified, e.g. in the phrase *the Mary whom you mentioned*, where the relative clause postmodifies the proper noun *Mary*. The indefinite article *a(n)* normally precedes only count nouns, but it can sometimes be found with a non-count noun if this is accompanied by either a premodifying adjective as in *an insatiable inquisitiveness* or by a postmodifying phrase or relative clause as in *a devotion to music, a devotion which nobody understood*. As we saw above, the indefinite article is the only one of the central determiners with which certain predeterminers can combine. It is for this reason that we choose the articles to help us to decide whether another determiner is a predeterminer, a central determiner or a post determiner. In a noun phrase, if a determiner can precede one of the articles it is a predeterminer, if it follows one of the articles it is a post determiner, and if it can replace one of the articles, it is a central determiner (cf. one use of *all, both, what!* and *such* above).

Demonstratives

Of the central determiners the demonstratives are the only ones which have a separate singular form (*this, that*) and a separate plural form (*these, those*). Normally the singular form is found before non-count nouns or singular count nouns and the plural form only before plural count nouns. However, we have seen that some nouns are semantically plural though their form is singular. These always take the plural demonstrative: *these cattle, those people*. We also saw that a formally plural noun phrase can sometimes be treated as a singular unit. In this case it takes a singular demonstrative, e.g. *this six dollars has to last till tomorrow*, where *six dollars = sum of six dollars*.

Possessives

Of all the determiners the possessives are the only ones which are differentiated for person, gender and number. The plural forms are less differentiated than the singular ones. Whereas the third person singular determiner has a masculine form *his*, a feminine form *her* and a neuter form *its*, the third person plural determiner has only one form for all three genders *their*. The first and second persons are not differentiated for gender, but show number differences: first person singular *my* (and in older English *mine* before a vowel, e.g. *mine eyes*), first person plural *our*. In Modern English the second person singular has a common form for both singular and plural: *your*. In older English there was a separate singular form *thy* (and *thine* before a vowel, e.g. *thine uncle*). Notice that the place of a possessive determiner in a noun phrase can be taken by a noun with genitive *-s*, e.g. instead of *her last three letters* we could say *Mary's last three letters*. It is for this reason that genitive nouns in this position are sometimes referred to as determiners.

Quantifiers

In the table on page 45 some of the quantifiers have been classified as central determiners and others as postdeterminers. Those that are listed as central determiners (*some, any, no, each, less, fewer, much, enough, several, either, neither)* cannot be used in a quantifying sense with another central determiner. They are always used alone, replacing one of the articles.

some, any

Both *some* and *any* are found before a non-count noun or before a plural count noun. Whereas *some* refers to an indefinite quantity or number in a **positive** context, *any* has this reference only in **negative** contexts or contexts where the speaker might expect a **negative reaction**, e.g. in questions, *if*-clauses, etc. The following examples should make this clear:

1. *Jason has brought some fruit and some flowers*. (We can see them)
2. *Do you want some cake?* (I expect you to say yes)
3. *Do they want any cake?* (The answer expected is no)
4. *Mary never has any money*. (Negative context with *never*)
5. *Did you see any people there?* (The person asking this question is not very hopeful of receiving a positive answer)
6. *If you have any complaints, speak now.* (The speaker either expects or hopes that there will be none)

no, neither

The central determiner *no* indicates a negative quantity or number of persons or things and can be used before any singular or plural noun, e.g. *They found no clue/no clues. No mail came today.* On the other hand, the central determiner *neither* restricts the negative quantity or number to only two persons or things and can be used only with a singular count noun, e.g. *She can use neither foot. Neither eye was injured.*

each, either

Similarly *each* refers to one of a number of individuals in turn, whereas *either* refers to one of only two: *Each child was praised. This shoe fits either foot.*

less, fewer

In careful English *less* is found only in front of non-count nouns (*less money, less attention*) and *fewer* is used before plural count nouns (*fewer apples, fewer mistakes*) or semantically plural nouns (*fewer people, fewer cattle*). In colloquial English, however, *less* often replaces *fewer* in both of these contexts. (Note that *much* in phrases such as *much less money, much less attention* is an adverb of degree meaning 'by far' and therefore *less* is a normal central determiner here, not a postdeterminer.)

much

In normal spoken English, *much* is found as a determiner only in negative contexts and always preceding a non-count noun: *They didn't have much incentive to work. There was never much time.* In affirmative contexts one of the more colloquial quantifiers is preferred, such as *a lot of, lots of, masses of, etc.* e.g. *She showed a lot of courage. There's lots of time.* In the latter example the quantifying expression *lots of* is not interpreted as a plural noun plus a preposition but as a determiner like *much*, as we can see from the singular verb agreement (*is*).

enough

The word *enough* is the odd man out amongst the central determiners as it occurs not only in premodifying position in a noun phrase, e.g. *enough money, enough weapons* but also in postmodifying position, e.g. *He has money enough. They have weapons enough to win.* This latter usage is found normally only in formal English.

several

The determiner *several* is used before a plural count noun to refer to a moderate number of persons or things: *Several musicians had flu. They ate several chocolates.* (Note that the same word after a central determiner in a sentence like *The men shook hands and went their several ways* is not a determiner but an adjective with the meaning 'separate, respective'.)

Mixed Quantifiers

The postdeterminers that are listed in the table on page 45 as quantifiers (*little, few, every, least, fewest, many, more, most*) are really mixed determiners. They can all be used as central determiners, replacing one of the articles or a demonstrative or possessive determiner, e.g. *He has little money. Few people like them. Every child knows that. Who did it with least effort? Which of them imposed fewest conditions? Many men smoke. More ships have arrived. Most shops open early.* However, as we shall see below, they can also appear after one of the other central determiners, in which position they must be considered as postdeterminers.

Wh-Determiners

Of the *wh*-determiners *what, which, whose, whatever, whichever* both *what* and *which* can be used before a singular or a plural noun as **interrogative determiners**, but the presupposition behind the question is different in each case. For example, if the assistant in a bookshop asks you *What book are you looking for?*, the question is general and asks about the kind of book. On the other hand the question *Which book are you looking for?* presupposes that that the conversation is about a limited set of books from which you are to mention one. The assistant would therefore use the question with *which*, if she pointed to one of the shelves of a bookcase or to a particular page in a book catalogue. The word *whose* is sometimes an interrogative determiner as in *Whose book is this?* and sometimes a **relative determiner** (i.e. introducing a relative clause) as in the phrase *the customer whose bag was searched.* Notice that *which* too can be a relative determiner in formal English (*She was reading the Times, for which newspaper her pupils had little respect*), whereas *what* never has relative function before a noun. Unlike the other *wh*-determiners, *whichever* and *whatever* are never used as interrogative or relative determiners. They do, however, show the same presupposition differences as we saw for *which* and *what* above. For example, the statement *We can supply whatever paper you need* refers to paper in general (in different amounts, of different kinds), whereas *We can supply whichever paper you need* presupposes that there is a specific number of different types of paper from which you can choose one.

4 Postdeterminers

General Notes

All of the words which we have listed as postdeterminers in the table on page 45 (**cardinal** and **ordinal numerals, general ordinals** and **quantifiers**) are in fact mixed determiners. They are usually found with a central determiner in front of them, i.e. in postdeterminer position, but they themselves can also occur as central determiners when they replace an article, a demonstrative or a possessive determiner. Furthermore, they are found combined with each other, i.e. there may be more than one postdeterminer in a single noun phrase, which never happens with predeterminers and central determiners. We shall see all these points illustrated below.

Cardinal Numerals

As central determiners, the cardinal numerals can be seen in a sentence such as *I have one brother and two sisters*, and as postdeterminers with a central determiner preceding them, in the noun phrases *this one important principle, my two cousins, which three children (do you mean?), every four days.*

Ordinal Numerals

The ordinal numerals normally occur only after a central determiner as in this first *book*, their second *journey*, whose fourth *son?* However, they are sometimes to be seen as central determiners in fixed expressions such as *first aid, first class, first hand, second rate, (to have) second thoughts, (a car) in third gear, (they were involved as) third parties (in wage negotiations).* Some ordinal numerals can sometimes be combined with a cardinal numeral or with the quantifier *few* in the same noun phrase: *the first three arrivals, two second prizes, the first few minutes.*

General Ordinals

The general ordinals *next, last, other* are common both as central determiners (*next week, last September, other ideas*) and as postdeterminers (*the next customer, his last wish, these other patterns, some other events, what other chance?*). They can also combine with cardinal numerals (*the next two trains, one last beer, three other players*) and with the quantifier *few*, as in *the next few days*. Notice that we have listed the word *another* under the postdeterminers as it contains the postdeterminer *other*. However, we could just as easily classify it as a central determiner, since it also contains the central determiner *an* and therefore cannot have another determiner in front of it. Like the other general ordinals it too can combine with a cardinal numeral or *few*, as in *another three whiskies, another few pages.*

Quantifiers

Examples of the quantifiers *little, few, every, least, fewest, many, more, most* as central determiners were given on page 49 (under Mixed Quantifiers). Here we can look at them as postdeterminers in combination with a central determiner or with another postdeterminer.

little, few

The word *little* is used as a postdeterminer (with the meaning of 'a small quantity of') after both articles before a non-count noun (*a little water, the little money we possessed*). Care must be taken not to confuse it with the adjective *little* (= 'small in size'), which can come in front of a singular or plural count noun: *a little girl, the little boys*. The postdeterminer *few* is used only with the plural of count nouns or with a (semantically) plural noun and can come after both articles, the demonstratives and the possessives (with the meaning of 'a small number of'): *a few ideas, the few people you know, these few vegetables, my few friends*. Whereas *little* forms no combinations with other postdeterminers, *few* as a postdeterminer combines with the general ordinals *last, other*, e.g. *their few last remarks, these few other doctors, a few other laws*. Notice that in the sentence *Few other women came* it is a central determiner, as no article precedes it now.

every

In our discussion of mixed determiners on page 49 we saw that *every* can often be used as a central determiner and sometimes as a postdeterminer. In the latter case it can only be preceded by a possessive determiner as in *his every wish (was fulfilled)*, but many speakers would prefer to replace this by *every wish of his*, where *his* is now a pronoun and *every* a central determiner. As a central determiner *every* combines easily with the general ordinal *other* and then always precedes a singular count noun: *every other year, every other person*. For some speakers it can combine with *other* as a postdeterminer after a possessive, e.g. *his every other word was 'bloody'*, but here too most people would prefer to say *every other word of his*. Notice that as a central determiner *every* can combine with a cardinal numeral or with *few* when these are followed by a plural noun in expressions of measurement where the measurement is regarded as a unit, e.g. *every three days, every few metres*. If the numeral is omitted the phrases are ungrammatical: **every days*, **every metres*. (See also 'measurements' on pages 25–26.)

least, fewest

As postdeterminers *least* and *fewest* are found only after the definite article: *without the least difficulty, she made the fewest mistakes*. Furthermore, they do not combine with other postdeterminers.

many, more, most

When the quantifiers *many, more, most* are postdeterminers, both *many* and *most* can have the definite article in front of them, as in *They could not answer the many questions that were asked. She has the most patience*. Only *many* can be used with a preceding possessive determiner: *his many virtues, their many observations*. We often find *more* as a postdeterminer after the quantifier *some* in an affirmative context (*we have bought some more wine*) and after *any* in a negative context (*they didn't want any more cheese*). It also combines with *many* before a plural count noun, as in *many more stamps* and with *much* before a non-count noun, as in *much more pleasure*. However, *much* and *many* here are better analysed as adverbs of degree. The *much* in *much more pleasure* does not go with *pleasure* (we are not talking about *much pleasure*): it modifies the determiner *more*. Even more convincing is the phrase *much less money*, which we saw on page 49 and where *much* modifies the determiner *less* and not the noun *money*. When we use this phrase we are not talking about *much money*. In both examples the word *much* goes closely with *more* or *less*, and has adverbial function telling us to what degree the money or the pleasure is more or less. A similar argument can be made for the adverbial status of *many* in *many more stamps*. Notice too that in all these cases *much* and *many* can be replaced by the adverb *far: far more stamps, far more pleasure, far less money*. It is nevertheless strange that an adverb should have one form (*much*) when it precedes *more* before a non-count noun and another (*many*) when it precedes *more* before a count noun. This is yet another example of the language working at two levels: on the formal level *much* and *more* are determiners, but on the functional level they behave like an adverb.

5 Postdetermining Adjectives

Adj or Det?

There is a small group of **adjectives** which in noun phrases can be found after a central determiner (usually the definite article) and in front of a numeral or quantifying postdeterminer. Among such adjectives are: *only, present, past, previous, remaining, following, same, usual.* Examples: *the* ***only*** *other people I asked, the* ***present*** *three days, the* ***past*** *few weeks, her* ***previous*** *two books, the* ***remaining*** *four dancers, their* ***following*** *last words, the* ***same*** *three dogs, these* ***usual*** *five banknotes.* In measurement expressions (see pages 25–26 above), the adjective *further* can be used in this postdetermining position after the indefinite article and preceding a numeral with a plural noun: *we need a* ***further*** *three hundred pounds.* Note that with the exception of *same* and *usual,* most of these adjectives are concerned with ordering things in time or space, and could therefore equally well be classified among the general ordinal postdeterminers. Like determiners they also precede all other adjectives in the noun phrase: *the* ***only*** *interesting people, her* ***previous*** *new English books, the* ***following*** *comical remarks.*

4 Pronouns

1 General Remarks

Definition

A pronoun, as its name ('pro' noun) suggests, is a word which replaces and refers to a noun or a noun phrase. Many of the pronouns have little meaning in themselves, but assume the meaning of the noun or noun phrase to which they refer. Consider, for example, the pronoun *it*. If you are suddenly asked *did you see it?*, you will have no idea what *it* refers to and will ask for clarification. The questioner will then have to supply the noun or noun phrase which *it* replaces, e.g. *the rainbow, that flash of lightning, the large bird that just flew past.* In the following sections we shall examine ten different kinds of pronoun: **personal, possessive, reflexive, emphatic, demonstrative, interrogative, relative, sentence relative, nominal relative** and **indefinite pronouns.** We shall look at the main characteristics of each type and where possible compare each pronoun with its determiner counterpart.

2 Personal Pronouns

Characteristics

Like the possessive determiners, the personal pronouns together with the possessive, reflexive and emphatic pronouns are the only words in English which are differentiated for grammatical person (first, second, third), gender (masculine, feminine and non-personal or neuter) and number (singular and plural). In addition, the personal pronouns are the only type which shows case differences. Each personal pronoun, apart from *you* and *it*, appears in two case forms: one form when it is in the **subject** or nominative case (i.e. when it is the subject of a verb) and another when it is in the **oblique** case (i.e. everywhere else, e.g. as the object of a verb or after a preposition). The following table will make these differences clear:

Table

(Number)	Singular					Plural		
(Person)	1	2	3			1	2	3
(Subject)	*I*	*you*	*he*	*she*	*it*	*we*	*you*	*they*
(Oblique)	*me*		*him*	*her*		*us*		*them*
(Gender)			M	F	N			

First Person Singular

The tradition of writing the first person pronoun with a capital letter dates back to medieval times. Written small, the single stroke in medieval manuscripts could be taken for part of another letter. For this reason the capital was used to make the pronoun more easily recognizable. The first person pronoun has a separate singular and plural form, each of which has a subject case (*I, we*) and an oblique case (*me, us*). In substandard speech, the singular oblique form is often used as part of a co-ordinate subject of a verb, e.g. **Me and the boss did it* instead of the grammatical *The boss and I did it.* As several generations of children have been taught that in co-ordinations the oblique form *me* should be avoided, it is not surprising that where it should be used, e.g. after a preposition (e.g. *for the boss and me)* we quite often hear the grammatically incorrect subject case form (e.g. *for the boss and *I*) even from educated speakers of standard English. Notice, however, that although many of the older prescriptive grammar books insisted that the subject case pronoun should be used after the verb *be*, as in *it is I*, modern usage prefers the oblique case here, e.g. *it's me*. On the other hand, in careful English the subject case form is used when a relative clause immediately follows, e.g. *It is I who made this promise.* What has just been said about the first person singular pronoun applies also to the other personal pronouns when used after *be*. The subject case pronouns in such sentences as *it is we, it was he, it is they, etc.* all sound stilted in educated spoken English and are usually replace by the oblique case pronouns: *it is us, it was him, it is them, etc.* However, they are preferable in written English when a relative clause follows: *It was we who told him. It was he who made the mistake. It is they who should be required to pay the bill.*

First Person Plural

The first person plural pronoun in English is both inclusive and exclusive, i.e. it can refer to the speaker and his hearer or hearers ('**inclusive *we***') and it can also refer to the speaker and to some person or persons other than the hearer or hearers ('**exclusive *we***'). In some languages inclusive and exclusive *we* are separate pronouns. Notice too that in archaic English, e.g. in royal documents, the monarch can use *We, Us* (written with an initial capital letter) to refer to himself/herself. This is usually called the '**royal *We***'. Written with a small letter, *we* is similarly used in formal English in books, newspapers or journals by an author or an editor referring to himself/herself and is then called '**editorial *we***'.

Second Person

In Modern English the second person pronoun *you* is the least differentiated pronoun. It has the same form for both singular and plural and this remains unchanged in the subject and oblique case. In older English, e.g. in Shakespeare's plays, there were separate second person pronouns for singular and plural and these had separate forms for the subject case (*thou, ye*) and the oblique case (*thee, you*). The old singular forms are still used in present-day northern dialects in England. The plural subject form *ye* can still occasionally be heard in the old-fashioned exclamation *ye Gods!* The original oblique case form *you* was later generalized and now replaces all the other historical differentiated second person forms.

Third Person

It will be noticed that only the third person singular pronouns have different forms for masculine (M), feminine (F) and non-personal (N), depending on whether the referent is male, female or neither. The masculine and feminine forms are further differentiated by each having a subject case form (*he, she*) and an oblique case form (*him, her*), whereas the non-personal pronoun *it* has the same form for both cases. Like the other Germanic languages, English has no gender differentiation in the plural. There is only one pronoun for all three genders, but it has a subject form (*they*) and an oblique form (*them*). Note finally that in Christian writings the third person singular masculine pronoun is written with a capital (*He, Him*) when it refers to God or to Christ. This rule also applies to the third person singular masculine possessive, reflexive and emphatic pronouns (*His, Himself*) and to the possessive determiner (*His kingdom*).

3 Possessive Pronouns

Characteristics

The possessive pronouns are historically the genitive case of the personal pronouns and therefore show the same person and gender distinctions, except that there is no non-personal third person singular pronoun corresponding to *it*. Whereas in reference to a male person we can say *That is his* (using the masculine third person singular possessive pronoun), we cannot say *That is *its* when we refer, for example, to something belonging to a cat. We must either say *That's the cat's* or else guess the sex of the cat and say *That's his* or *That's hers*. As was the case with the personal pronoun, the distinction between masculine, feminine and neuter is not made in the plural and only one form (*theirs*) serves for all three persons. The following is a full list of the possessive pronouns:

Table

	1	2	3M	3F	3N
Singular:	*mine*	*yours*	*his*	*hers*	*(–)*
Plural:	*ours*	*yours*	....	*theirs*	....

Comparison with Determiners

Notice that *his* is the only possessive pronoun which shares the same form with a determiner: (determiner + noun) *She made his bed*, (pronoun) *His came later*. With the exception of *mine* all the other possessive pronouns look like the corresponding determiner with an *s* added. Examples:

1. (Determiner + Noun) *This is my pullover*.
(Pronoun) *And that is mine too*.
2. (Determiner + Noun) *We've inspected your house*.
(Pronoun) *They 'll buy yours*.
3. (Determiner + Noun) *I like her hair*.
(Pronoun) *Jane's is better than hers*.
4. (Determiner + Noun) *Our room is large*.
(Pronoun) *Ours is cosier*.
5. (Determiner + Noun) *Their lawns are not so well mown as John's*.
(Pronoun) *But I like theirs better*.

4 Reflexive and Emphatic Pronouns

Table

In English the reflexive pronouns and the emphatic pronouns have the same forms, and these are differentiated for number and gender in the same way as the personal pronouns. They are listed in the following table:

	1	2	3M	3F	3N
Singular:	*myself*	*yourself*	*himself*	*herself*	*itself*
Plural:	*ourselves*	*yourselves*	....	*themselves*	....

Charac-teristics

The reflexive and the emphatic pronouns differ from the personal pronouns in being unmarked for case: they have only one form for both subject and oblique case. Another difference is that the second person has both a singular and a plural form. Normally, we can tell a reflexive pronoun from an emphatic pronoun by its stress pattern and by its function and importance in the sentence. Whereas the reflexive pronouns normally carry no stress at all, the emphatic pronouns are always stressed on the final syllable. Both pronouns refer back to the subject of the verb in the sentence, but whereas the reflexive pronoun is either the object of the verb or of a preposition, the emphatic pronoun does not usually occupy one of these positions. So if the reflexive pronoun is omitted, the sentence usually sounds incomplete e.g. *They prided (themselves) on their sportsmanship, She looked at (herself) in the mirror*, whereas if the emphatic pronoun is left out, the sentence is grammatical and still makes sense, e.g. *Alfred gave her the money (himself), Jane (herself) washed the car.*

Exceptions

Unfortunately, there are a number of verbs which allow the reflexive pronoun to be omitted with no change of sense, when it is their grammatical object. For example: *Did they wash/shave/dress (themselves)this morning? He pushed (himself) into the room.* This never happens with verbs which take a preposition, but rather strangely, some verbs, notably those followed by a preposition indicating position, do not permit a reflexive pronoun after the preposition but use the corresponding personal pronoun instead. This seems always to happen when the verb has a direct object. For example, we can only say *She put the cushion <u>behind/beside</u>* ***her*** (where the noun phrase *the cushion* is the direct object of the verb *put*, and the personal pronoun *her* now refers back to the subject *she*) and not *She put the cushion behind/beside *<u>herself</u>* (where the reflexive pronoun would seem grammatically more logical). Other examples with positional prepositions are *He pulled the plate <u>in front of</u>* ***him****, She pushed me <u>away from</u>* ***her****, I threw the cloak <u>around</u>* ***me*** and the commonly heard question: *Have you got any money <u>on</u>* ***you****?*

Both Pronouns Together

In German, which uses an emphatic pronoun that is formally different from the reflexive pronouns, it is possible to have both types of pronoun present in the same sentence. For example, *ich rasierte mich selber* means literally *I shaved myself* (reflexive) *mysélf* (emphatic), i.e. I myself did the shaving of my face, not somebody else. If English permitted both types of pronoun in the same sentence, the result would be two identical pronouns standing side by side and differing only in stress. As we see from the ungrammatical literal translation, the reflexive pronoun *myself* is unstressed whereas the emphatic pronoun *mysélf* is stressed.

This repetition is avoided in English by deleting one of the two pronouns. We might be tempted to say that it is the unstressed reflexive pronoun that is deleted, but it would be more logical from a grammatical point of view to assume that the reflexive pronoun (which normally cannot be omitted) is kept and that it receives the stress of the deleted emphatic pronoun. The correct translation of the German sentence is thus: *I shaved mysélf.* Another example, this time with the reflexive pronoun after a preposition, is *Mary baked a cake for hersélf* instead of the ungrammatical **Mary hersélf baked a cake for herself* or **Mary baked a cake for herself hersélf.*

Ourself

An oddity among the possessive and emphatic pronouns is *Ourself*, the archaic pronoun belonging to the 'royal *We*', which is used by the King or Queen in formal documents (see page 55). The first person plural possessive *our* is combined with the singular form *self.* Notice that the emphatic and reflexive pronoun corresponding to 'editorial *we*', used in books and newspapers, has the regular form *ourselves.*

5 Demonstrative Pronouns

this/these, that/those

The demonstrative pronouns are identical with the demonstrative determiners, except that they always occur alone and never come in front of a noun. Like the determiners, *this* and *that* have each a plural form *these* and *those* respectively, but are not differentiated for person. The words *this* and *these* (whether used as pronouns or determiners) always refer to a thing or things close to or strongly associated with the speaker, i.e. with the first person singular or plural, whereas *that* and *those* refer to a thing or things at a distance from the speaker or not associated in any way with him or her. If I ask the question *Do you want <u>this</u>?*, the pronoun must refer to something which I, the speaker, am holding or pointing to or which has some connection with me, e.g. I have just mentioned it or fetched it. On the other hand, in the question *Do you want <u>that</u>?* the pronoun must refer to something which is not connected or associated with me, e.g. something which is not near me (the speaker) but perhaps near the listener or even somewhere else, or which the listener has in his hand or has just talked about.

Comparison with Determiner

The following sentences will make the difference between the demonstrative determiner and the demonstrative pronoun clear:
6a. (Dem. Determiner + Noun/Pronoun) *You sleep in <u>this bed</u> (here) and I'll sleep in <u>that one</u> (over there).*
6b. (Dem. Pronoun) *<u>This</u> is my brother and <u>that</u> is her sister.*

7a. (Dem. Determiner + Noun) *If you buy those socks, Mary can buy these gloves.*
7b. (Dem. Pronoun) *Did they ask for these or for those?*
8. (Dem. Determiner + Pronoun) *I think she chose this one.*
Note that the singular demonstrative determiner can be followed by the indefinite pronoun *one*, as in example 6a above (*that one*) and in example 8 (*this one*). On the other hand, careful speakers always avoid *ones* after the plural demonstrative determiner and use the demonstrative pronoun instead, as in example 7b (*these*, not **these ones*, and *those* not **those ones*). In colloquial spoken English, however, the starred forms can sometimes be heard.

6 Interrogative Pronouns

Characteristics

In English there are three interrogative (or question) pronouns: one for persons (*who*), one for things (*what*), and one for both persons and things (*which*). The latter two differ in meaning. The pronoun *which* refers to one or more persons or things from a particular group or set and is therefore specific in meaning (e.g. *Which of these two girls is Mary? These books are interesting. Which would you like?*). The pronoun *what*, on the other hand, has more general reference and is therefore vaguer in meaning (e.g. *I'd like to give you a present. What would you like?*). Both *what* and *which* are not differentiated for case, each having only one form for both subject and oblique case. The personal interrogative pronoun, on the other hand, has three case forms, *who* being used for the subject case, *whom* for the oblique case, and *whose* for the genitive case. Note that *whom* is used only in formal or careful English: in normal spoken English, it usually sounds too stilted and is replaced by *who*, which is then used for both the subject and oblique cases. Both *what* and *which* have no special genitive form and therefore need the help of the preposition *of* to form this case. These distinctions are shown in the following table:

Table

	Persons	Things	Persons/Things
Subject	*who*	*what*	*which*
Oblique	*who(m)*	*what*	*which*
Genitive	*whose*	*(of what)*	*(of which)*

Comparison with Determiners

The only form of the personal interrogative pronoun which also serves as a determiner is the genitive *whose*:
9. (Determiner + Noun) *Whose money is this?* (Pronoun) *Whose is this?*
The interrogatives *what* and *which*, on the other hand, can both be used as determiners or pronouns:

10. (Determiner + Noun, Subject Case) *What news has arrived from the Balkans? Which house is famous?* (Pronoun) *What has happened? Which came yesterday?*
11. (Determiner + Noun, Oblique Case) *What information have you got? Into what language was the letter translated? Which CD did she buy? Which pocket did he put it in?* (Pronoun, Oblique Case) *Which did she buy? Which did he put it in? What have you got? What are you looking for?*
12. (*of* + Determiner + Noun, Genitive) *Of what play could this be the title? Of which child did they take no notice? Of which field was the gate open?* (Pronoun, Genitive) *Of what could this be the title? Of which did they take no notice? Of which was the gate open?*

Which one?

Note that, in contrast to *whose* and *what*, the word *which* can be followed by the indefinite pronoun *one* and is then a determiner. Thus in place of the pronoun *which* in the examples in 11 above, we could also say: *Which one did she buy? Which one did he put it in?* The use of *one* after the determiner is characteristic of colloquial English. For this reason, the two sentences in 12 above beginning with *of* + the pronoun *which* would sound strange if we added the word *one* to them, because the word order with a preposition + *which* at the beginning of the sentence belongs to formal English. The sentences would then contain a mixture of two styles: (?) *Of which one did they take no notice?* (?) *Of which one was the gate open?* On the other hand, the first of these two sentences is perfectly acceptable with *one*, if the colloquial word order with the preposition at the end of the sentence is used: *Which one did they take no notice of?*

7 Relative Pronouns

Table

	Persons	Things
Subject Case	*who*	*which*
Oblique Case	*who(m)*	*which*

Characteristics

In modern English there are only two relative pronouns (*who, which*), both of which are normally undifferentiated for case. In formal English, however, the pronoun *who* takes the form *whom* when it is the object of the verb in the relative clause or when it comes after a preposition. If the relative pronoun has a person as its antecedent, i.e. if it refers back to a noun phrase, noun or pronoun denoting a person, then *who* is used. If the antecedent is a thing, the relative pronoun *which* is used.

Examples

The following sentences show the two pronouns with different functions in both formal and neutral style:

13. *We know the actress who plays the role of Mrs Smythe.* [Here the antecedent (*the actress*) is a person and the relative pronoun is the subject of the verb *plays* in the relative clause. The pronoun *who* can be used in both styles here.]

14. *The person whom they met was the Prime Minister.* [The use of *whom* for the object of the verb *met* in the relative clause shows that the sentence is in formal style. If *whom* is replaced by *who* the style is neutral. When the relative pronoun is not the subject of the relative clause, it is often left out altogether in neutral style: *The person (0) they met was the Prime Minister.* This omitted pronoun *(0)* is sometimes referred to as the 'zero relative pronoun'.]

15. *The officer of whom you are talking is now on leave.* [The antecedent is again a person and, as in 14, the use of *whom* indicates formal style. Furthermore, the position of the preposition *of* immediately in front of the relative pronoun is also characteristic of formal English. In this case in neutral style the pronoun is usually omitted *(0)* and the preposition placed at the end of the relative clause: *The officer (0) you are talking of is now on leave.*]

16. *They read the letter which arrived yesterday.* [The antecedent is now a thing (*the letter*) and, as subject of the verb *arrived* in the relative clause, can be referred to by the relative pronoun *which* in both styles.]

17. *Some countries which they visited were in Asia.* [Again we have a non-personal antecedent (*some countries*) referred to by the relative pronoun *which*. As it is here the object of the verb in the relative clause (*visited*), the pronoun would be retained in formal style. In neutral style it would normally be omitted: *Some countries they visited were in Asia.*]

18. *Many of the plants to which Pliny refers cannot be identified.* [As in 15 above, the position of the preposition in front of the relative pronoun makes this sentence sound formal. In neutral style the preposition would be relegated to the end of the relative clause and the relative pronoun either kept or left out: *Many of the plants (which) Pliny refers to cannot be identified.*]

that

In neutral and especially in colloquial English, relative clauses can also be introduced by *that*. Some grammarians refer to this word as another relative pronoun, but it is probably better to follow the example of others who prefer to call it a **relative particle**, since it does not behave like the two relative pronouns. As we saw in the examples above, both *who* and *which* can be used with a preposition in front of them. This is not possible, however, with *that*. It is ungrammatical to say *the book from *that he was reading*, though *the book that he was reading from* is perfectly acceptable. Furthermore, whereas *who* must have a person antecedent and *which* an impersonal one, *that* can be used to refer to both persons and things. Thus *that* functions more like an indeclinable particle, one which announces 'This is the beginning of a relative clause!', just as a question mark tells us 'That was a question!'.

8 Sentence Relative Pronouns

Characteristics

Another use of the relative pronoun *which* in English is to refer back to the whole of the sentence preceding it or to part of that sentence. When used in this way, it is called a **sentence** (or **sentential**) **relative** and has the meaning 'and this'.

Examples

19. *He had lost the key, which (= and this) was annoying for everyone.* Here the relative pronoun does not have a noun phrase or noun as its antecedent, but the whole of the sentence in front of it. To show what the antecedent is, we could paraphrase 1 by saying: *His having lost the key was annoying for everyone*, or alternatively *That he had lost the key was annoying for everyone.*
20. *When he was single Adam always smoked a pipe, which (= and this) he never did when he was married.* In this example the sentence pronoun *which* refers to only part of the sentence preceding it: here it is 'the smoking of a pipe' which he never did when he was married. Notice that *always* and *Adam* are not included in the antecedent.

Warning

Speakers of German should be careful **not** to use *what* as a translation of their native sentence relative "*was*". In English only *which* is used for this purpose and *what* is ungrammatical.

9 Nominal Relative Pronouns

Characteristics

The final kind of relative pronouns which we need to examine are the **nominal relative pronouns:** *whoever, whatever, whichever, what*. They are given this name because unlike the other relative pronouns they do not have an external antecedent. The noun phrase antecedent of each is included in the meaning of the pronoun. The following examples will make this clear.

Examples

21. (*whoever = the person who*) *There's a prize for whoever wins.*
22. (*whoever ... to = the person to whom*) *Whoever he gave the money to never thanked him.*
23. (*whatever = every thing, action, etc. which*) *Whatever she did was always a success.*

24. (*whichever = every thing, object, etc. which*) *These are French and those are German. You can take whichever you like.*
25. (*what = the thing which*) *What he feared most was gossip.*
Note that *whatever* refers to every thing, action, etc. in general, whereas *whichever* refers to every thing, action, etc. from a defined set. Notice too that in formal English the nominal relative *what* can be replaced by *that which,* e.g. *That which he feared most was gossip.*

Comparison with Determiner

Each of the three nominal relative pronouns *whatever, whichever, what* can also be used as a determiner:
26. (Determiner + Noun) *Whatever suggestion we made was always wrong.*
27. (Determiner + Noun) *They can drink out of whichever glass they like.*
28. (Determiner + Noun) *We supplied them with what food we could.*

10 Indefinite Pronouns

Characteristics

The final group of pronouns needing our attention are the **indefinite pronouns**, most of which are also quantifiers. They are called indefinite because the number of persons or things to which they refer can usually be given only approximately, and not exactly. When we deal with each separately below, we shall see that some of the indefinite pronouns have a positive meaning or are found only in an affirmative context, whereas others have a negative meaning or are found only in a negative context. It will be convenient to divide them into nine sets.

Set 1

Set 1 consists of the pronouns:
all, each, everybody, everyone, everything.
Like most of the words listed in the other sets below, both *all* and *each* are pronouns when followed by *of* (+ Noun Phrase), e.g. *all of the children, each of the cakes*, but determiners if the preposition is omitted, e.g. *all the children, all children, each cake.* In formal English *all* can be used as a pronoun in other contexts where no preposition follows, e.g. *All listened in silence. They ate all that was put in front of them.* In neutral and colloquial style *all* is replace here by *everybody, everyone* or *everything*; e.g. *Everybody/Everyone listened in silence. They ate everything that was put in front of them.*

Set 2

Set 2 contains the pronouns:
much, many, more, most.
Just as the determiner *much* modifies a non-count singular noun and the determiner *many* a plural count noun, so the pronoun *much* can only refer to a non-count noun and the pronoun *many*

only to a plural count noun. In one respect the pronouns *much* and *many* behave like adjectives: they have a comparative and a superlative form (*more, most*), and they can be modified by the intensifying adverb *very* (*very much, very many*). All four words in Set 2 are quantifying pronouns and are found both with and without the preposition *of* (+ Noun Phrase), e.g. *This clock is not worth very much. Nobody said much to Uncle Bill. Not very much of this opera has survived. Many of the people thought he was mad and many thought he was a genius. We already have six guests and more are coming tomorrow. We need more of those blue envelopes. These people are very poor and most have lost all their relatives. Most of them are refugees.*

Formal versus Non-Formal Style

In contexts containing a negative word, both of the pronouns *much* and *many* are heard in both formal and non-formal style, e.g. *He had never shown much appreciation of their efforts. Our cat likes mice but hasn't caught many recently.* The use of *much* in affirmative contexts is usually limited to formal style: *Much of the decoration aroused her interest and much she would have liked to examine in greater detail. There was much to discuss.* In non-formal style, *much of* is normally replaced by *a lot of*, and *much* by *a lot* or sometimes *plenty*, e.g. *A lot of the decoration interested her. There was plenty to talk about.* In affirmative contexts *many* is not quite so formal as *much*, but in spoken English it too is usually replaced by *a lot (of)* or by *plenty (of)*, e.g. *A lot of the people thought he was mad. We didn't see a single mouse yesterday but the cat has caught plenty today.*

Set 3

In Set 3 we find the following pronouns:

few, fewer, fewest; little, less, least

Like *much* and *many* in Set 2, the words *few* and *little* whether functioning as determiners or as pronouns behave in some respects like adjectives: they both have comparative and superlative forms (*fewer, fewest; less, least*) and they can be qualified by intensifying adverbs like *very, extremely, rather*, etc. The pronouns *few, fewer, fewest* are used to refer to a plural noun, and the pronouns *little, less, least* are used to refer to a non-count singular noun. All six words function as pronouns when they are followed by the preposition *of* + Noun Phrase, when they are the subject or object of the verb in their clause or when they are the object of a preposition. Consider the following examples:

Examples

29. *(Very) Few of the inhabitants had heard the explosion and (very) little of the damage was made know to the public.*

30. *Fewer of the customers had read the announcement than was expected and therefore less of the product was sold.*

Note that when *fewest* and *least* are followed by *of* + Noun Phrase they usually require *the* in front of them:

31. *The son inherited* <u>*the fewest*</u> *of his father's good looks. That's* <u>*the least*</u> *of my problems.*

When *few* and *little* are in subject or object position and not followed by *of* + Noun Phrase, they sound a little formal and are usually replaced in spoken English by *not many* and *not much* respectively:

32. (Subject) *Many people disliked him and* <u>*few*</u> *(not many) shared his opinions.* <u>*Little*</u> *(not much) was said about this to his relatives.*

33. (Object) *Though their garden was full of flowers, they had* <u>*few*</u> *to give away and said* <u>*little*</u> *to their neighbours.* The spoken English version of this sentence would probably be: *Their garden was full of flowers, but they didn't have many to give away and didn't say much to their neighbours.*

When *least* and *fewest* are in object position, the use of *the* in front of them is usually optional:

34. *On his death Smith left* <u>*(the) least*</u> *of all to his own children. They made very few films in America and* <u>*(the) fewest*</u> *in Canada.*

All six words in Set 3 can be used as pronouns after prepositions:

35. (After Preposition) *She had many servants, but he had to make do* <u>*with few/with fewer*</u>. *Terence acted in very few of these films, but his wife appeared* <u>*in the fewest*</u>. *We must be content* <u>*with little/with less*</u>. *They listened to little jazz and their son* <u>*to the least*</u>.

Note that in spoken and informal English there is a tendency to replace *fewer* (both as a pronoun and as a determiner) with *less* when it refers to or is in front of a plural count noun or a noun with plural meaning (e.g. *people, cattle*). This usage is, however, avoided by careful speakers:

36. (Informal *less* instead of *fewer*) <u>*Less*</u> *(people) came to the concert than last year, so they sold* <u>*less*</u> *(tickets) than expected.* Careful style: *Fewer (people) ... fewer (tickets) ...*

a few, a little

Whereas *few* and *little* have a negative meaning ('not many' and 'not much'), the same pronouns take on a positive meaning when preceded by the article *a*. Thus *a few* means 'a certain number', while *a little* means 'a certain amount'. When used in this way, neither of them has a comparative or superlative form and neither can be modified by an intensifying adverb, but they occur in all the same grammatical contexts as *few* and *little*, i.e. they are found before *of* + Noun Phrase, in subject and object position in a clause, and as the object of a preposition, as can be seen in the following examples:

Examples

37. (*of* + Noun Phrase) <u>*A few of those raisins*</u> *and a* <u>*little of this rum*</u> *would greatly improve the cake.*

38. (Subject) <u>*A few*</u> *arrived yesterday.* <u>*A little*</u> *goes a long way.*

39. (Object) *If you like these biscuits, take* <u>*a few*</u>. *I examined the sugar and then put* <u>*a little*</u> *in my tea.*

40. (After Preposition) *They looked at a few but did not buy them. We have too much furniture, we must get rid of a little.*

Set 4

This set contains only the pronouns:

several, enough

Like the other quantifying indefinite pronouns, both *several* and *enough* can be followed by the preposition *of* + Noun Phrase, e.g. *Several of the children have left. We've heard enough of that nonsense.* Or they can be used alone: *They have several growing in their garden. She cooked enough to feed a regiment.*

Set 5

Comprised in this set are the pronouns:

some, others, another, somebody, someone, something

Unlike *somebody, someone,* which can only refer to persons, and *something,* which can only refer to things, the first three of the pronouns in this set can refer to both persons and things. Only *some* and *another* can be followed by *of* + Noun Phrase, whereas all of them can be used alone.

Examples

41. (*of* + Noun Phrase) *Some of the women wore blue gowns, and some of the men red trousers. I'd like another of those cakes please.*
42. *When the guests came, some played chess and others played darts. All the rooms in the castle were too big, but some were bright and others were pleasantly furnished.*

Notice that the pronoun *some* (like its determiner counterpart) and the pronouns beginning with *some-*, i.e. *somebody, someone, something,* are found only in affirmative contexts. In negative contexts they are replaced by *any* or a pronoun beginning with *any-* (see Set 6 below). In questions, the use of *some, somebody, someone, something* suggests that the questioner expects an affirmative answer, whereas the use of *any, anybody, anyone, anything* suggests that the questioner is more uncertain and would not be surprised by a negative response. Compare:

43a. *We have made some tea. Would you like some?* [The speaker is making a friendly offer and expects you to say yes.]
43b. *She'd made some tea. Did she offer you any?* [The speaker is making a neutral statement here and would not be surprised if you said no.]
44a. *Can somebody help me?* [The speaker is looking at the people around him and hoping that one or more of them will say yes.]
44b. *Can anybody help me?* [The speaker is not optimistic about getting help and would not be surprised if nobody responded to his question.]

Set 6

The pronouns in this set are:

any, anybody, anyone, anything

Apart from the interrogative contexts with non-affirmative expectations, which we have just seen in the discussion of Set 5 pronouns, all the pronouns in Set 6 are restricted to contexts which either contain a negative word or a word with 'negative feel', i.e. adjectives beginning with *un-* (e.g. *unhappy, unlikely*) or adverbs such as *seldom* or *rarely* (both of which are equivalent to *not often*). When used in this way, the *any* pronouns are the non-affirmative counterparts of the *some* pronouns in Set 5. Some grammarians call the *some* pronouns **assertive** and the *any* pronouns **non-assertive**.

Examples

45. (Negative Context) *She hadn't read any of the notices and therefore didn't know anybody at the meeting and couldn't suggest anything to help them.*
46. (Context with 'Negative Feel' Word) *They had a large number of relatives but rarely invited any to their home. The film started an hour ago and it is unlikely that they will let anybody go in now. I was uncertain whether anything had been stolen.*

'Not Important Which/Who'

The pronouns in Set 6 can also be used to refer to both count and non-count nouns with the meaning 'it is not important which or who'. For example, in reference to things we can say: *Here are the screws. You can use any of them. The paint is over there and you can use any of that too.* Or in reference to persons: *Any of you should be able to answer this question. Which girls can I ask?... Any.*

Set 7

This set contains only the pronoun *one*, but with three different meanings and functions:
one (Numeral), ***one*** (Replacive), ***one*** (Impersonal)

Numeral *one*

As a numeral pronoun, *one* can refer to both persons and things, can be followed by *of* + Noun Phrase, or stand alone, e.g. *One of the boxes belonged to one of my sisters, and one belonged to my aunt. I have one and she has two.* In this function *one* behaves like any of the other numerals.

Replacive *one*

The replacive pronoun *one* is used in a noun phrase beginning with a determiner to replace a count noun when this noun would otherwise have to be repeated (often with the addition of an adjective or with a contrasting adjective). In this sense the pronoun has a plural form *ones*. For example: *If you like pearls, let me buy you this pink one. You polish the large knives and I'll clean the small ones.* Replacive *one* is also the indefinite pronoun which we saw used in spoken English after the singular demonstrative determiners (*this one, that one*) and after the interrogative determiner (*which one?*). In non-formal style it is also found after the indefinite determiner *each* and after the indefinite determiner *any* when this means 'it is not important which'. In the latter case it is written separate from the determiner to avoid confusion with the indefinite pronoun *anyone*, e.g. *All these roses smell good! You* *can pick any one you like* (Determiner + Pronoun) *and give it to anyone* (Pronoun). Note that in careful English the plural replacive *ones* is not used after *any* nor after *these* and *those*. Instead the simple pronoun is preferred, i.e. *any* (not **any ones*), *these* (not **these ones*), *those* (not **those ones*).

Impersonal *one*

The impersonal pronoun *one* has the meaning 'people in general' and can be used as the subject or object of a verb or can come after a preposition. It has a genitive form *one's* and a reflexive (or emphatic) form *oneself*. Its is used mainly in formal English: in non-formal style it is replaced by the personal pronoun *you*. **Examples:** *If one* (Subject) *wishes to make one's* (Genitive) *will with a lawyer, he will ask one* Object) *to sign it in his presence. One* (Subject) *must sign it oneself* (Emphatic) *and not get somebody else to do it for one* (After Preposition). The repetition of *one, one's, oneself* in a sentence or a sequence of sentences, as in the two preceding examples, makes for a rather heavy style. In American English *one* is usually replaced by *he, him, his* or *himself* after the first use of the impersonal pronoun, e.g. *When one cleans his teeth, he should use a hard toothbrush. One should not commit himself to action that may harm him.* As the pronoun *he* and its various forms could also refer to another person and not *one*, most speakers prefer the personal pronoun *you* in such sentences.

Set 8

In this set we have just the two pronouns:

either, neither.

Both also function as determiners when they precede a noun in a noun phrase. As a pronoun, *either* means 'one or the other of two', and *neither* is its negative counterpart. The use of *either* in a negative context is not as emphatic as the use of *neither* alone. For example, the sentence *Adam couldn't find either of his socks* insists less strongly on the absence of the socks than *Adam could find neither of his socks*, but the difference is not great. In formal English, when both pronouns are in subject position and followed by *of* + a plural noun, they take singular agreement with the verb, and singular personal or possessive pronouns are used to refer to them, e.g. *Neither of the men has paid his taxes.* In non-formal English, the verb usually agrees with the plural noun in the *of*-phrase, and plural personal or possessive pronouns are used instead of singular ones, e.g. *Neither of the men have paid their taxes.* The same stylistic difference is seen also with co-referential reflexive and emphatic pronouns: (Formal) *Has either of the women artists painted herself in her own garden?* (Non-Formal) *Have either of the women artists painted themselves in their own gardens?*

Set 9

The final set includes all the remaining negative indefinite pronouns:

none, nothing, nobody, no one

Although *no one* is written as two separate words, it is always treated as a single pronoun with the same meaning as *nobody.* Both pronouns can only refer to persons, whereas *nothing* can only refer to things. On the other hand, *none* can refer to both persons and things and is the only member of this set which can be followed by *of* + Noun Phrase. When used in this latter construction with a plural noun, it behaves like *either/neither*, taking a singular verb and singular pronouns in formal style and a plural verb and plural pronouns in non-formal style, e.g. (Formal) *None of the houses has its windows open.* (Non-Formal) *None of the houses have their windows open.* When used alone, all four pronouns can be found as the subject or object of a verb or come after a preposition:

Examples

48. (Subject) *Bombs were dropped but none exploded. In fact, nothing happened and nobody was hurt.*
49. (Object) *They had many guests and we had none. We saw nothing and we heard no one.* [Both these sentences are formal in style. In non-formal English they could be replaced by: *They had a lot of guests and we didn't have any. We didn't see anything and we didn't hear anyone.*]
50. (After Preposition) *All the students wanted to meet him, but he spoke to none (of them). He was pleased with nothing and friendly to nobody.* [These two sentences are also formal. A non-formal version of them would be: *All the students wanted to meet him, but he didn't speak to any of them. He wasn't pleased with anything and wasn't friendly to anybody.*]

Final Note

All the indefinite pronouns which end in *-body, -one* or *-thing* (*anybody, anyone, anything, everybody, everyone, everything, somebody, someone, something, nobody, no one, nothing*) always have singular verb agreement in both formal and non-formal style. However, in formal English they are always followed by singular pronouns, whereas in non-formal English plural pronouns are preferred. Compare: (Formal) *Has anybody lost his gloves?* (Non-Formal) *Has anybody lost their gloves?* (Formal) *Everybody was asked to bring his own food.* (Non-Formal) *Everybody was asked to bring their own food.* Note that the non-formal plural pronouns are gaining more and more ground in these constructions in modern English as they are neutral with regard to the sex of the persons referred to. The formal construction with the masculine singular pronouns seems to suggest a world in which only males are of importance.

5 Prepositions

1 General Remarks

Charac-teristics

Prepositions are words such as *after, in, with, about,* which are placed in front of a noun, a noun phrase or a pronoun to form a **prepositional phrase**. The constituent which follows the preposition in a prepositional phrase is usually referred to as the **object of the preposition**. Prepositions are used to show how this object is connected with another constituent in the sentence. They can indicate a variety of relationships such as time (*after, before, during*), place or direction (*in, under, below, through, over*), manner or means (*with, by means of, through*), reason or cause (*because of, on account of*), purpose or intention (*for*), and many more. Strictly speaking a preposition consists of a single word, but it is customary for some more complex structures also to be called prepositions. The latter usually consist either of a single-word preposition preceded by some other element such as an adjective or adverb (*because of, near to, close to, ahead of, away from, out of, according to*) or of a single-word preposition plus a noun plus another single-word preposition (*on account of, in front of, in spite of, on top of, with reference to*). When the noun in complex prepositional structures of this second type is also accompanied by the definite article (*on the underside of, at the rear of, in the vicinity of*), it is better not to treat these structures as prepositions. A series of words such as *on the underside of the table* is better analysed as Prep + Noun Phrase + Prep + Noun Phrase rather than as Complex Prep + Noun Phrase (*on the underside of the table*). However, some very common combinations, such as *in the middle of, at the bottom of,* are often treated as complex prepositions.

2 Position of Preposition

Normal

We saw above that English prepositions are usually placed in front of a noun, a noun phrase or a pronoun. They can sometimes also occur in front of a gerund (the noun form of a verb ending in *-ing*) or in front of a clause which functions as a noun phrase. Let us look at some examples illustrating all these possibilities.

Examples

1. (Prep + Noun) ***after*** *dinner*; (Prep + Noun Phrase) ***in*** *the early morning*; (Prep + Pronoun) ***behind*** *them*, ***with*** *everybody*.
2. (Prep + Gerund) *I'm looking forward* ***to*** *seeing the film.* ***After*** *offending his sister, he wasn't content* ***with*** *apologizing and insisted* ***on*** *helping her.*

3. (Prep + Noun Clause) *We talked* **about** *what they had done. The soldier reported to his superior officer* **on** *how he had escaped.*
[In the examples in 3 we can see that the clause after each preposition functions like a noun, because we can substitute an appropriate noun phrase for it, e.g. *We talked* ***about*** *their actions. The soldier reported ...* ***on*** *his (method of) escape.*]

Stranded Prep

Sometimes prepositions are separated from their object and then appear in final position in their clause. Let us call prepositions in this position **stranded prepositions**. In spoken English, stranded prepositions are regularly found in direct and indirect questions and also in relative clauses, i.e. at the end of clauses which are introduced by one of the so-called *wh*-words: *who, which, what, where.* In formal English, stranded prepositions are usually avoided, though in some cases, as we shall see below, there is no alternative. Consider the following examples:

Examples

4. (Direct Question) *What are you looking for? Where did it go to?*
[Since direct questions are rarely used in formal English, these examples sound stilted with formal word order: (?)*For what are you looking?* (?) *To where did it go?*]
5. (Indirect Question) *We know who Jack wanted to dance with. You asked where the runners had started from. I wonder what he opened the safe with.*
[When indirect questions, such as these, are part of sentences with neutral or colloquial vocabulary, or with personal pronouns such as *I, we, you,* which are typical of spoken language, the style is more natural if a stranded preposition is used. Here too, the same sentences with the preposition in front of the *wh*-word usually sound unnaturally formal or stilted: (?) *We know with whom Jack wanted to dance.* (?) *You asked from where the runners had started.* (?) *I wonder with what he opened the safe.* On the other hand, an indirect question in a sentence with more formal vocabulary and grammar, such as *They could no longer remember with whom she had attended the party* is perfectly acceptable with the preposition in front of the *wh*-word.]
6. (Relative Clause) *This is the box (which) he took the key from. He introduced us to some people (who) we had spoken to already last week.*
[Notice that in spoken English a relative clause with a stranded preposition sounds even less formal if the relative pronoun is also omitted. It is also important to note that the stranded preposition does not have to be the very last word in its clause. It can be followed by an adverbial expression (e.g. *already, last week*), as in the last of these two examples. When the preposition precedes the pronoun *who,* as in formal English, the pronoun always assumes the form *whom,* e.g. *He introduced us to some people to whom we had already spoken last week.*]

Unavoidable Final Position

We mentioned above that even in formal style there are some constructions in which the preposition must be separated from its object and put at or near the end of its clause. This happens in (1) certain passive constructions, (2) in certain *wh*-clauses, i.e. certain clauses which begin with a *wh*-word, and (3) after certain adjectives requiring *to*.

Passive

Unavoidable stranded prepositions are found in passive constructions in which the object of the preposition has become the subject of the verb, e.g. *These problems have been dealt with before. More dedication has been called for by the government. His efforts were laughed at.* Compare these with their active counterparts: *Someone has dealt with these problems before. The government has called for more dedication. They laughed at his efforts.*

***wh*-Clauses**

Stranded prepositions are also found in *wh*-clauses when these depend on a verb which also takes a preposition, e.g. *He asked about who we had given the money to. They politely passed over what she had laughed at. We looked after whoever we lived with. They lived off whatever they could come by.* All of these examples are unacceptable with the preposition in front of its object, since this would make it clash with the preposition governing the *wh*-clause: **He asked about to whom we had given the money. *They politely passed over at what she had laughed. *We looked after with who(m)ever we lived. *They lived off by whatever they could come.*

Adj + *to* + Infinitive

Certain adjectives, such as *hard, difficult, awkward, easy, impossible* can be followed by *to* with an infinitive. When this infinitive is a verb which requires a preposition, sometimes the object of this preposition can become the subject of the whole sentence and the preposition is then left stranded. For example, instead of *It was hard to think of a present for Jane*, where the infinitive *to think* (after the adjective *hard*) requires the preposition *of*, the noun-phrase object of this preposition can be removed to subject position and replace the pronoun *it*. The sentence now reads: *A present for Jane was hard to think of.* Other examples of this kind are: *The problem was difficult to cope with. The hook is awkward to get at. The boy's excuse was easy to see through. This rubbish is almost impossible to dispose of.*

3 Required Prepositions

General remarks

For foreign language learners, prepositions always present a serious problem, because their use differs so greatly from language to language and the learner cannot therefore easily guess which preposition should be used. In English we find a variety of prepositions which are required (1) after **adjectives**, (2) after **nouns**, and (3) after verbs. Let us examine a few examples of each of these in turn.

After Adjectives

The two most common prepositions required after adjectives are *to* and *of*, but others such as *about, by, for, on, upon, towards* and *with* can also be found.

Adj + *to*

Some adjectives require the preposition *to* when they are used predicatively. In the following sentences a few of these adjectives with their prepositions are shown underlined: *They were not accustomed to the climate. He's not averse to a good cigar. She lived close to her parents and was very devoted to them. These children are prone to exaggeration. The two tales are related to each other and similar to an ancient legend. The timetable is subject to alteration.*

Adj + *of*

Among the adjectives requiring *of* in English is **one group** which **needs** the **special attention** of German learners of English, since the corresponding German adjectives all require *für*. These are the adjectives: *characteristic, typical, symbolic, symptomatic, representative, true.* **Examples:** *Stalin trusted his wife implicitly, though this was not characteristic of the man. The lion is symbolic of strength. Their jealousy was symptomatic of their low self-esteem. His behaviour was typical of the urban area he came from. Furniture of this kind is not representative of modern European taste. Alan had charming manners and this was also true of his sister.*

Others

The following sentences illustrate some of the **other adjectives requiring the preposition *of*** when they are used predicatively: *The teacher was not aware of his mistake. She was capable of very hard work and rather fond of chocolates. His letter was full of long words which were devoid of any sense. His father said that this particular song always seemed reminiscent of his youth. They all seemed hopeful of success.*

Adj + Other Preps

A number of adjectives require prepositions other than *to* or *of*, and in many of these cases the speaker has the **choice of one of two prepositions**. Among the commonest of this category are: *anxious for/about, angry with/at, furious with/at, dependent on/upon, parallel with/to, reliant on/upon.*
Examples: *We were anxious for her safety. The refugees were anxious about their relatives. The teacher was angry/furious at the noise and angry/furious with the children. She did not want to seem dependent/reliant on/upon her father's support. The road runs parallel with/to the canal.*

Others

Many of the adjectives of the kind mentioned in the foregoing paragraph are **adjectives derived from verbs** and therefore require the same preposition or prepositions as the verb does.

They are usually past participles or present participles: *filled with, descended from, connected with/to, pleased with/about, delighted with/about, lacking in*. However, some are derived from verbs in other ways, e.g. the two adjectives *dependent* (< *to depend on/upon*) and *reliant* (< *to rely on/upon*), which we saw above, and also *separate* (< *to separate sth. from*), which differs only in the pronunciation: adjective = ['sepərət], verb = ['sepəreɪt]. One particularly common verbally derived adjective is *different*. In careful English the adjective behaves like the verb and takes the preposition *from*: *Braque's painting is different from (< differs from) Picasso's*. However, instead of *from* we often hear *to* in spoken British English and *than* in spoken American English, although many people frown on this use.

After Nouns

Like adjectives, certain nouns can only be followed by a certain preposition. Among the commonest of these prepositions are: *for, on, to, with* and *of*. Many of these nouns also have a corresponding verb. The verb may be a transitive verb, i.e. one which has a direct object and is not followed by any preposition, or else the verb and its noun both take the same preposition. Note that nouns with similar meanings often take the same preposition. In the discussion below, restrictions on space will allow us to mention only a few of the nouns in each category.

Noun + *for*

We can distinguish the following groups of nouns requiring *for:*
(1) Nouns derived from a transitive verb: (semantically related) *admiration for (< to admire s.o./sth.), desire for (< to desire sth.), love for/of (< to love s.o./sth.), regard for (< to regard s.o./sth. highly), respect for (< to respect s.o./sth.)*; (semantically unrelated) *cure for (< to cure s.o./sth.), demand for (< to demand sth.)*.
Examples: *They were not surprised at the wife's great love for her mother and her deep respect for her husband's parents. My regard for these politicians would be boundless if only they had a little less desire for power.*
(2) Semantically related nouns of miscellaneous origin: *aptitude for, cure for, hunger for, remedy for, responsibility for, taste for, thirst for.*
Examples: *His appetite for hard work was matched by her thirst for knowledge. He had a marked taste for loud shirts and ties.*

Noun + *on*

Most of the nouns which take the preposition *on* are of varied origin. Among the commonest are: *attack on, claim on, comment on, concentration on, dependence on, effect on, insistence on, reflection on, restriction on, tax on.*
Examples: *You have no claim on our assistance. We need more concentration on details. Their insistence on immediate payment caused a great deal of unrest. The tax on alcohol has been raised again.*

Noun + *to*

Nouns which require the preposition *to* can be broadly divided into two groups:
(1) Nouns derived from or related to a transitive verb: *answer to, approach to, damage to, introduction to, resistance to, solution to, threat to.*
Examples: *This is not the answer to your question (cf. This does not answer your question). This paragraph is the introduction to a new book (cf. This paragraph introduces a new book). Accusing them is no solution to the problem (cf. Accusing them will not solve the problem). The new factory was a threat to people's health (cf. The new factory threatened people's health).*
(2) Nouns derived from verbs after which *to* is also required: *allusion to, attachment to, reply to.*
Examples: *His allusion to their poverty caused distress (cf. He alluded to their poverty). The doctor was on special attachment to the clinic (cf. The doctor was attached to the clinic). They made no reply to his question (cf. They did not reply to his question).*

Noun + *with*

A small group of nouns of varied origin require the preposition *with*. The commonest of these are: *dealings with, dissatisfaction with, encounter with, familiarity with, intimacy with, quarrel with.* A number of nouns can take both *with* and *between*. Among these are: *connection with/between, contrast with/between, correspondence with/between, link with/between.*
Examples: *The army's dealings with the prisoners caused much public dissatisfaction with the generals. His connection with the Socialists was well known but the link between his party and the Communists surprised many of us.*

Noun + *of*

Of the many nouns which take *of* after them, there is one group which should be particularly noticed by German learners of English, since the corresponding German nouns all take *für* (cf. Adj + *of*, page 73): *a characteristic, an example, an indication, an indicator, a proof, a sign, a symbol, a symptom.*
Examples: *It is a characteristic of parrots to imitate human voices. This is another example of their strength and an indication of their potential dangerousness. They were searching for a convincing proof of his new theory. The dove has always been a symbol of peace. Violence is a sign of (a symptom of) the unrest in modern society.*

Noun + Other Preps

The following examples show a few nouns which take a preposition other than those dealt with above: *They had no control over those who committed crimes against humanity. The father's constant anger at his son's behaviour caused the boy to have a grudge against the whole family. The politician's sudden departure from the meeting was a reaction against the persistent heckling of the audience. One quotation from Dickens was said to illustrate the author's freedom from bias. The debate on the state of the economy was marred by the speakers' frequent relapses into sarcasm.*

After Verbs

In our discussion above of the prepositions required after certain nouns, we encountered a number of verbs which take the same preposition as the noun. Let us now look at some more verbs and list them according to the preposition they take.

Verb + *to*

The commonest preposition after verbs is *to*. Some of the verbs which belong to this group are: *add to, adhere to, allude to, amount to, appeal to, attend to, belong to, lead to, object to, refer to, relate to, resort to.*

Examples: *Their noisy entrance only added to the confusion. If we had adhered to the rules of the game we could have won. The officer alluded to the huge sums of money needed and later appealed to the public to give generously. Her remarks led to a heated discussion, in which many strongly objected to the council's policy but fortunately nobody resorted to violence.*

Verb + *of*

Another common group of verbs take the preposition *of*. Some of these are: *complain of, conceive of, consist of, despair of, learn of, think of, tire of.*

Examples: *She often complained of headaches. They have now conceived of another plan which consists of only two points. She despaired of ever reaching them, when she learnt of their fate. Can't you think of another topic, I'm tired of this one.*

Verb + *for*

Among the verbs requiring *for* are: *appeal for, care for, hope for, long for, pay for, strive for.*

Examples: *The workers have appealed for more pay. We will have to care for our sick mother ourselves or hope for more help.. She longed for a holiday in Miami but would her father pay for it? Most countries are striving for peace.*

Verb + *from*

A few verbs take the preposition *from*. Among these are: *detract from, emerge from, shrink from, stem from, suffer from.*

Examples: *The yellowed pages of the manuscript did not detract from its value. One fact emerged from this discussion: they would not shrink from using pressure on their customers. The disease from which they suffer stems from years of poor working conditions.*

Verb + *with*

A few verbs take the preposition *with*. Among these are: *associate with, contend with, cope with, flirt with, sympathize with, agree with.*

Examples: *Her name is associated with many great works of art. Among the greatest difficulties with which they had to contend were poverty and filth. Jim could not cope with Julie's reactions and preferred to flirt with another girl. We sympathize with your aims but do not agree with your analysis.*

Verb + Other Preps

The following are a few of the verbs which require a preposition other than those illustrated above: *look after, react against, hint at, shoot at, alternate between, differentiate between, profit by/from, believe in, culminate in, end in/with, indulge in, result in, depend on/upon, improve on/upon, insist on/upon, spy on/upon, contribute towards/to.*

Examples: *The nurses found it difficult to look after the patient properly, as he reacted against all their efforts to keep him in bed. The general hinted at the problem of shooting at targets in the dark. The weather constantly alternates between sunshine and rain. Their manager has profited by our mistakes, but our firm has profited from the new changes in the tax laws. Her session with the psychiatrist ended in/with tears. They were always spying on/upon their neighbours, which naturally contributed to bad feelings between the two families.*

After Transitive Verbs

All the examples above of prepositions after various verbs have been with intransitive verbs. There are, however, some verbs which need a **preposition after their direct object**. The following list shows a few of these transitive verbs with their particular preposition: *regard sth./s.o. as, mistake sth./s.o. for, prevent sth./s.o. from, deprive sth./s.o. of, remind s.o. of, rid sth./s.o. of, accustom sth./s.o. to, compare sth./s.o. to/with, entitle s.o. to, owe sth. to, associate sth./s.o. with, confront s.o. with, trust s.o. with, base sth. on/upon.*

Examples: *They regarded the doctor as a friend. We mistook the man for her husband and therefore did not prevent him from seeing her again. The neighbours' loud parties deprived her of her sleep. The house reminded him of an old castle. After they had rid all the rooms of mice and vermin, they had to accustom their eyes to the darkness. We can compare these plays to/with Shakespeare's. The ticket entitled the children to one free meal every day. He still owed a large sum of money to his mother-in-law. We usually associate kangaroos with Australia. When the police confronted the young man with the evidence, he confessed to the crime. She was very honest, so they knew they could trust her with the money. They based their trust on her honesty.*

Others

Note that a few verbs require a **different preposition depending on whether the direct object is a person or a thing**: *entrust sth. to, entrust s.o. with, present sth. to, present s.o. with, supply sth. to, supply s.o. with.*

Examples: *They entrusted the repairs to the car mechanic. They entrusted the car mechanic with the repairs. The Head Master presented the best pupil with a book prize. The Head Master presented a book prize to the best pupil. They supplied all the details of the crime to the local policeman. They supplied the local policeman with all the details of the crime.*

6 Verbs

1 General Remarks

Definition

A verb is one of a class of words used to say what a person or thing is doing, or to describe the state a person or thing is in, or what is happening to that person or thing.

Semantic Characteristics

Semantically, verbs can be divided into lexical (full) verbs and auxiliary (helping) verbs. **Lexical** verbs are either dynamic or stative. A **dynamic lexical** verb is one which expresses the particular action a person or thing is performing, e.g. *run, jump, help, make, encourage*. Dynamic verbs can be used in both simple and progressive tenses (see page 85 below). A **stative lexical** verb is one which expresses the state that a person or thing is in: *be, become, feel, know, mean, realize, seem, suppose*. Stative verbs can only be used in the simple tenses and not in progressive tenses. **Auxiliary** verbs are either primary or modal. A **primary auxiliary** verb is one which is used together with a lexical verb to show aspectual differences, such as those seen in the continuous, perfect and emphatic forms of the verb. In English there are three: *be, have, do*. We can see them in use in the following forms: *is running, has run, has been running, does run*. A **modal auxiliary** verb is one which is used with a lexical verb to show the speaker's intentions or wishes, or to help him or her to make offers, suggestions or requests. English has the following modal auxiliary verbs: *can, could, shall, should, will, would, may, might, must, ought to*. An intention or wish is seen in the following sentence: *He shall go to London!* And an offer, suggestion or request in the sentence: *Can we help you?*

Lexical Verbs

Let us look first at lexical or full verbs and examine some of their general morphological characteristics. All lexical verbs can occur in one of **five forms:**

1. a **base form**: *help, wish, stop, try; feel, mean, know, sing, see.*
2. an **-s form**: *helps, wishes, stops, tries; feels, means, knows, sings, sees.*
3. an **-ing form**: *helping, wishing, stopping, trying; feeling, meaning, knowing, singing, seeing.*
4. a **past tense form**: *helped, wished, stopped, tried; felt, sang, saw*
5. a **past participle form**: *helped, wished, stopped, tried; felt, sung, seen*

Base Form

The base form is the one under which the verb is listed alphabetically in dictionaries and which is found with *to* in front of it in the infinitive. In the infinitive form without *to*, the base form occurs after all the modal auxiliary verbs (except *ought*) as well as after the primary auxiliary *do*, e.g. in the emphatic sentence *They* **do** *go!*, the negative command *Don't go!*, and the questions *Do/Don't they go?* It is also used for all persons of the simple present tense except the third person singular (*I/you/we/they sing*) and for the imperative form of the verb (*Stop! Try!*). In the examples in the preceding paragraph the four verbs before the semicolon are typical regular verbs, i.e. they have regular morphological forms, whereas those following the semicolon are irregular verbs, i.e. they have irregular past tense and past participle forms.

-*s* Form

The -*s* form consists of the base form to which the suffix -*s* has been added. If the base form ends in a single written vowel (e.g. *go*) or a sibilant sound (e.g. *cross, buzz, wish, watch)* the suffix is then extended to -*es* (e.g. *crosses, buzzes, goes, wishes, watches*). If the base form ends in a consonant plus the letter *y* (e.g. *try*), the *y* is changed to *ie* before the -*s* suffix (*tries*). The -*s* form is characteristically used to show the third person singular of the present tense. This is the only tense in English in which the verb form is differentiated for the categories of person (third) and number (singular). For the one exception to this rule, see the verb *be* on page 95.

-*ing* Form

The -*ing* form consists of the base form plus the suffix -*ing* and is characteristically used as the present participle, either alone or more often preceded by forms of the primary auxiliary *be* to form the so-called **progressive** (or **continuous**) tenses (see **Progressive Aspect** below, page 85), as in *am going, has been going, etc.* It is also used to form the gerund (verbal noun), as in *His smoking in bed annoyed them.* Note that when the -*ing* suffix is added, base forms ending in *e* usually lose this letter (*smoke* > *smoking*), whereas those with a final *y* keep this *y* (*try* > *trying*). If a base form ends in a stressed single written vowel followed by a single consonant (*rob, hit, begín*), the final consonant is doubled when the suffix -*ing* is added (*robbing, hitting, begínning*), provided that the single written vowel remains stressed (cf. *prefér, préference* where the stress pattern has changed).

Past Tense Form & Past Participle Form

For regular verbs, both the past tense and the past participle forms consist of the base form plus the suffix -*ed*. For this reason they are sometimes referred to as **the -*ed* forms of the verb**. The past participle form can be used either alone or more commonly preceded by the primary auxiliary *have* to form the perfect tenses, i.e. present perfect: *has stopped*, future perfect *will have stopped*, and past perfect (= pluperfect) *had stopped* (see **Perfect Aspect**, page 86 below). As with the -*ing* form, here too when the suffix -*ed* is added after a stressed single written vowel plus a final single consonant, the consonant is doubled (*stóp > stópped; rebút > rebútted*), provided that the single written vowel remains stressed (cf. *góssip > góssiped*, where the final syllable of the base form is never stressed). Notice that some irregular verbs often have two distinct forms, one for the past tense and one for the past participle: *sang, sung (< sing), knew, known (< know), went, gone (< go)*. Other irregular verbs may have the same form for past tense and past participle as the base form: *cut, cut (< cut), shed, shed (< shed), thrust, thrust (< thrust)*.

Modal Auxiliary Verbs

Unlike the lexical verbs and the three primary auxiliary verbs (*be, have, do*), all six of the modal auxiliaries (*can, shall, will, may, must, ought*) are morphologically severely restricted. Furthermore, they also do not have the same syntactic patterns as lexical verbs. The following six differences should be noted.
Morphologically, they all have

1. **no *-s* form**
2. **no *-ing* form**
3. **no past participle form.**

Syntactically, they all have

4. **no *do*-support in Questions and Negations**
5. **no *to* in front of a following infinitive** (except *ought*)
6. **their own base form in Tag Questions** (instead of being picked up by one of the primary auxiliaries).

Morphology

Let us look first at the morphological differences. With regard to the first, we may note that the modal auxiliaries all use the base form without the suffix *-s* for the third person singular of the present tense, e.g. *he/she/it can* (not **cans*), *he/she/it will* (not **wills*), etc. The fact that the modal auxiliaries have no *-ing* form and no past participle means that they can form only two tenses: the simple present tense and the simple past tense. However, only four of them (*can, shall, will, may*) have a past tense form: *could, should, would, might*. Historically, the modal auxiliaries *must* and *ought* are derived from the past tense of two Old English verbs (*motan* 'to be allowed' and *agan* 'to possess'), which probably accounts for them having only one form. In modern English *must* is used as a present tense form and *had to* serves as its past tense form: compare (present) *Bess must (has to) go now* with (past) *Bess had to go yesterday*. Similarly, *ought* is also used as a present tense form (*you ought to leave now*), but forms its past with a perfect infinitive (*you ought to have gone yesterday*). (For **Perfect Aspect** see page 86 below).

Syntax

Syntactically, both the primary and the modal auxiliary verbs differ from lexical verbs in using an historically older method of forming questions and negations.

Q's & Negs

Whereas a lexical verb such as *work* needs ***do*-support**, i.e. must introduce the primary auxiliary *do*, in order to form questions and negations (e.g. *Do/Did they work?*, and not **Work they?* **Worked they?*. Or *They do/did not work* and not **They work/worked not*), the **modal auxiliary verbs** merely reverse the positions of the verb and the subject for the question (*we can > can we?, she will > will she?*), and place the negative particle *not* immediately after the modal for the negative (*he could > he could not (couldn't), they will > they will not (won't)*. The **primary auxiliaries** also follow these same two patterns, as we see from the examples *Do they (work)? They do not (don't) (work). Have the scouts gone? The scouts have not (haven't) gone. Is the water boiling? The water is not (isn't) boiling.* It should be noted that when the negative particle *not* is **not stressed**, it loses its vowel and is then suffixed to the auxiliary verb, which then often has an irregular form with irregular spelling and irregular pronunciation: *can not < cannot < can't, will not > won't, shall not > shan't, etc.*

Tag Q's

Another syntactic way in which auxiliary verbs behave differently from lexical verbs is in the formation of so-called **tag questions**. In English we can make a statement such as *The men all know* and then ask the listener whether he or she agrees by adding a word or expression such as *Right?* (In German we could say *nicht wahr?*, in French *n'est-ce pas?* or in Spanish *no es verdad?*) In addition to this method, English also has a special syntactic mechanism, namely **the tag**, which can be attached to the end of the initial statement. If the **lexical verb** in the initial statement is in the **simple present** or **simple past** form, then the tag consists of the **negated** present or past form of ***do* followed by a pronoun** picking up the person of the subject of the verb. Thus from the present tense sentence above, we obtain the tag question *The men all know, don't they*, where *do* picks up the present tense lexical verb *know*, and the pronoun *they* picks up the subject noun phrase *the men*. From the corresponding past tense form of the same sentence we obtain the tag question *The men all knew, didn't they*, where *did* picks up the past tense form *knew*. If we now look at the **auxiliary verbs**, we see that for them the pattern is different. **Instead of the present or past tense form of the auxiliary being picked up by *do* or *did* in the tag, the auxiliary verb itself is repeated there.** For example, we cannot say *The men all can, *don't they?* We must say *The men all can, can't they?* Similarly, the ungrammatical sentence *The men all could, *didn't they?* must be replaced by the grammatical sentence *The men all could, couldn't they?* We may observe that the rule for the repetition of the auxiliary in tag questions explains why lexical verbs which are not in the present or past tense form are always picked up in the tag question by the primary or modal auxiliary which accompanies them: *Elvis is smoking, isn't he? Jane has come, hasn't she? The books had been sold, hadn't they? They must pay, mustn't they? You would have been seen, wouldn't you?*

No *to* before Infinitive

The last of the syntactic differences between lexical verbs and auxiliary verbs is seen in their behaviour before a following infinitive. Whereas lexical verbs such as *begin, want, hope* all require *to* in this position (*I begin to understand, I want to know, I hope to win*), all the modal auxiliaries (with the exception of *ought*) take a **bare infinitive** after them (i.e. an infinitive without *to*): *can see, will break, shall hear, may think*, but *ought to object*.

Marginal Modal Auxiliaries

There are two verbs, *need* and *dare*, which sometimes behave like modal auxiliary verbs and sometimes like lexical verbs. There may be differences of meaning or style between these two uses of the verbs. They are found as modal **auxiliary** verbs in **Questions, Negative Sentences**, and in **Tag Questions** and then only in the **present tense**. Elsewhere they function only as lexical verbs. Let us examine each of the above-mentioned three contexts using explained examples, where (a) shows the verb used as a modal auxiliary and (b) as a lexical verb.

Qs with *need/dare*

1(a) *Need I say how pleased I am?* (b) *Do I need to say how pleased I am?* These two sentences do not have equivalent meanings. The first (with no *do*-support and no *to* before the infinitive) is a rhetorical question which does not expect an answer and which means 'I am very pleased', whereas the second is a genuine question asking the addressee for advice.
2(a) *Why need it be today?* (b) *Why does it need to be today?* There is little difference between these two sentences, except that (a) sounds more formal in style. Notice that as a modal auxiliary, the verb in (a) not only lacks *do*-support and *to* before the following infinitive, but also the *-s* suffix for the third person singular. In (b) this latter suffix is given to the supporting *do* and then *to* is necessary before the following infinitive.
3(a) *Dare I mention her name?* (b) **Do I dare to mention her name.* The first sentence is rhetorical and as such formal in style. The second makes no sense, as you cannot ask a genuine question of another person about what you yourself dare, since only you know the answer.
4(a) *How dare he make such a suggestion!* (b) **How does he dare to make such a suggestion?* The first sentence here is a typical exclamation in which the speaker is indignant about the behaviour of others. Such formulaic sentences always begin with *How dare you/he/she/they ...*, but notice that **How dare I/we ...* is unaccept-

able, since you cannot be indignant about yourself. The second sentence (4b) as a genuine question again makes little sense, since only 'he' can give the reasons for his daring and no other person.

Neg. Sentences with *need/ dare*

5(a) *He needn't do it today.* (b) *He doesn't need to do it today.* For most speakers these two sentences are equivalent in meaning and style.
6(a) *Nobody need tell her.* (b) *Nobody needs to tell her.* These two are also equivalent in meaning and style. Note that as the subject is now a negative word, there is no *do*-support in (b) and therefore the lexical verb *need* must take the third person singular suffix *-s*.
7(a) *He need only say the word and I'll come.* (b) *He needs only to say the word and I'll come.* There are some adverbs in English which have a negative feeling about them, e.g. *only, hardly, scarcely, etc.* (see Broad Negative Adverbs, page 104). Both *need* and *dare* can be used in this context either as a modal auxiliary or as a lexical verb with little difference in meaning and style. A similar pair of sentences with *dare* are:
8(a) *I hardly dare think about it.* (b) *I hardly dare to think about it.*

Tag Qs with *need/dare*

In negative sentences with an affirmative tag, *need* can be found either as a modal auxiliary or as a lexical verb, e.g.
9(a) *We needn't go, need we?* (b) *We don't need to go, do we?*
The use as an auxiliary sounds a little old-fashioned in British English and is usually not found in modern American English. Notice that an affirmative sentence with a negative tag can only be formed with the lexical verb:
10(a) **She need pay, needn't she.* (b) *She doesn't need to pay, does she?* The first sentence (with *need* as a modal auxiliary) is unacceptable, as *need* in the main clause is not negative.

2 Categories of the Verb

General Note

Having looked at the basic morphological forms of verbs and at some of their syntactic features, it is now time for us to consider in more detail the use to which these are put in the grammar. One of the most important characteristics of verbs is that they are able to show contrasts **of tense, aspect, voice, mood, person** and **number**. These are referred to by grammarians as **categories of the verb**. We shall find that in English some are reflected in the morphological forms of the verb, some are indicated by the use of auxiliary verbs, and some by the use of special word order. Let us now examine what is meant by each of these categories and provide some examples of their use.

Tense

Tense is a category used by grammarians to refer to the form which a verb takes in order to indicate chiefly the **time of the action or of the state expressed by the verb**. Grammarians usually distinguish three basic tenses: a **present**, a **future** and a **past** tense. In many languages (e.g. Latin, French, Spanish) the verb has a different set of endings for each of these. In English the lexical verb has only two tenses of this kind, i.e. where only the base form with or without suffixes is employed: the present (*jump, jumps*) and the simple past (*jumped*). Other tenses are formed by using an auxiliary verb together with a form of the lexical verb, e.g. the future by means of *will/shall* followed by the base form as in (*I/we*) *shall jump,* (*he/she/it*) *will jump.* Where necessary, grammarians may subdivide the three basic tenses into further tenses, e.g. future perfect (*will/shall have jumped*), past perfect or pluperfect (*had jumped*), etc.

Real Time and Tense

It is very important to notice that when we talk about the present **tense** or the past **tense**, we are referring to forms of the verb and not necessarily to a specific time. The relation between real time and tense is often more complicated than was suggested in the preceding paragraph. The tense forms of a verb may be used to refer to a time other than that suggested by the name of the tense form. For example, in English the **present tense** form of the verb may sometimes refer to **future time**: *Tomorrow we fly to Paris.* The simple **past tense** form may sometimes be used to refer to **present time**, as in *If they wrote today, the letter would reach him in time*, or in *I'd rather Albert came now than tomorrow.* Sometimes the **past tense** may even be used to refer to **future time**: *If John shaved his beard off tomorrow, I'd invite him to dinner.* Notice that the past tense form of the modal auxiliaries is often used in this way. There is little difference between the sentence *Can you come tomorrow?* and *Could you come tomorrow?* The real time referred to in each is the same (future) but the use of the past tense form *could* instead of the present tense form *can* makes the second question more tentative. We shall see below that when the tense of the verb does not correspond with the real time, then usually other categories such as aspect or mood are involved.

Aspect

Aspect is the name given to a verbal category which refers to **a way of looking at the time of an action**. It typically serves to indicate the beginning or completion, the duration or the repetition of an action. In some languages this characteristic may be expressed by inflections on the verb. For example, Latin has a suffix *-scere* with the meaning 'begin to' which forms verbs such as *maturescere* (< *maturus* 'ripe') 'to begin to be ripe', i.e. 'to become ripe', *tremiscere* (< *tremere* 'to tremble') 'to begin to tremble'. Other languages may employ other mechanisms. We can distinguish three important types of aspect: **progressive, perfect** and **habitual**.

Progressive Aspect

English makes use of its auxiliary verbs to show aspectual differences connected with the continuousness, progression or duration of an action. Thus in contrast to the simple present tense as seen in the sentence (*Max*) *speaks*, we can also say (*Max*) *is speaking*, where the auxiliary verb *be* is used together with the *-ing* form of the lexical verb to show that the action is still continuing. We see the difference clearly when we compare the sentence *If Max speaks now, they will hear him* with the sentence *Be quiet when Max is speaking*. In the first sentence only the act (of speaking) is of importance, whereas in the second sentence attention is focussed on the continuousness (progression or duration) of the speaking. In this latter case, the *be + -ing* forms of the English verb are used to express what grammarians call the **progressive** (or **continuous**) **aspect**. Other languages may not be interested in these aspectual differences. French and German, for example, have only one form (*Max parle, Max spricht*) with the same meaning as the two English forms *Max speaks* and *Max is speaking.*

Terminology

Notice that grammatical terminology is rather confusing here, as it often uses the name of the aspect to refer to a verb form or a tense. Thus a form such as *is speaking* is usually referred to as the progressive or continuous **tense** of the verb *speak* compared with the simple present **tense** (*speaks*). It is for this reason that some grammarians prefer to reserve the term 'progressive' or 'continuous' for the name of the aspect and to call the *-ing* tenses the **expanded tenses**. These are not limited to the expanded present in English: we can also have the expanded past (*was speaking*), the expanded future (*will be speaking*), the expanded perfect (*has been speaking*), the expanded past perfect (*had been speaking*). The *be + ing* forms of the lexical verb can also be seen after modal verbs: *may be going, might have been going, etc.*

Dynamic versus Stative

It is important to remember that only dynamic verbs (see page 78) have expanded forms, i.e. can be used to express the progressive or continuous aspect. They denote actions which the speaker can consider as progressing or continuing over a period of time. Thus with dynamic verbs (e.g. *do, say, break, jump*), we can ask the diagnostic question *What are they doing?* and the answer could be *They are going, saying something, breaking something, jumping.* On the other hand, stative verbs (e.g. *know, suppose, mean*) denote states and not actions and therefore do not normally have expanded forms. Here the question *What are they doing?* does not make any sense. It cannot be answered, for example, by saying **They are knowing/supposing/meaning some-*

thing. This is why we can only say *I know he did it* (not **I am knowing he did it*) or *I suppose you are right* (not **I am supposing you are right*) or *This word means* ... (not **This word is meaning* ...).

Perfect Aspect

Another type of aspectual difference which English verbs can express may be seen in the sentences *Alice arrived* and *Alice has arrived.* The simple past tense of the lexical verb in the former sentence tells us that Alice's arrival took place in the past and is over and finished with now, whereas the present perfect tense in the latter sentence, i.e. the auxiliary verb *have* used with the past participle of the lexical verb, indicates an **action which started in the past but which has present relevance**. For example, we can now see Alice's car stopping outside our house or maybe her luggage is now standing in the hall of the hotel we are staying in. This aspect is best referred to as the **perfect aspect**, since it is associated with the perfect tense in English. Some linguists refer to it as the perfective aspect, but this is confusing, because this term is used for a completely different kind of aspect in Slav languages such as Russian and Polish, where the verb has two different forms: one for an action that has been completed and is therefore considered in its entirety (perfective) and one for an action which is not yet finished (imperfective).

Habitual Aspect

Finally, let us note that sometimes English also uses the **simple** form of the verb for aspectual purposes. For example, in the right context the simple present tense often **indicates a habit**, i.e. an habitual action, one which a person often does but which he or she is not necessarily doing at the present moment. If we say *Jack smokes a pipe*, we are referring to his habit and not to his present actions, but if we say *Jack is smoking a pipe*, using the *be + -ing* (progressive) form of the verb, then the act of smoking must be taking place now while we are speaking. The use of the simple present tense to indicate an habitual action illustrates what grammarians refer to as the **habitual aspect**. Note that if the habit belongs to the past, English usually then employs the past tense verb *used to*, as in *Jack used to smoke a pipe*. This verb cannot be used to indicate a present habit: it is ungrammatical to say **Jack uses to smoke a pipe.*

Voice

Voice is a verbal category which refers to a form or set of forms of the verb showing the **relation of the subject** of that verb **to the action** denoted by the verb. In English we can distinguish between an **active voice** and a **passive voice**.

Active Voice

The term **active voice** is used by grammarians to refer to the form of a verb whose **subject** is the **agent** (or performer) **of the action** denoted by the verb. For example, in the sentence *The child dropped the glass*, the verb *dropped* is in the active voice, as the subject (*the child*) is the agent, i.e. the person who does the dropping.

Passive Voice

The term **passive voice** refers to the form of a verb in which the **subject** of the verb is the **recipient** or the **undergoer of the action** denoted by the verb. For example, in the sentence *The glass was dropped by the child*, the subject (*the glass*) is not the performer but the undergoer or sufferer of the action of the verb: it was the glass which underwent or suffered the breaking. A verb in the **passive voice** is formed by using the auxiliary verb *be* with the past participle of the lexical verb. In our sentence, the form *was dropped* is the **passive form** of the verb *drop*. Note that the agent is still present in this sentence, not as the subject but as a prepositional phrase beginning with *by*. One of the stylistic advantages of the passive voice is that, if the agent prepositional phrase is omitted, we can talk about an action without mentioning who did it. This is useful if we do not know or are unwilling to reveal the identity of the performer of the action.

Recipient Passive

Unlike many languages, English also has the possibility of forming a recipient passive, where the **subject is now the recipient** or **beneficiary** of the action of the verb, i.e. the person who receives or benefits from the direct object (see page 152). Put more simply, the indirect object (see page 154) of the active verb is made the subject of the passive verb. For example, from the active sentence *Tom gave the money to Sue*, where *Sue* is grammatically the indirect object and semantically the recipient, we can form a recipient passive sentence *Sue was given the money by Tom*, where *Sue* is now grammatically the subject but semantically still the recipient. Note that *Tom* (in the prepositional phrase *by Tom*) also remains semantically the agent (the performer of the action of the verb) but is grammatically no longer the subject of the verb. For stylistic or other reasons, recipient passive sentences can also be made agentless, just as normal passive sentences can, by omitting the prepositional phrase with *by*, e.g. *Sue was given the money*.

Mood

Mood is a verbal category involving the speaker's attitude towards the action expressed by the verb. There are three important moods: the **indicative**, the **imperative** and the **subjunctive** mood. They may be characterized as follows:

1. If the **action expressed by the verb** is **regarded as a fact**, the verb is put in the **indicative** mood.
2. If the action is **regarded as a command**, the verb is put in the **imperative** mood.
3. If the action is **regarded as a wish or desire, as a possibility, or as a matter of supposition**, the verb is put in the **subjunctive** mood.

These moods are expressed in different ways by different languages. Some, like Latin, use inflected forms of the verb, some may use syntactic devices, some make use of modal auxiliary verbs, and others may employ a combination of these methods. English falls into the latter class. Let us examine how it expresses each mood.

Indicative

English has no special verb forms or auxiliary verbs to mark the indicative mood. It prefers to leave the verb unmarked. For example, if an action is considered to be a fact, any of the simple tenses or those formed by means of the primary auxiliaries can be used without any change. The absence of marking for the indicative mood, compared with the special marking for the imperative and subjunctive moods, is in fact a way of marking the verb. We have already seen this principle applied to tense and aspect. Consider the following pairs of sentences:

1. *They help us. They are helping us.* (Simple Present – Progressive Present)
2. *They helped us. They were helping us.* (Simple Past – Progressive Past)
3. *They have helped us. They have been helping us.* (Simple Perfect – Progressive Perfect)
4. *They had helped us. They had been helping us.* (Simple Past Perfect – Progressive Past Perfect)

Here we can clearly see the principle of the **unmarked** verb **contrasting with** the **marked** verb in regard to aspect and tense. In each pair the first sentence is unmarked for the progressive aspect, whereas the second is marked by the use of the expanded form (*be* + the *-ing* form) of the lexical verb. Similarly, the sentences in 1 and 2 are unmarked for the perfect aspect, whereas those in 3 and 4 are marked by the use of *have* + the past participle. We also see that the sentences in 2, 3 and 4 are all marked for past tense by the presence of the past tense form or of the past participle, whereas those in 1 indicate the present tense by being unmarked. In the same way, compared with the sentence *Help us!*, where the imperative mood is signalled by the absence of the subject pronoun *you*, or with the sentence *He should help us*, where the modal auxiliary signals the subjunctive mood, all the sentences in 1- 4 are in the indicative mood as they show no special marking for the imperative or the subjunctive. As we observed above, they are in fact marked by being unmarked!

Imperative

The imperative mood is the mood reserved for commands. These are marked in different ways in English depending on whether the recipient of the command is the first, second or third person of the verb. There are no special forms of the verb for the imperative mood. Commands are shown either by the omission of a subject pronoun or by the use of *let*. The second person imperative is by far the most common kind.

2nd Person without Pronoun

As mentioned above, the **second person imperative** is usually marked by the absence of the second person subject pronoun, i.e. **the bare base form** of the verb is used **for both singular and plural**. Thus the commands *Save them!, Wash it!* can be addressed to one person or to more than one. We can see that it is the second person subject pronoun which is omitted, as the reflexive imperative verb can only take a second person reflexive pronoun. We can only say *Wash yourself!* or *Wash yourselves!* but not *Wash *himself! Wash *ourselves!* The negative form of the command is introduced by *don't*, e.g. *Don't wash yourself! Don't shout!* In more formal English *don't* can be replaced by *do not*, e.g. *Do not forget the tragic plight of these people!*

2nd Person with Pronoun

The bare second person imperative with just the base form can usually only be used when the speaker is in a position of authority, e.g. officer to soldier, parent to child, teacher to pupil. The command can be **softened** by reintroducing the subject pronoun: *You drink some tea and then you'll feel better!* Rather surprisingly the same mechanism can also make the command **more forceful**: *You drink your tea or you'll be punished!* Only the context can make the intended meaning clear. Like the second person command without a pronoun, the command with the pronoun (whether softened or threatening) can also be made negative by using initial *don't*, e.g. *Don't you get cold, will you! Don't you spill your tea or I'll get cross!* Note that *do not*, the uncontracted form of *don't*, is ungrammatical here: **Do not you get cold ...! *Do not you spill your tea ...!*

3rd Person Command

English marks the third person singular of the imperative mood by employing the **bare base form**, which then contrasts with the base form + the suffix *-s* of the indicative mood. For example, *Mary take the tray and Ellen carry the teapot!* is an order, whereas *Mary takes the tray and Ellen carries the teapot* is statement of fact. When the subject of the third person imperative verb is plural, there is no formal difference between the imperative and the simple indicative present. Only the context and perhaps the intonation make it clear what the speaker intends. However, the addition of the softening interjection *please* shows that the sentence which it accompanies is a command, e.g. *Mary and Jack take the trays and Ellen and Bill carry the teapots, please.* Without *please* the sentence could be either a command or a statement. The negative form of the third person command is introduced by *don't*. It is not common but can be heard in commands with the pronoun *anybody* as the subject, e.g. *Don't anybody move! There's a snake on the carpet!* Uncontracted *do not* is not possible in this kind of command: * *Do not anybody move!*

1st Person Commands

A speaker can address a command to himself or herself or to a group of people including the speaker. Such **first person commands** are introduced by the word ***let***. This is followed by **the subject in the oblique (object) case**, preceding **the bare infinitive** of a lexical verb. Although *let* in this construction looks like the imperative of the verb *to let* meaning 'to allow', it usually does not have this meaning here. It is probably better to consider it as an **imperative particle**, which has little in common with the lexical verb from which it was historically derived. It can be used with both the singular and the plural of the first person, as in *Let me think! Let me see! Let me close the window! Let us pray! Let us be silent for a moment! Let us forget the past!* The negative form of first person commands is formed by adding *not* immediately before the base form of the lexical verb, e.g. *Let me not waste time! Let us not be afraid!*

Jussive

A **third person** imperative can also be formed with *let* and may be referred to as the **jussive imperative**. Unlike the third person commands described above, which are aimed directly at the addressee (the listener), jussive commands are spoken to an addressee but aimed indirectly at somebody else. **Examples:** *If he wants money, let him earn it! Let every man do his duty. Now that they are older, let the children speak for themselves.* The negative form of a jussive command is made in the same way as first person commands by adding *not* in front of the base form of the lexical verb, e.g. *If it is the truth, let her not be afraid to tell it! Let them not hesitate for a moment!*

Note on *let* Commands

Stylistically, all imperatives with *let* (except for those beginning with *let me*) sound antiquated or rather elevated. One might expect to encounter them in older versions of the Bible or in rhetorical speech. Notice, however, that this does not apply to the *let us* type when contracted to *let's*, which is very common in colloquial English: *Let's have fun today and go to the zoo! Let's help father dig the garden!* That the *let* in this contracted form of the command is different from the *let* which means 'allow' is shown by the fact that the latter cannot be followed by the contracted form of *us*, i.e. we can only say *Open the door and let us come in!* and **not** *Open the door and *let's come in!*

Formulaic Commands

There are a few archaic expressions in English in which an old present subjunctive (see next paragraph) has been preserved in place of the modern *let* construction. Some of these are: *God save the Queen. Long live the President! Suffice it to say that ....* The fact that these are fossilized formulae is emphasized by the word order of the last two, where the subject comes after the verb instead of in front of it.

Subjunctive

English makes sparse use of special forms of the verb to indicate the hypothetical nature of a speaker's utterance. The only clearly subjunctive form of the regular English verb is found in the third person singular of the present subjunctive.

Present Subjunctive

The **base form** is used **bare for all persons** of the present subjunctive. The *-s* suffix, which is characteristic of the third person singular of the present indicative, is missing. (For the special subjunctive forms of the irregular verb *be*, see Past Subjunctive and *were* below and also The Verb *be* on page 95 below). The present subjunctive occurs mostly in formal English, especially in *that* clauses and is commoner in American English than in British English. Thus in formal contexts we can hear sentences such as: *It has been suggested that he/I come at midday. It is essential that the child/you leave now. The wish has been expressed that the candidate/they appear in person.* The negative form of the present subjunctive makes no use of *do*-support, but adds *not* immediately in front of the verb, e.g. *It is essential that the child not leave now. Her most fervent wish is that we not tell her brother.*

should

In normal spoken and written British English, the subjunctive mood in these sentences is indicated by the use of the modal auxiliary *should*, e.g. *It has been suggested that he/I should (not) come at midday. It is essential that the child/you should (not) leave now. The wish has been expressed that the candidate/they should (not) appear in person.* Sometimes this use of *should* with the bare base form is referred to as a subjunctive substitute.

Past Subjunctive

The past subjunctive is commonly found in both written and spoken English in **hypothetical** ('unfulfilled') **conditional clauses** (see page 133), e.g. *He would forgive you, if he knew. If I tried now, I would fail. If you spoke to her politely, she would help you.* It also occurs **in idiomatic expressions** such as: *It is (high) time you found a wife.* Notice that in form the past subjunctive is identical with the simple past indicative.

were

The only verb that has past subjunctive forms distinct from those of the past indicative is the verb *be*, which uses *were* for both the first and third persons singular. This ***were*-subjunctive** is chiefly employed in formal English **in hypothetical conditional clauses** and in a few other constructions (such as **wishes**) which also have hypothetical meaning. In spoken English the past subjunctive *were* is often replaced in the first and third person singular by the indicative form *was*. **Examples:** *If she were/was my daughter, I* *would help her. He wouldn't spend his holidays abroad even if he <u>were/was</u> rich. She strutted into the room as if she <u>were/was</u> the Queen in person. I wish I <u>were/was</u> in Rome now! If only Jane <u>were/was</u> not here in this dreadful city! I would rather I <u>were/was</u> not invited.* The following examples show conditions and wishes where persons other than the first and third singular function as subject (i.e. where the subjunctive is indistinguishable from the indicative form of the verb): *If they <u>were</u> not my daughters, I wouldn't help them. We wouldn't go abroad, even if we <u>were</u> rich and <u>had</u> a lot of time. You look as if you <u>were</u> very unhappy, as if you <u>thought</u> I had insulted you.* Some of the constructions with hypothetical meaning in which it is possible to use subjunctive *were* can be replaced by less formal sounding grammatical alternatives. Thus, the sentence *I would rather I were not invited* could be rephrased with an infinitive: *I would rather not be invited.*

Emphatic *do*

Emphasis is not usually thought of as being a mood of the verb, but as a stylistic device. However, it has in common with the moods the fact that it can be considered as a way of looking at the action of the verb. Furthermore it is at least for the simple present and simple past tenses in English formed by the use of the same primary auxiliary *do*, which is needed for *do*-support in the formation of questions and negative sentences. Notice that it is also a phonetic phenomenon as the emphatic *do*-forms of the verb must be stressed, e.g. *I **dó** like your hat!* instead of the unemphatic simple present *I like your hát*. Emphatic sentences are particularly common as contradictions. Thus if somebody claims that you have not written to them, you can contradict them with the emphatic simple past sentence *But I **díd** write to you – yesterday!* For other tenses and moods, i.e. those formed by means of auxiliary verbs, emphatic sentences are always made by stressing the latter: *We **wíll** go! I **cán** do it! He **shóuld** know the answer! They **múst** come!* Emphatic *do* is found not only in the indicative mood, but also in the imperative. Here, however, the emphasis has a softening rather than a strengthening effect. If I really want you to take a piece of cake, I can say ***Dó** have a piece of cake!* The offer is gentler than *Have a piece of cáke!* but it insists on your putting any unwillingness aside. Other examples are ***Dó** tell me! **Dó** visit us!* Emphatic *do* is not usual in the subjunctive mood. If there is need to emphasize the subjunctive verb in a sentence such as *It is necessary that the child <u>like</u> it*, then we cannot say *It is necessary that the child *dó like it*. Emphasis is achieved by merely stressing the subjunctive verb itself (i.e. ***líke***).

Person & Number

Although person and number are two separate categories, it will be convenient to treat them together. Neither plays a very big role in the morphology of the English verb, though in some languages both are very important. Let us look first at **person**. This category is concerned with the **roles** of persons or things **in a conversational exchange**. All languages distinguish a **first person** (the speaker or speakers), a **second person** (the addressee or addressees), and a **third person** (one or more persons or things referred to by the speaker in his exchange with the addressee). The category of person is most clearly seen in English in the personal pronouns and determiners: 1st person: *I, me, my, mine, we, us, our, ours*; 2nd person: *you, your, yours*; 3rd person: *he, him, his, she, her, hers, it, its, they, them, their, theirs*. The category of **number** is manifested in English by the two-way contrast between **singular** and **plural**, which we find among the personal pronouns and also the demonstrative pronouns (*this/these, that/those*) and among almost all nouns (*dog/dogs, dish/dishes*). For verbs, however, apart from *be* (see page 95), number is of little importance. Number and person distinctions are found only in the simple present tense of lexical verbs, where the *-s* form of the verb for the third person singular, as in *(he/she/it) speaks*, contrasts with the base form for all the remaining persons of the singular and the plural, as in *(I/you [sg]/we/you [pl]/they) speak*. As we saw above, even this distinction in the present tense is missing in the morphology of the modal auxiliary verbs, as they have no separate form for the third person singular. Moreover, the past tense of both lexical and auxiliary verbs (except *be*) also shows no distinctions for person or number.

Verbal Agreement

Despite the fact that English makes little use of the category of number in the morphology of its verbs, the role of this category is nevertheless important in the agreement that is found between a third person subject and the verb, since it is here (in the present tense) that the difference between the singular and the plural verb forms can be clearly heard. We have already dealt with some cases of surprising or problematic agreement in connection with subjects which are special types of nouns (see Unmarked Plurals, Collective Nouns, Fractions, pages 24–26). We can complete the picture here, by mentioning the kind of agreement which is often found in present-day English in connection with the indefinite pronouns *somebody, someone, anybody, anyone, everybody, everyone, nobody, no one*. When these are in subject position, the verb must agree with them by assuming the third person singular form, e.g. *everybody agrees, someone refuses*. In **formal** English, any pronoun which refers back to the indefinite pronoun subject must be **masculine singular**, e.g. *When somebody introduces himself, he gives his name. If anybody loses his ticket, he has to pay for a new one. Nobody has hurt himself, has he?* In

non-formal English, however, many people feel that this use of masculine pronouns discriminates against women, and therefore prefer third person **plural pronouns**, since these can refer to either sex. When this is done, the verb still retains its singular agreement after the indefinite subject pronoun, but in a following sentence or clause whose subject refers back to that pronoun by using *they*, both verbal and subsequent pronoun agreement is plural, e.g. *When somebody introduces themselves, they give you their name. If anybody loses their ticket, they have to pay for a new one. Nobody has hurt themselves, have they?*

3 Types of Verb

General Remarks

In addition to the categorization of verbs into lexical versus auxiliary verbs and into dynamic versus stative verbs according to their semantic characteristics (see page 78), we can also differentiate verbs according to their morphology into **regular** versus **irregular** verbs, and according to their syntactic behaviour into **prepositional**, **phrasal** and **phrasal-prepositional** verbs.

Regular versus Irregular

There are a little over 170 verbs in English whose past tenses and past participles are formed irregularly. As these are listed in any good Foreign Learner's Dictionary of English, e.g. CIDE, DCE, OALD, we need only mention a few of these here with their main characteristics.

American versus British

Occasionally there are differences between American English (AE) and British English (BE). For example, the verbs *dive* and *plead* have a regular form for past tense and past participle in BE (*dived, dived; pleaded, pleaded*), but an irregular form for both in AE (*dove, dove*, pronounced: [douv]; *pled, pled*). In the case of *fit*, where BE has the regular forms (*fitted, fitted*), AE uses the unchanged infinitive form for past tense and past participle (*fit, fit*). AE also uses the unchanged infinitive form *spit* for past tense and past participle, whereas BE has *spat* for both. More commonly AE prefers regular forms (*dwelled, dreamed, kneeled, smelled, spoiled*) whereas BE prefers irregular ones (*dwelt, dreamt*, pronounced: [dremt], *knelt, smelt, spoilt*). Sometimes, the irregular forms are partially different in each variety of English. For example, the verb *get* has the same irregular past tense form *got* in BE and AE, but a different past participle in each (BE: *got*, AE: *gotten*). Note that this AE past participle is preserved in BE in prefixed forms of *get: begotten, forgotten.* Two verbs (*eat, shine*) have the same irregular past tense form *ate, shone* in both varieties of English but the pronunciation is different: BE: [et], AE: [eɪt]; BE: [ʃɒn], AE: [ʃoʊn].

Types of Irregularity

Among all the verbs which have the same irregular forms in AE and BE we can distinguish three main kinds:

1. Those which have **only one form** for infinitive, past tense and past participle. These are usually verbs that end in *t* or *d*, e.g. *cast, cast, cast; cut, cut, cut; let, let, let; shed, shed, shed, etc.*
2. Those which have **two forms**: one for the infinitive and a single different form for past tense and past participle, e.g. *bind, bound, bound; dig, dug, dug; feed, fed, fed; hear, heard, heard; sell, sold, sold, etc.* Note that *have* as a lexical verb with the meaning 'possess' belongs in this category: *have, had, had.*
3.Those which have **three forms**: one for the infinitive, another for the past tense and a third for the past participle, e.g. *arise, arose, arisen; bear, bore, borne; drink, drank, drunk; eat, ate, eaten; forgive, forgave, forgiven; speak, spoke, spoken, etc.* Note that the past tense of *go*, which belongs in this third category (*go, went, gone*), has been borrowed from the old verb *wend*, now only heard in archaic or rhetorical speech in the expression *to wend one's way*. This use of a different root, e.g. a form borrowed from another word, in order to complete a paradigm is referred to as **suppletion**.

The Verb *be*

Of all the verbs of English, *be* is the **most irregular**. In the singular of the **present tense**, it is the only verb which has **different forms for all three persons**:

1st Person *(I) am*; 2nd Person *(you) are*; 3rd Person *(he/she/it) is.*

In archaic English we can sometimes hear the older second person singular form of the present: *(thou) art.* Notice that suppletion also plays a role here: although *am, art, are* can be considered to have the same root, *is* has a totally different one. We see a further case of suppletion in the past tense forms, which all have a different root from those of the present. The verb *be* is the only English verb whose simple **past tense** forms are **differentiated for number:**

Singular *(I, he/she/it)* <u>*was*</u>, but Plural *(we, you, they)* <u>*were*</u>.

Note that the archaic second person singular form *(thou)* <u>*wast*</u> has been replaced in modern English by the second person plural form which now serves for both singular and plural.

Present Subjunctive of *be*

The verb *be* is unique in English in having a special form for the present subjunctive, namely the base form *be* undifferentiated for person and number. Thus in formal and rhetorical language we find sentences such as: *If <u>he</u> <u>be</u> a man, let him resolve the problem himself. I will do it, if <u>it</u> <u>be</u> in my power. It is essential that <u>you</u> not <u>be</u> placed under pressure.* In less formal style this subjunctive form would normally be replaced by the present indicative in the first two examples (*If he <u>is</u> a man ..., ... if it <u>is</u> in my power*) and by the auxiliary *should* with the infinitive of *be* in the last example (*It is essential that you should not be placed under pressure*). Notice that in formulaic commands of the kind *God be praised* (see page 90), the *be* form is usually analysed as a subjunctive rather than as an imperative.

Past Subjunctive of *be*

There is only one past subjunctive form of *be*, namely *were*. No differentiation is made for person and for number. The past subjunctive can still be found in adverbial clauses with hypothetical meaning which begin with *if, as if, as though,* and also in noun clauses after verbs of wishing, supposing, etc. However, it is frequently replaced in modern English by the past indicative. **Examples:** *If his brother were/was here, he could give us more details. She spoke to them as if she were/was their mother. The child snored as though it were/was fast asleep. I wish I were/was in Paris now. Suppose he were/was president, what difference would that make?* There are two fixed expressions in which modern English always has the past subjunctive and not the past indicative. One is *as it were (= so to speak)*, used when speakers wish to indicate that words are not being used in their exact sense, e.g. *He was, as it were, taken by her charm* (i.e. *infatuated by her*). The other is *if I were you*, used especially when giving advice to another person, e.g. *If I were you, I'd use a smaller hammer.*

Prepositional, Phrasal & Phrasal-Prepositional Verbs

The last important category of verbs that we need to look at are those which consist of a verb root (base form) plus a preposition or an adverbial particle or both a particle and a preposition. Some grammarians refer to all three kinds of verb as phrasal verbs, but it is more useful (as we shall see when we come later in this book to sentence constituent analysis) to distinguish the three types from one another as **prepositional verbs, phrasal verbs**, and **phrasal-prepositional verbs**.

Prep. Verbs

Not every verb which is followed by a preposition is a prepositional verb. Some verbs, like *go, run, travel* or *put, place* can be followed by almost any preposition: *She ran into/ out of/ through/ down/ up/ round the garden. He put the book on/under/beside/above/ behind/in front of the table.* Verbs of this kind will not be referred to as prepositional verbs. We shall reserve the term for a verb which requires one particular preposition (occasionally there is a choice between two) in order to complete its meaning. Usually the verbs of this kind are idiomatic, i.e. the sense is arbitrary and cannot be deduced from the meaning of the verb root plus the meaning of the preposition, as it can for the verbs *ran* and *put* in our two example sentences above. Thus *She ran into the garden yesterday* describes an act of running into a specific place, but *She ran into her cousin yesterday* does not describe an act of running in a particular direction, but has the idiomatic meaning of *She happened to meet her cousin yesterday*, i.e. *She met him or her by chance.* This meaning is attached to *run* only when it is followed by the preposition *into*. We can tell that *into* is a preposition here, because if we replace the noun phrase *her cousin* by the corresponding pronoun (*him/her*) then *into* comes before the pronoun (i.e. it is pre-posed): *She ran <u>into</u> <u>him/her</u> yesterday.* The verb *run into* used in this specific sense is a prepositional verb. We have already mentioned quite a number of these verbs in our discussion of prepositions on pages 76–77 above. Let us re-examine a few of them here.

Examples

1. *They <u>objected</u> strongly <u>to</u> the council's decision.* We can see from this sentence that *object to* is a prepositional verb, because (a) *object* can only be followed by the preposition *to* when it has this meaning of 'protest against', and because (b), if the noun phrase following *to* is replaced by the corresponding pronoun (*it*), the word *to* remains in front of the pronoun: *They objected <u>to</u> <u>it</u>.* We shall see below that this latter condition is especially important as phrasal verbs often look exactly like prepositional verbs but require a different position for the pronoun.

2. (a) *She often complained <u>of/about</u> <u>headaches</u> (... <u>of/about</u> <u>them</u>)* (b) *The headaches (which) she often <u>complained</u> <u>of/about</u> were always severe.* In the (a) sentence the verb is clearly a prepositional verb because *complain* must be followed by one of the two prepositions *of* and *about* when it has this meaning of 'moan' or 'grumble', and because each of the prepositions retains its position when the noun following it (*headaches*) is replaced by the corresponding pronoun (*them*). In the (b) sentence, the verb is now in a relative clause in which the preposition is stranded, i.e. it has been left at the end of its clause instead of coming in front of a relative pronoun at the beginning of the clause (see page 71 above). To decide whether *of* or *about* are prepositions here, we must either see whether they can be moved to a position **in front of** the relative pronoun (e.g. *The headaches <u>of which</u>/<u>about which</u> she often complained ...*) or we must take the verb *complain* out of its clause and form a sentence such as 2(a) where the noun or noun phrase after *of* or *about* (here *headaches*) is replaced by the corresponding pronoun (e.g. *She complained <u>of</u> <u>them</u>/<u>about</u> <u>them</u>*). In both cases if *of* or *about* remain in front of the relative pronoun or the personal pronoun, then *complain of/about* is a prepositional verb. To illustrate this principle again let us consider the following example:

3. *The book I was <u>looking</u> <u>at</u> fell onto the floor.* If we restore the relative pronoun and try putting *at* in front of it, we get an acceptable sentence: *The book <u>at</u> <u>which</u> I was looking fell onto the floor.* The

word *at* seems thus to be a preposition. To make sure, we can try the other test and take *complain* out of its relative clause and form a simple sentence replacing the noun phrase after *at* by the corresponding pronoun: *I was looking at it*. Again *at* is in front of the pronoun, showing that the word *at* is a preposition. Finally, to decide whether *look at* is a prepositional verb in example 3, we observe that *look at* has the meaning 'examine' here and that this meaning is only possible when *look* is combined with the preposition *at* and no other preposition. This being so, *look at* must be a prepositional verb.

Phrasal Verbs

If we now turn to phrasal verbs, we discover that they look very like prepositional verbs but behave differently. They too are often idiomatic and consist of a **verb root** combined with another word. However, this second word is now not a preposition but an **adverbial particle** (some grammarians refer to it merely as an adverb). In order to understand this, let us look at the typical phrasal verb *send back*. In a sentence such as *They sent back the letter*, we have a verb form (*sent*) followed by the word *back* in front of a noun phrase. The word order is the same as for a prepositional verb, but if we replace the noun phrase after *back* (namely *the letter*) by the corresponding pronoun (*it*), we notice that the **pronoun must precede** *back* and can no longer follow it: *They sent it back*. This means that *back* cannot be a preposition here, because prepositions must be pre-posed with respect to a pronoun. The word *back* is an **adverbial particle** and the combination *send back* is a **phrasal verb**. Other phrasal verbs are: *call off, cut down, hand over, put on, ring up, take out*. In the following example sentences, each phrasal verb is shown in three versions: first with a noun or noun phrase after the adverbial particle, then with the corresponding pronoun, and finally with the noun or noun phrase object **preceding** the adverbial particle (a pattern which is impossible for prepositional verbs):

4. (a) *The Government called off the elections (= cancelled)*. (b) *The government called them off*. (c) *The Government called the elections off*.
5. (a) *The forester cut down the tree (= felled)*. (b) *The forester cut it down*. (c) *The forester cut the tree down*.
6. (a) *They handed over all the prisoners (= returned, surrendered)*. (b) *They handed them all over*. (c) *They handed all the prisoners over*.
7. (a) *She put on a coat (= dressed herself in)*. (b) *She put it on*. (c) *She put the coat on*.
8. (a) *We rang up her father (= telephoned to)*. (b) *We rang him up*. (c) *We rang her father up*.
9. (a) *John took out a coin and paid (= extracted, withdrew)*. (b) *John took it out* ... (c) *John took a coin out* ...

Intransitive Phrasal Verbs

All the prepositional verbs and phrasal verbs which we have discussed above have been followed by an object (the noun or noun phrase which in our test could be converted into the corresponding pronoun). There are some two-word verbs, however, which are intransitive, i.e. they do not admit an object, e.g. *turn in (= go to bed), turn up (= arrive)*. These can only be phrasal verbs, i.e. the second word in them must be an adverbial particle, since a preposition must have an object. Let us compare them for a moment with the prepositional verb *argue with*. We cannot say **They argued with*, but only *They argued with somebody*, since the preposition *with* is incomplete without a pronoun or noun phrase object. The situation is quite different with the two phrasal verbs *turn in* and *turn up*. Both make good sense without an object: *Now I must turn in. When did they turn up?* Other intransitive phrasal verbs are: *run away, boil over, break out, crop up, go ahead, hang back, hold on, lash out, nod off, pine away, rise up, stand out, tail off, tune in, wear off.*

Mixed

There are a number of verbs whose second word can be either a preposition or an adverbial particle. They are of **two types**: (a) those which must take an object when followed by the preposition but which are intransitive when followed by the adverbial particle, and (b) those which take an object in both cases. Examples:

Type (a)

10. (Prep. Vb:) *The teacher came across another mistake.* (Phras. Vb:) *The meaning of his words did not come across.*
11. (Prep.Vb:) *The children gathered around the old man.* (Phras.Vb:) *I'd like everbody to gather around, so that I can explain the plan.*
12. (Prep.Vb:) *They pushed past the doorkeeper and entered the room.* (Phras. Vb:) *He swore at them as they pushed past.*

Other type (a) verbs are: *come down, cross over, do without, fall off, go up, hang around, join in, move about, spill over.*

Type (b)

13. (Prep. Vb:) *She couldn't get down the stairs (= descend).* (Phras.Vb:) *She couldn't get the pot down (= lift down).*
14. (Prep.Vb:) *The train passed through the tunnel (= travelled through).* (Phras. Vb:) *The cashier passed the money through (= handed it through the window of the cashdesk).*
15. (Prep.Vb:) *The girl looked through the window.* (Phras. Vb:) *She took the letters and looked them through (= examined them briefly).*

Type (b) verbs are not as common as type (a) and they usually show a change in the meaning between the two uses.

Phrasal-Prepositional Verbs

Some verbs are three-word verbs, i.e. they consist of a verb root plus an adverbial particle plus a preposition. Most of them are idiomatic, i.e. their meaning cannot be derived from the basic meaning of the verb root. The preposition is always last, as we can see when we change the noun phrase object into the corresponding pronoun. For example, with the phrasal-prepositional verb *do away with* we can form the following two sentences: *They did away with their old furniture (= got rid of). They did away with it.* Of the two words *away* and *with*, only *with* has a noun phrase or pronoun directly after it. Only this word can therefore be the preposition; *away* must be the adverbial particle. Other typical phrasal-prepositional verbs are: *boil down to, catch up with, come up against, face up to, go in for, grow out of, look down on, look forward to, make off with, put up with, run off with, talk down to.*

7 Adverbs

1 General Remarks

Definition

The word class **adverb** consists of a very heterogeneous collection of words whose basic function is to add some information to the verb, i.e. about the time, place, manner, etc. of the action of the verb, e.g. *yesterday, here, slowly*. However, 'adverb' is a rag-bag category into which grammarians and dictionary makers also put many words which do not fit into the other grammatical classes. Thus there are some adverbs which modify an adjective or another adverb or even a sentence, and some which connect sentences together. We shall see examples of all of these types below.

Morphology

Many adverbs cannot be recognized by their shape, though adverbs of manner (which are usually derived from adjectives and tell us how something is done) mostly end in the suffix *-ly*, e.g. *slowly, happily, quietly*. We must be careful, however, not to jump to conclusions. Not all words ending in *-ly* are adverbs: some are adjectives, e.g. *friendly, godly, heavenly, lonely, lovely, ugly, queenly, motherly, etc.* No single-word adverbs can be formed from these adjectives, but they can be made into adverbial phrases, such as *in a friendly way, in a godly manner, in a heavenly fashion.* Most adverbs of manner and frequency are gradable like adjectives, i.e. they have a comparative with *more*, a superlative with *most*, and can be preceded by an intensifier such as *very*, e.g. *more slowly, most slowly, very slowly; more often, most often, very often*. Some monosyllabic ones, however, form the comparative with the suffix *-er* and the superlative with the suffix *-est*: *hard (he worked harder, hardest), fast (she ran faster, fastest), long (we waited longer, longest), soon (they came sooner than expected)*. The superlative of *soon* is rare but can be heard in the proverb *least said, soonest mended*. The two manner adverbs *badly* and *well* have irregular comparatives and superlatives: *they worked badly, worse, worst; they spoke well, better, best*.

→ 6 different irregular ones

2 Classification

Semantic

Adverbs can be classified on semantic grounds into eight broad classes (1) **manner**, (2) **place**, (3) **time**, (4) **degree**, (5) **focussing** (6) **interrogative**, (7) **linking** adverbs, (8) **sentential** adverbs. We will consider each of these classes in detail below.

Manner

A manner adverb typically answers the questions ***How?, In what manner?, In what way?***, when asked of the verb which the adverb modifies. Thus, as we saw above, manner adverbs tell us how the action of the verb is performed. For example, with regard to the sentence *The bird sang beautifully*, if we ask the question *How did the bird sing?* the answer is given by the manner adverb *beautifully*. Since manner adverbs describe actions, they can be used only with dynamic verbs and not with stative verbs. We have also seen that they are frequently derived from adjectives by means of the suffix *-ly* (*beautiful > beautifully, wise > wisely, bright > brightly, pure > purely, etc.*). In consequence, they form a very large class of adverbs.

Place

Just as manner adverbs answer the question ***How?***, so place adverbs answer the questions: ***Where? In, at or to what place?*** Unlike manner adverbs, they cannot easily be recognized morphologically as they do not end in *-ly*. Typical place adverbs are *abroad, here, there, indoors, outdoors, underneath, below, above, down, inside, outside*. We see some of these illustrated in the following example sentences:

Examples

1. *Judy has left her country and gone abroad to Spain.*
2. *James was sitting indoors in order to avoid the hot sun.*

Notice that some of these adverbs of place can also be used as prepositions:

3. (a) *The cat is not on the table! - Look underneath!* (adverb) (b) *The cat was underneath the table.* (preposition + prepositional object)
4. (a) *Sue was in the post office, so the boys waited outside.* (adverb) (b) *They left their bicycles outside the post office.* (preposition + prepositional object)

In our discussion of phrasal verbs (page 98) we noted that a verb root is combined in each case with an adverb, which we preferred to call an adverbial particle. Many of these were originally adverbs of place, but their present meaning is obscure and has no relation to space. A few examples will make this clear.

5. (*give in*) *They lost the fight and had to give in (= surrender).*
6. (*fall through*) *All their plans have fallen through (= failed).*
7. (*slip up*) *This is wrong. We must have slipped up somewhere (= made a mistake).*
8. (*stand in*) *Her boss is ill, so she is standing in for him (= temporarily doing his job).*
9. (*watch out*) *Watch out! (= be careful) That ladder is dangerous.*

Time

Adverbs of time are best divided into three categories, depending upon the questions which they answer. We can distinguish between adverbs of **specific time**, of **frequency** and of **duration**.

Specific Time

The adverbs in this category answer the question ***When?*** or ***At what time?*** A few common ones are: *now, then, tomorrow, yesterday, afterwards, before.* Notice that the nouns for the days of the week can also be used colloquially as specific time adverbs: *We'll be arriving Monday.* In less colloquial speech the prepositional phrase on Monday would be required here. Particular attention must be paid to the specific time adverb *presently*. Besides its obvious meaning of 'now, at the present moment', as in *Jane is presently working in Edinburgh*, it can in both British and American English rather confusingly mean 'soon, later', although for some speakers this usage is a little old-fashioned now, e.g. *I'll bring the book presently, after I've washed the car.*

Frequency

Adverbs in this category answer the question ***How often?*** A few of these are: *often, occasionally, repeatedly, frequently, seldom, never, once, twice*. Some adverbs are ambiguous: both *never* and *once* can refer to specific time or to frequency, e.g.

10. (a) **(Specific Time)** *He never recovered from his accident (= not at any time)* (b) **(Frequency)** *They have never answered our letters*. In the (a) sentence it makes no sense to ask *How often did he recover?* but only to ask *When did he recover?* On the other hand, the (b) sentence is more likely to be the reply to the question *How often have they answered your letters?* than to the question *When did they answer your letters?* but the latter could also be asked here.

11. (a) **(Specific Time)** *She was once a famous author but nobody reads her books now (= at a specific time in the past)*. (b) **(Frequency)** *We visited them once and never again (= only one time).*

Notice that in colloquial speech the plural forms of the nouns for the days of the week (*Mondays, Tuesdays, etc.*) can be used as frequency adverbs, but usually only at the beginning of a sentence. They then have the meaning 'every Monday', 'every Tuesday', etc., for example *Mondays we always do the washing*. However, here too there is some ambiguity, as *Mondays* could also be the answer to the question *When do you do your washing?(= On what days?)*

Duration

Adverbs of duration answer the question ***For how long?*** A few of them are: *briefly, temporarily, momentarily, fleetingly, overnight, perpetually, always.* A couple of examples will make their use and meanings clear:

12. *They stopped off briefly in Berlin (= stayed for a short time).*

13. *I wondered fleetingly whether they really did have enough money to pay the bill (= for a brief moment).*

Some of these adverbs can be ambiguous between duration and frequency. Consider *always* in the following examples:

14. (a) *She always came on Thursdays.* (b) *I shall always think of you when I see this chair.* In the (a) sentence, *always* is the answer to the question *How often did she come on Thursdays?* The adverb is clearly an adverb of frequency here. On the other hand, in the (b) sentence *always* is the reply to the question *For how long will you think of me when you see this chair?* Here it is clearly an adverb of duration, but the other question *How often will you think of me …* also seems to make sense too, and in answer to this, *always* must be an adverb of frequency. There is nothing disturbing about this ambiguity: languages are often fuzzy in some areas.

Degree

Degree adverbs answer the question ***To what degree?*** Typical examples of this kind of adverb are: *almost, nearly, quite, highly, extremely, very.* Some of these can be used to modify a verb provided that the action of the verb permits degrees of fulfilment, e.g. *She almost fainted* (some of the signs of fainting were present but not all of them); *He nearly died of fright* (his death did not occur but he was only a few degrees away from it); *They quite enjoyed the concert though the orchestra did not play its best* (their enjoyment was not to the full degree but close to it).

Intensifiers & Downtoners

Some degree adverbs are mainly used to modify adjectives or other adverbs. They either intensify the degree of the quality which the adjective or adverb denotes **(intensifiers)** or they tone the quality down **(downtoners)**. The last three of the adverbs given as examples in the preceding paragraph are intensifiers: *highly, extremely, very.* The meaning of these intensifying adverbs is 'to a (very) high degree', e.g. *highly indignant, extremely pretty, extremely often, very carefully.* Many intensifiers are restricted to colloquial speech, as in *awfully clever, terribly serious, frightfully rich, fearfully old-fashioned*; others, as in *amazingly intelligent, surprisingly often, absurdly expensive*, can be used in more formal style. The meaning of the downtowners, on the other hand, is 'not to a high degree, but only to a fairly high degree'. The adverbs *almost, nearly, quite* from the preceding paragraph when used to modify an adjective or an adverb are downtoners, e.g. *almost certain, nearly dark, quite easily.* Other examples can be seen in *fairly small, relatively open-mindedly, (I'm) pretty sure.*

Negative Adverb *not*

There is one particular degree adverb which is concerned with negative degrees. This is the negative adverb *not*, which when modifying adjectives and adverbs means 'to no degree', e.g. *not certain, not dark, not easily.* It can also be used unrestrictedly with all types of verb, even if the meaning does not easily permit degrees of perception, e.g. *She did not sing, They did not break it, We might not see them.*

Broad Negative Adverbs

One interesting group of degree adverbs (which are also concerned with negativity) are the **broad negative adverbs**. Formally these do not look negative, but when we analyse their meaning we find that it contains a negative element. Members of this group are *seldom, rarely* (both = 'not often'), *hardly, scarcely, barely* (all = 'almost ... not', 'almost ... no') and *only* (= 'nobody but', 'nothing but', 'nowhere but', etc.). Adverbs of this kind may also be referred to as **negative-feel adverbs**, as they are also behave as if they were grammatically negative, e.g. they **require** (a) the **non-assertive** (i.e. non-affirmative) **pronouns** and **determiners** *any, anybody, anything* (see pages 66–67), (b) an **affirmative tag** in tag questions, and (c) **inversion** of the subject and verb (see pages 147–149). A few examples will make this clear.

15. (a) *They **seldom** had any* (not **some*) *money and **rarely** visited anybody* (not **somebody*). (b) *They **seldom** had any money, did they?* (not **didn't they?*). (c) ***Rarely** did they visit their relatives* (not *Rarely *they visited*).

16. (a) ***Hardly** anything* (not **something*) *was eaten.* (b) ***Scarcely** any of the guests ate anything, did they?* (not ** didn't they*). (c) ***Barely** had she left the house* (not *Barely *she had left*) *when the police arrived.*

Only

It should be observed that *only* is primarily a focussing adverb (see below) and that, perhaps for this reason, it does not have all the characteristics of the other broad negative adverbs. Thus, although it can be used with a non-assertive pronoun or determiner in statements, as in *Only the girls* (= 'nobody but the girls`) *had any money*, we also find the same sentence with an assertive pronoun or determiner: *Only the girls had some money.* In tag questions it does not usually have a negative feel about it at all: *Jane bought only one book, didn't she?* (not **did she?*). Or: *Only Jane bought a book, didn't she?* (not **did she?*). Compare these two tag questions with their equivalents: *Jane did not buy more than one book, did she?* and *Nobody but Jane bought one book, did they?* Notice, however, that when *only* begins a sentence as part of an adverbial phrase, then like all negative adverbs in sentence-initial position, it requires inversion of the subject and verb, e.g. *Only in Iceland* (= 'nowhere but in Iceland') *did he wear a fur coat* (not **he wore*). *Only in spring* (= 'at no other time than in spring') *will these plants bear flowers* (not **these plants will*).

Focussing Adverbs

Another class of adverbs which can perhaps be thought of as related to the degree adverbs are the focussing adverbs. These are of two kinds: **selecting** and **restricting**. Selecting adverbs focus on a particular group of persons or things from a larger group: among these are *chiefly, especially, mainly, mostly, particularly, primarily*. Restricting adverbs focus attention on only one person or thing as the centre of interest: among these are *only, just, solely,* *exclusively, purely.* Both kinds of focussing adverb can be used with nouns or noun phrases, adjectives and prepositional phrases, as we see in the following examples.

17. *They liked reading books, particularly detective novels* (**Selecting**, with **Noun Phrase**) *but their other interests were mainly political* (Selecting, with Adjective).
18. *Fires were lit mainly in winter, especially by the peasants.* (In both cases **Selecting**, with **Prepositional Phrase**)
19. *It was simply a matter of politeness* (**Restrictive**, with **Noun Phrase**)*: they should not have offered us only tea* (**Restrictive**, with **Noun**) *and food that was just lukewarm* (**Restrictive**, with **Adjective**).
20. *They acted purely out of self-interest* (**Restrictive**, with **Prepositional Phrase**).

Interrogative Adverbs

The interrogative adverbs are a small group of adverbs which, with the exception of *how*, all have *wh-* at the beginning of them: *when, where, why.* As their name suggests, they are all used to introduce questions. We find them, for example, in direct questions: *When did he go? Where are the keys? Why are you laughing? How do they know?* And also in indirect questions: *She wondered when he had gone. They wanted to know where the keys were. He asked us why we were laughing. We inquired how they knew.* Care must be taken not to confuse the interrogative adverb *when* (= 'at what time') with the conjunction *when* (= 'at the time at which'). Compare 21 and 22.
21. **(Interrogative Adverb)** *I asked them when she came. (= 'At what time did she come?')*
22. **(Conjunction)** *I asked them when she came. (= at the time at which she came).*
Note that if the clause beginning with the conjunction *when* is put first, the sentence remains grammatical: *When she came I asked them.* This cannot be done, however, with the clause beginning with the interrogative adverb *when*.

Linking Adverbs

The class of linking adverbs is used to make logical links between sentences. Among its members we find: *so, consequently, therefore, thus, similarly, furthermore, moreover, however.* The following sequence of three sentences illustrates the use of two of them: *Our house has been broken into twice. So we have moved to another area. However, we didn't lose very much.* Linking adverbs are most often found as the first word in a sentence, but most of them can also occur later, usually after the first sentence constituent (e.g. subject, adverbial phrase), and are then often separated off from the rest of the sentence by commas, e.g. *All the ministers were punctual. The President, however, came late.* The adverb however can also come in final position: thus the last sentence could read *The President came late, however.*

Sentential Adverbs

Those adverbs which indicate the viewpoint of the speaker are usually referred to as **sentential adverbs**. They are of two kinds: (a) those which show the **speaker's attitude** to what he or she says, and (b) those which state the **speaker's field of reference**, i.e. which make clear the context in which the speaker's words are to be understood. Like the linking adverbs, both kinds usually come first in the sentence but can sometimes appear in later positions.

Attitude

Typical attitude adverbs are: *apparently, interestingly, luckily, obviously, possibly, perhaps*. Consider the following examples:
23. *Apparently (= As far as I know), he is not married.*
24. *Interestingly (= I think it is interesting to know), the house is still for sale.*
25. *Perhaps (= I think it is possible), I can help you.*
Note that the attitude sentential adverb *actually* introduces a statement which the speaker considers surprising for the listener or the opposite of what the listener my expect:
26. *Do you know that young man? – Actually, he's my brother!*
Notice also that some attitude sentential adverbs (*naturally, frankly, surely)* can also be adverbs of manner. In the latter case they are usually in medial or even in final position in the sentence. Compare the following pairs of sentences:
27. (a) **(Sentential Adverb)** *Naturally (= of course), he spoke to them.* (b) **(Manner Adverb)** *He spoke naturally to them* or *He spoke to them naturally* (in both cases = *in a natural manner*).
28. (a) **(Sentential Adverb)** *Frankly (= I am being frank with you), I don't believe a word he says.* (b) (**Manner Adverb**) *I told him frankly (= in a frank manner) that I detested them.*
29. (a) **(Sentential Adverb)** *Surely (It cannot be true that), you are not going to give them the money.* (b) **(Manner Adverb)** *The goat planted its feet surely (= in a sure manner) on the rocky ledge.*

Field of Reference

Typical sentential adverbs showing the speaker's field of reference are *biologically, economically, historically, militarily.* When used in this way, they can always be replaced by adverbial phrases such as *from a biological (economic, historical, military) point of view* or be expanded to *biologically (economically, historically, militarily) speaking*, e.g. in the following sentences:
30. *Historically, this character was insignificant, although he is the hero of the novel.*
31. *Militarily, the dropping of atom bombs makes little sense.*
Notice that in colloquial speech it is possible to make sentence adverbs of this kind by adding the suffix *-wise* to nouns. For example,

32. *<u>Employment-wise</u> (= With regard to employment), these jobs should never have been created.*
33. *<u>Money-wise</u> (= As far as money is concerned), they are better off now than they used to be.*

8 Conjunctions

1 General Remarks

Definition

Traditionally, conjunctions have been defined as a class of uninflected words which are used to connect words, phrases, clauses or sentences. They are usually put into two classes: **co-ordinating** conjunctions such as *and, or* and **subordinating** conjunctions such as *although, as, because.* To these may also be added **correlative** pairs such as *both ... and.* As this is the terminology used by almost all the modern dictionaries and by most school-book grammarians, we shall continue to use it here. However, it should be pointed out that many modern grammarians find this terminology confusing and prefer to reserve the term *conjunction* just for co-ordinating conjunctions. This is because the wide meaning of the verb *conjoin* (= 'join, connect together') has been restricted in transformational grammar to refer to the grammatical process of connecting together only items belonging to the same grammatical class, i.e. co-ordinate items. As this excludes linking words which subordinate, the traditional subordinating conjunctions have to be given a new name. Those which introduce subordinate **adverbial** clauses (see pages 131–137) are referred to by these grammarians as **subordinators**, e.g. *although, as, because*, and those which introduce subordinate **noun** clauses are called **complementizers**, e.g. *that, whether.* Below we shall use the older terminology to classify the conjunctions under the three main headings: co-ordinating, subordinating and correlative conjunctions; but we shall make use of the more modern terminology to subclassify subordinating conjunctions.

2 Co-ordinating Conjunctions

Characteristics

The co-ordinating conjunctions (often referred to nowadays merely as conjunctions) are a very small set of words which, as we saw above, connect together items that have the same grammatical status. There are **only five** single-word co-ordinating conjunctions: *and, or, nor, but, yet.* Sometimes the combination *or else* is treated as a compound co-ordinating conjunction.

and, or

The conjunctions *and, or* can be used to link two or more items of equal status from any one grammatical category, e.g. nouns (*men and women and children*), noun phrases (*the oranges or the lemons*), adjectives (*hot and cold [food]*), adjective phrases (*very small or relatively large [objects]*), adverbs (*happily and lovingly*), adverb phrases (*much more quickly or much more safely*), prepositions (*in and around and under London*), clauses (*They all stood up when she entered or when she left*), sentences (*Sometimes they played music and sometimes they went for walks in the country*). The compound conjunction *or else* is mostly use to link alternative grammatical units when the speaker is not certain that the first is correct: *They often rented a cottage in Devon or else in Cornwall.*

nor

The conjunction *nor* is more restricted in use. It is most often found as the second member of the correlative pair *neither ... nor* (see 'correlatives' below), but it can be heard alone in sentences which begin with a negative statement, such as *The ring was not very expensive, nor was it very valuable.* Unlike *and, or, but* the conjunction *nor* can be preceded by another conjunction. Thus the second half of the example in the preceding sentence could also read: ... *but nor* (or ... *and nor*) *was it very valuable.* Notice that *nor* requires inversion of subject and verb, i.e. *was it* instead of the normal word order *it was.*

but, yet

The conjunctions *but, yet* are used to introduce items which are contrary to expectation or which offer a contrast. Unlike *and, or* they cannot link together more than two items. For example, *The child was clever but obstinate. Her brother was rough-mannered, yet very likeable.* They are often found after a negative statement: *They were not rich, but they had enough to live comfortably. She did not have a pretty face, (and) yet most people found her very attractive.* Note that, as in this last example, the conjunction *yet* can be immediately preceded by *and* with no change in the meaning, whereas *but* cannot be used in this way.

3 Subordinating Conjunctions

Subordinators

We saw above that the traditional class of subordinating conjunctions is divided by many modern grammarians into subordinators and complementizers. **Subordinators** are those which **introduce adverbial clauses**. It is not surprising to find that some of the types of adverbial clause which subordinators introduce are closely related to the corresponding types of adverb whose classification was discussed on page 101. As adverbial clauses will be dealt with in detail in Chapter 4 (see pages 131–137), we need only to list here the most characteristic subordinators for each type of adverbial clause and to provide a few example sentences.

Types of Sub-ordinator

1. **Manner:** *as, as if.* Examples: *She spoke very slowly, as she always did. The food tasted as if it had been burnt.* Notice that though *as if* consists of two words it is usually treated as a single (compound) subordinator.
2. **Place:** *where, wherever.* Example: *Put it where/wherever you can find it again.*
3. **Time:** *when, after, before, until.* Examples: *The chair collapsed when he sat on it. They left after they had dined. We waited until the clock struck again.* There are also a number of compound subordinators in this group: *as long as, as soon as, now that, etc.*
4. **Reason:** *as, because, since.* Examples. *They treated him with great respect, as he was very old. You hesitated because you were uncertain. Since you have done no wrong, they cannot punish you.*
5. **Condition:** *if, unless.* Examples: *He will succeed, if he works hard. They will go bankrupt, unless they improve their output.*
6. **Concession:** *although, though.* Example: *We were happy although our friends had abandoned us.*
7. **Purpose:** *so that, in order that.* Example: *The teacher spoke slowly so that/in order that the children could understand.*
8. **Result:** *so that, with the result that.* Example: *We arrived very early, so that/with the result that we got good seats.*
Note that compound subordinators of the type *in order that, with the result that* are sometimes referred to as **phrasal subordinators**, as each contains a prepositional phrase.

Comple-mentizers

When the subordinators have been subtracted from the traditional class of subordinating conjunctions, we are left with two (*that, whether*), which **introduce the noun clause object of a verb**. As an object of this kind can also be referred to as the complement of the verb, some modern grammarians use the term **complementizer** to refer to these conjunctions. *That* is used to introduce indirect statements, whereas *whether* introduces indirect questions. In colloquial speech *whether* can usually be replaced by *if*, which must then also be classified as a complementizer. The following sentences provide examples of their use: *Andrew knew that he had done wrong. I wonder whether/if she has received my letter. They asked me whether/if I knew the way to the inn.* Notice that *if* can sometimes be ambiguous between the complementizer and the conditional subordinator. For example in *They said they would ask him if he knew the way*, only the context can make clear whether *if he knew the way* is what they wanted to ask him (*if = whether*) or the condition on which they would ask him (*if = on condition that*).

4 Correlative Conjunctions

Co-ordinating

There is a small group of conjunctions which always occur in pairs, but not adjacently. Some of these, e.g. *both ... and, either ... or, neither ... nor*, are used to link together grammatical units of the same kind, but whereas normal co-ordinating conjunctions occur only **between** the two items that are conjoined (conjuncts), the first member of the correlative pair is placed **in front of** the first conjunct, while the second member comes between the two conjuncts. For example: *Both the cheese and the wine were excellent. You can pay either in cash or by cheque. This Government neither protects nor supports its citizens.* Conjunctions of this kind we can call **simple co-ordinating correlative conjunctions**. There are some, however, which consist of two words before each part of the correlation: *not only ... but also, just as ... so too* (or: *so also*). For example: *They travelled to India not only in winter, but also in summer. Just as Helen started her career very early, so too has her daughter.* These conjunctions may be referred to as **compound co-ordinating correlative conjunctions.**

Sub-ordinating

Correlative subordinating conjunctions are rare in English, but we can draw attention to the pair *whether ... or*, which is used to introduce a pair of subordinate noun clauses. For example: *She was not sure whether he really wanted to help her or was merely making fun of her.* Notice that in spoken English *whether* in this correlative pair is often replaced by *if*, as in *I'm not certain if they own the house or just rent it.* Speaking against this analysis of *whether/if ... or* as correlative subordinating conjunctions is the fact that the *or* in these pairs can normally be optionally followed by *whether* (or *if*), e.g. *I'm not certain whether* (or: *if*) *they own the house or whether* (or: *or if*) *they just rent it.* This suggests that the *whether* (or *if*) before the two conjuncts is the normal subordinating conjunction and that *or* between them is the normal co-ordinating conjunction, which in this case links together two subordinate clauses introduced by *whether* or *if.* Notice, however, that if *whether* or *if* is repeated, the second conjunct must be a full clause with its subject expressed, whereas when *or* alone follows *whether,* this is not the case. We can see this very clearly when the second conjunct consists merely of the word *not,* e.g. *We don't know whether he came or not.* Here only *or* alone can precede the second conjunct. We cannot say *We don't know whether/if he came or *whether not/*if not.* This seems to support the analysis of *whether/if ... or* as correlative subordinating conjunctions.

5 Confusion of Conjunctions with other Word Classes

with Wh-Adverbs

Sometimes only the sense can tell us whether the *when* at the beginning of a clause following a verb of asking is a subordinating conjunction or an interrogative adverb. For example, the sentence *I asked when he came* is ambiguous out of context. If my question was *When did he come?*, then *when* in *I asked when he came* must be the interrogative adverb introducing the noun clause which tells us what I asked. However, if the *when* in the sentence *I asked when he came* means 'at the time at which', then it is here a subordinating conjunction introducing an adverbial clause of specific time. In this latter case only, the *when*-clause can also precede the main clause: *When he came, I asked.*

With Relative Adverbs

A similar ambiguity occurs in the sentence *I had forgotten the time when I missed my train.* If we can place the *when*-clause at the beginning of the sentence (*When I missed my train, I had forgotten the time)*, it is an adverbial clause telling us the specific time when my forgetting of the time of day occurred. Here the *when* introducing the adverbial clause is a subordinating conjunction. However, the original sentence could also refer to 'an occasion on which I had missed my train'. If this is what I had forgotten, then the *when*-clause is now a relative clause modifying the noun *time*, and *when* is a relative adverb introducing this relative clause.

9 Interjections

1 General Remarks

Definition

Interjections (*oh! ah! hey! ouch! hooray! etc.*) are a small class of words which normally do not enter into any syntactic or grammatical relations with other words in a sentence. As their name suggests, they are interjected, i.e. 'thrust into' the utterance, without affecting its grammar. Their primary purpose is to express emotion and they are therefore usually exclamations or parts of exclamations.

2 Characteristics

Types

Since interjections are a peripheral word class, they do not deserve much attention in grammatical analysis. However, it is important for us to be able to recognize them. Most of them are conventionalized reactions to external stimuli, e.g. *ouch* or *ow* (said when something causes pain), *gosh* or *golly* (mild surprise), *wow* (amazement or admiration), *whoops* (said as a mild excuse when one has spilt something or almost had an accident with something). Some are phonetically odd, as they contain very rare sounds or sounds which occur nowhere else in the language, e.g. *ugh* (expressing disgust) may be pronounced [ʌx] with a final velar fricative sound commonly heard for the spelling *ch* in German in words such as *machen, Kuchen, Loch*. In another pronunciation of this word [ɯə], we hear an unrounded high back vowel found nowhere else in English, followed by shwa [ə], the sound at the end of the most common pronunciation of the definite article *the*. Some interjections are used as greetings, e.g. *hi, hello, goodbye*; some as expressions of pleasure, e.g. *hooray, cheers, yippee*. Others are said when a person is annoyed or angry about something, e.g. *bother, blast, damn*. Many of the interjections in this last group, including *blast* and *damn* are offensive to many people for religious reasons; others such as *shit, fuck* are equally offensive, as they are considered obscene. It is therefore not surprising that a number of the members of this group and of others too are euphemisms: *darn (< damn), shoot (< shit), golly (< God), gosh (< God), crikey (< Christ)*.

Limited Syntactic Relations

Although we have characterized interjections as members of a word class which does not enter into grammatical relations, there are a few members, notably of the group expressing anger, which permit limited syntactical relations. These are usually of the kind: verb + noun (or pronoun) object, e.g. *Damn this weather! Blast it!* Note also *Hey John! Hey you!* used when calling to a person.

Sometimes Initial

Interjections are most commonly found as separate entities outside of sentences and are then followed by an exclamation mark. However, some occur quite often as the initial element in a sentence, and are then divided from the rest of the sentence by a comma, e.g. *Ah, that was good! Oh, I had no idea you knew! Hey, stop that! Well, let me see. Heavens, I've missed my train again.*

Final Remarks

With interjections we have dealt with the last of the nine word classes. Before we turn our attention away from the word level and in the following chapters consider units on higher levels of grammatical analysis, let us conclude this chapter by looking briefly at the phenomenon of multiple class words in English.

10 Multiple Class Words

1 General Remarks

Background

Since Modern English in the course of its development from Old English has lost almost all of its inflections, it is not surprising that the word class of most English words is not easily recognizable from the shape of the individual word. The absence of typical word-class inflections means that a word from one class can be used relatively easily in another class, with the result that the same word can belong to two or more classes. Although the transfer of a word from one class to another with no morphological change (technically called **conversion** or **zero derivation** or **functional shift**) may present problems for the foreign learner, this process is a very valuable grammatical mechanism which greatly enhances the flexibility of the language.

2 Types of Multiple Class Word

Clear Derivation

We can distinguish between two types of multiple class word: those with clear derivation, i.e. where it is clear to the modern speaker which of the word classes that the word now appears in was the original one, and those with obscure derivation, i.e. where this is no longer clear. Examples with clear order of derivation can be found especially with nouns and verbs. There is little doubt that the verbs *dog, doctor, butter* in the following sentences are derived from the corresponding nouns: *They dogged me* (= 'followed me like a dog') *all day with their questions. Somebody has doctored the evidence* (= 'dishonestly altered it' so that it appears better, as a quack doctor does with his medicine). *He buttered* (= 'spread butter on') *the toast.* Similarly, in the following examples the nouns *eats, edit, update* are obviously derived from original verbs: *Bring in the eats* (= 'food'). *Save the edits* (= 'items that have been edited'). *We need an update on the hurricane in Florida* (= 'newer information').

Obscure Derivation

Let us now consider two examples (*over* and *up*) where the order of the derivation of the word classes is obscure. In each example sentence below, the word class to which the item in question belongs is shown in brackets at the beginning.

Example 1

(Adverbial Particle):*They fell over.*
(Adjective) *The war is over.*
(Preposition) *They threw the rope over the wall.*
(Noun) *In English cricket an over is a set of six balls bowled from the same end of the pitch.*
Although *over* used as a noun in the technical language of cricket is obviously the most recent addition to the word classes in which the word is found, we can only guess at the order of derivation of the others. Even if we look the word up in a historical dictionary such as the Oxford English Dictionary, which shows the date of the first written records for each meaning of a word, we still cannot decide.

Example 2 An even more impressive example of a multiple class word where it is not easy to determine which word class was the original one is the word *up*, as we see in the following sentences:
(Adverbial Particle) *Prices have gone up again.*
(Adjective) *The sun is up now. What's up? Take the up train.*
(Preposition) *He climbed up the ladder.*
(Noun) *We take no notice of the ups and downs of life.*
(Verb) *He upped (= got up) and hit me. Prices have upped again.*
(Interjection) *Up! Up!* (said to make a tame animal stand on its rear legs).
Here both the noun and verb uses of *up* sound a little exotic and can therefore safely be considered later additions to the word's repertoire, but with regard to the others the picture is not at all clear and again it is difficult to say which word class gave rise to the others.

Conclusion We can finish this brief examination of multiple class words by pointing out that though most cases of conversion from one word class to another are useful to the language, there are some which may occasionally lead to ambiguity. One of these is the conversion of the conjunction *than* in present-day spoken English to a preposition. For example, in formal style where *than* can only be a conjunction, there is no ambiguity between the two elliptical sentences *She spoils her children more than we* and *She spoils her children more than us.* In the first sentence, we spoil her children too but less than she does, whereas in the second, she spoils us but less than her children. In spoken English, however, *than* can be used as a preposition and must then be followed by a pronoun in the oblique case. Now, the second sentence is ambiguous as it can be used with the meaning of the first, just as *He is bigger than they (are)* can be replaced in spoken English by *He is bigger than them.*

3 CHAPTER Phrases

1 Types of Phrase

1 General Remarks

Levels of Analysis

In the course of our examination of the different word classes of English and their characteristics, we have often been compelled to place items on the word class level in a higher context in order to show their characteristic environments (neighbours) and behaviour. This higher level of analysis was sometimes the phrase level and sometimes the sentence level. It is now time for us to look in a little more detail at entities on the phrase level.

2 Characteristics of Phrases

Definition

A phrase is usually considered to be a group of two or more words which form a grammatical unit within a clause or sentence. A phrase may function as a constituent of a clause or sentence or it may be a part of another constituent. For example, in *The green suit is too small* the underlined noun phrase is the subject of the sentence, but in *the man in the green suit* it is part of a prepositional phrase within another noun phrase. In *She is very attractive* the underlined adjective phrase is the subject complement of the sentence (see pages 159–163), but in *his very attractive secretary* it is part of a noun phrase.

Limitations

Not all of the nine word classes discussed in Chapter 2 are readily expandable into phrases. We thus find only five **main** kinds of phrase: **noun phrase, adjective phrase, adverb phrase, prepositional phrase and verb phrase**.

General Characteristics

Every phrase must consist of a **head word** (see page 11), which gives its name to the type of phrase, e.g. the noun in a noun phrase (*the poor boy*), the adjective in an adjective phrase (*very funny, hungry for love, capable of understanding*), the adverb in an adverb phrase (*extremely rapidly, ever so carefully*), the preposition in a prepositional phrase (*under the bridge, notwithstanding the difficulties*) and the main verb in a verb phrase (*had opened, will have been eating*). Sometimes in some kinds of grammatical analysis, the term *phrase* may be applied to a single word, when the headword stands alone (i.e. is a noun, adjective, adverb or verb without any modification). This is usually done when the grammarian is particularly interested in the phrase level analysis of the rest of the sentence or clause (see *[waited]*$_{Verb\ P}$ in the last example on page 172).

3 Noun Phrases

General Remarks

A noun phrase (NP) consists of a **head noun** (from now on printed in bold type in the examples) and some form of **modification**. If the modification comes in front of the head noun it is called **premodification**; if it comes after the head noun it is called **postmodification**.

NP with Premodified N

The simplest type of noun phrase with a premodified noun is where the noun is preceded by an article or another determiner, e.g. *a*$_{Det}$ ***dog***, *the*$_{Det}$ ***horse***, *this*$_{Det}$ ***child***, *some*$_{Det}$ ***sugar***, *my*$_{Det}$ ***hat***. A simple noun phrase of this kind can be expanded by adding one or more adjectives to the premodification, e.g. *a*$_{Det}$ *ferocious*$_{Adj}$ ***dog***, *the*$_{Det}$ *strong*$_{Adj}$ *young*$_{Adj}$ ***horse***, *this*$_{Det}$ *clever*$_{Adj}$ *little*$_{Adj}$ ***child***. A premodifying adjective may itself be premodified by an adverb, e.g. *a*$_{Det}$ *[remarkably*$_{Adv}$ *ferocious*$_{Adj}$*]* ***dog***, *an*$_{Det}$ *[extremely*$_{Adv}$ *strong*$_{Adj}$*]* *young*$_{Adj}$ ***horse***. The premodification can also consist of another noun (N) or a gerund (*-ing* noun form of a verb), e.g. *a bronze*$_{N}$ ***dog*** *(= made of bronze), a walking*$_{Gerund}$ ***stick*** *(= used for walking)*. In place of the initial determiner the premodification may begin with a genitive noun: *William's ferocious* ***dog***, *Mary's [extremely strong] young* ***horse***.

Patterns 1 & 2

In summary we can say that a noun phrase (NP) with premodification is found in the following two basic patterns:

Pattern 1 [(Det) + Adj + Noun]$_{NP}$
Pattern 2 [(Det) + Noun + Noun]$_{NP}$

The determiner may be missing with some kinds of head noun, e.g. *brown*$_{Adj}$ ***sugar***, *iron*$_{N}$ ***doors***. As we saw above, the adjective position in Pattern 1 may be occupied by more than one adjective or by a premodified adjective. Similarly the noun position in Pattern 2 may also be occupied by a simple noun or a premodified one. Thus besides *a bronze dog*, we may also find *a Chinese bronze* ***dog*** *(= made of Chinese bronze)*. Very rarely, other word classes may take the position of the premodifying adjective or noun in Patterns 1 and 2, e.g. an adverb as in *the then*$_{Adv}$ *Prime* ***Minister*** or even a sentence (S) as in *the author's ['I hate you']*$_{S}$ ***poems***.

NP with Postmodified N

The head noun in a noun phrase may also be followed by various modifying elements. The most common kinds of postmodification are a prepositional phrase (Prep P), a long adjective phrase (Adj P) or a relative clause (Rel Cl), i.e. in the following patterns:

Pattern 3 (Det) Noun + [........]$_{Prep\ P.}$

Pattern 4 (Det) Noun + [........]$_{Adj\ P}$
Pattern 5 (Det) Noun + [........]$_{Rel\ Cl}$

Pattern 3

In noun phrases of the kind shown in Pattern 3, the commonest type of postmodifying prepositional phrase is probably one beginning with the preposition *of* followed by a noun or noun phrase, as in the complex NPs

*the **King** [of$_{Prep}$ England]$_{Prep\ P}$*
*a **pound** [of$_{Prep}$ best butter]$_{Prep\ P}$*

but other prepositions are possible, e.g. as in

***evidence** [against$_{Prep}$ his enemies]$_{Prep\ P}$*
*his **difficulty** [in$_{Prep}$ expressing himself]$_{Prep\ P}$*

Note that in the last example, the preposition (*in*) governs a noun phrase consisting of a gerund (*expressing*) with its object (*himself*). We shall see more examples of these prepositional phrases below (page 122).

Pattern 4

In noun phrases of the Pattern 4 type, the postmodifying adjective phrase may consist of an adjective followed by a prepositional phrase, as in

***criminals** [capable$_{Adj}$ [of murder]$_{Prep\ P}$]$_{Adj\ P}$*
*an **atmosphere** [heavy$_{Adj}$ [with smoke]$_{Prep\ P}$]$_{Adj\ P}$*

or of a verbal participle often followed by a prepositional phrase, as in

*a **ring** [made [of pure gold and rubies]$_{Prep\ P}$]$_{Adj\ P}$*
***industrialists** [swimming [in money]$_{Prep\ P}$]$_{Adj\ P}$*

Sometimes we find the head noun postmodified by a series of co-ordinated adjectives (especially in poetical English), as in

*(He wore) a **beard** [long and white and unkempt]$_{Adj\ P}$*

In less poetic style the adjectives would come in front of the head noun, but since English does not usually allow co-ordinated adjectives in premodifying position, the conjunctions would be omitted:

*(He wore) a long white unkempt **beard***

A rarer example of a Pattern 4 noun phrase is found where the head noun is followed by a single adjective which is always used in postmodifying position. We have already encountered some of these when we discussed adjectives in Chapter 2 (see pages 40–41), e.g.

*the **President** elect, the **heir** apparent, the **person** opposite*

Pattern 5

A very common type of noun phrase is one in which the head noun is postmodified by a relative clause. Since a relative clause is really a clause with adjectival function, this pattern is in effect a variation of Pattern 4. Examples are:

*the **meat** [which she bought]$_{Rel\ Cl}$, the **house** [they lived in]$_{Rel\ Cl}$*
*the **people** [for whom you work]$_{Rel\ Cl}$*
*the **man** [that was killed]$_{Rel\ Cl}$*

In some analyses it is assumed that Pattern 4 NPs are derived from relative clauses containing some form of the verb *be* by omitting the relative pronoun and the verb. This would rather neatly account for the examples given above, e.g.

__criminals__ (who are) capable of murder
an __atmosphere__ (which was) heavy with smoke
a __ring__ (which is) made of pure gold and rubies
__industrialists__ (who are) swimming in money
a __beard__ (which was) long and white and unkempt

It also accounts for some patterns which we have not mentioned above, e.g. with an adverbial expression as postmodification:

the __factory__ (which is) [<u>over there</u>]$_{Adv\ P}$

Unfortunately, however, there are relative clauses whose verb can only be used in simple tenses not containing the verb *be*, and yet the present participle of *be* is still found introducing the postmodifying adjective phrase in noun phrases of the Pattern 4 type. This is always the case when the verb in the relative clause is stative and not dynamic (see page 78). Consider the following two noun phrases:

__tax-payers__ [owning a house]$_{Adj\ P}$ (< who own a house, **not** **who are owning a house)*
a __room__ [measuring five metres by four metres]$_{Adj\ P}$ (< which measures five metres by four metres, **not** ** which is measuring five metres by four metres)*

Stative verbs like *own* and *measure*, whose present participles we see in these two noun phrases, cannot be used in the expanded (continuous) tenses. Therefore the postposed adjective phrase cannot in these cases have been derived by omitting the relative pronoun and the verb to *be* from an original relative clause.

NP with Pronoun Head

Sometimes phrases are found which consist of a **pronoun** as head word, followed by some kind of **postmodification**. These are usually treated as noun phrases, since pronouns stand for nouns and since the postmodification follows the same patterns (3, 4 and 5) as for noun phrases. Thus we can have a pronoun with a prepositional phrase (***somebody*** *of importance*), or with an adjective or adjective phrase (***nobody*** *important*, ***anyone*** *able to swim*), or with a participle (***something*** *made of copper*, ***anything*** *lying on the floor*) or with a relative clause (***somebody*** *who believes in ghosts*).

4 Adjective Phrases

General Remarks

Adjective phrases consist of an **adjective as head noun** (shown in bold type in the examples below) accompanied by some form of **modification** (pre- or postmodification or both). Attributive adjective phrases, like simple attributive adjectives, can appear before or after a noun in a noun phrase. As we saw in the discussion of noun phrases above, premodified adjective phrases occur as premodifiers before a head noun, whereas postmodified adjectives occur as postmodifiers after a head noun. The only notable exception to this rule is the noun phrase with a pronoun headword. Since all modification must follow the pronoun, this type of noun phrase can have the pronoun postmodified by a premodified adjective phrase, e.g. *[**somebody** [extremely **young**]$_{Adj\ P}$]$_{NP}$*. Adjective phrases can also occur alone in predicative position after the verb *be* or another linking verb, e.g. in the sentences: *Elizabeth was [extremely **young**]$_{Adj\ P}$. The workmen seemed [very **tired**]$_{Adj\ P}$.*

Adj P with Premodified Adj

The usual kind of premodification in adjective phrases is with an adverb of degree such as *very, extremely, intensely, rather, quite, fairly* or the comparative or superlative adverbs *more* or *most*, e.g. *very **handsome**, extremely **kind**, intensely **interesting**, rather **funny**, quite **nice**, fairly **expensive**, more **restful**, most **suspicious***. Occasionally other types of adverb are found such as adverbs of time or frequency, especially when the head word is a participle used adjectivally, e.g. *[<u>recently</u> **discovered**]$_{Adj\ P}$* (as in the noun phrase: *a recently discovered document*), or *[<u>often</u> **overwhelming**]$_{Adj\ P}$* (as in the noun phrase: *the often overwhelming difficulties*). Sometimes the adverb premodifying the adjective may be joined to it by a hyphen, e.g. *<u>never</u>-**ending*** (as in *their never-ending complaints*). Here it could be argued that this is a compound adjective, rather than an adjective phrase.

Adj P with Postmodified Adj

The postmodification of an adjective is often referred to as its complement or complementation. In Chapter 1 (pages 42–43) we distinguished three main patterns of adjective complementation:

Pattern 6 Adj + Prep P
Pattern 7 Adj + *to* + Infinitive (= Infinitive Clause)
Pattern 8 Adj + *that/whether* + Clause (= Noun Clause)

The many examples of these three patterns given there showed the adjective phrase in predicative position (i.e. after *be* or another linking verb). These same three patterns are also found when the adjective phrase is used attributively (i.e. modifying a noun in a noun phrase). In this latter case the adjective phrase can only appear in postmodifying position, as English does not permit an adjective with its complement to premodify a noun.

Pattern 6

In the discussion of Pattern 2 noun phrases above we have already seen some examples of adjective phrases of the Pattern 6 kind with a prepositional phrase postmodifying the adjective. As these adjective phrases were all attributive, it will suffice here to give just a couple of examples of this pattern, where the adjective phrase is used predicatively:

*The students are [**anxious**$_{\text{Adj}}$ [about$_{\text{Prep}}$ their results]$_{\text{Prep P}}$]$_{\text{Adj P}}$*
*The teacher became [**impatient**$_{\text{Adj}}$ [with$_{\text{Prep}}$ the child]$_{\text{Prep P}}$]$_{\text{Adj P}}$*

Pattern 7

Although the adjective in a Pattern 7 adjectival phrase looks as if it is followed by a prepositional phrase beginning with the preposition *to*, the complementation following it is in fact a **non-finite** clause consisting of *to* + an infinitive, i.e. a verb which is not marked for tense or for the grammatical person of the subject, but which has a subject and may have an object. The subject is often not present but can be understood from the context. This will become clear if we examine the following examples:

*Sally will be [**happy**$_{\text{Adj}}$ [to come]$_{\text{Inf Clause}}$]$_{\text{Adj P}}$*
*Bill seems [**hesitant**$_{\text{Adj}}$ [to accuse Tim]$_{\text{Inf Clause}}$]$_{\text{Adj P}}$*
*Joan looked [**glad**$_{\text{Adj}}$ [to hear the news]$_{\text{Inf Clause}}$]$_{\text{Adj P}}$*

In the first sentence, the verb *come* in the infinitive clause is unmarked for tense or person, cannot have an object and has no overt subject, but it is clear that the person who will come is Sally. Thus, grammatically, *Sally* is not only the subject of the verb *will be* but also of *come*. The situation in the second sentence is comparable. In the infinitive clause *to accuse Tim* the verb *accuse* has an object *Tim* (i.e. Tim is the object of the possible accusation, the person whom Bill will perhaps accuse) and, although the infinitive clause has no overt grammatical subject we know that semantically the subject is *Bill* (i.e. Bill is the person who will do the accusing). Similarly, in the infinitive clause *to hear the news* in the third sentence, the verb *hear* has an object *the news* and it is clear that, although there is no overt subject in the infinitive clause, the person who did the hearing was Joan. Thus *Joan* is not only the subject of *looked* but also of the infinitive *hear*.

Pattern 8

In Pattern 8 the adjectival phrase consists of an adjective followed by the conjunction *that* or *whether* introducing a **finite** clause, i.e. a clause which has an overt subject and may have an object, and in which the verb can be marked for the person of the subject and for tense. (See pages 157–158 for an explanation of the missing preposition before these finite noun clause complements of adjectives.) Adjective phrases of the Pattern 8 kind are most commonly found after *be* or another linking verb (i.e. in predicative position), e.g.

*The child is [**annoyed**$_{\text{Adj}}$ [that it has no milk]$_{\text{N Clause}}$]$_{\text{Adj P}}$*

They can also be used attributively when the noun they postmodify is used in a general sense, e.g.

*Candidates [**uncertain**$_{\text{Adj}}$ [whether their applications have been received]$_{\text{N Clause}}$]$_{\text{Adj P}}$ must ask the secretary.*
*Fathers [**proud**$_{\text{Adj}}$ [that their sons and daughters have been successful]$_{\text{N Clause}}$]$_{\text{Adj P}}$ are often rather boastful.*

General Remarks

In the discussion of adverb phrases it is particularly important to distinguish between form and function. For example, some phrases can have adverbial function, although they are formally not adverb phrases. Consider the following sentence: *The boys are sitting here$_{Adv}$ and she is sitting [in the garden]$_{Prep\ P}$*. In the second half of this sentence, the phrase *in the garden* is functionally equivalent to the adverb *here* in the first half, but formally it is a prepositional phrase introduced by the preposition *in*. We shall not be concerned with such phrases here, but shall concentrate our attention on those which are both formally and functionally adverbial, i.e. which have an adverb as their head word.

Types

In structure, adverb phrases are very similar to adjective phrases. The head adverb (shown in bold type below) can optionally take premodification, postmodification or both.

Adv P with Premodified Adv

As in adjective phrases, the premodification of the head word can be an adverb of degree. Examples of an adverb premodified in this way are: *very* ***rapidly***, *extremely* ***kindly*** *rather* ***unpleasantly***, *quite* ***softly***. Sometimes even two degree adverbs can occur, e.g. *far too* ***closely***. Note that the degree adverbs *enough* and *indeed* do not follow this pattern. They must always come after (i.e. postmodify) the head word, and in addition *indeed* requires the intensifying adverb *very* before the head word, e.g. ***cleverly*** *enough,* ***soon*** *enough; very* ***clearly*** *indeed, very* ***slowly*** *indeed.* (Both *enough* and *indeed* show similar behaviour in adjective phrases.)

Adv P with Postmodified Adv

Since adverbs (unlike adjectives) do not take prepositions after them, there is no adverb phrase pattern corresponding to Pattern 6 for adjective phrases. However, adverbs (like adjectives) can be followed by an infinitive clause as in Pattern 7 provided the head word is preceded by the degree adverb *too*. Thus, corresponding to the adjective phrase *too* ***hot*** *[to eat]$_{Inf\ Cl}$*, we find adverb phrases such as *too* ***slowly*** *[to be seen]$_{Inf\ Cl}$*, *too* ***quietly*** *[to be heard]$_{Inf\ Cl}$*. Adverbs can also be postmodified by a finite clause provided that they have the appropriate premodification. Thus, with premodifying *as*, the head adverb can be followed by a clause introduced by a second *as*, e.g.

(We came) [as ***quickly*** *[as we could]$_{Adv\ Cl}$]$_{Adv\ P}$*

(You can phone) [as ***often*** *[as you like]$_{Adv\ Cl}$]$_{Adv\ P}$*

Similarly, an adverb can be postmodified by a clause introduced by the conjunction *than* provided that the adverb has a comparative suffix or is premodified by the adverb *more*, e.g.

*(She arrived) [***sooner*** *[than he had expected]$_{Adv\ Cl}$]$_{Adv\ P}$*

(The parson preached) [more ***eloquently*** *[than he had ever preached before]$_{Adv\ Cl}$]$_{Adv\ P}$*

Charac-teristics

As we have seen many times in previous chapters and in this, a prepositional phrase consists of a **preposition as the head word** (shown in bold type in the examples below) followed by the **complement of the preposition**. Until now we have called this complement the 'object of the preposition' or 'prepositional object', but to prevent terminological confusion with the objects of the verb (see Chapter 5 pages 152–159 for direct, indirect and prepositional objects), we shall henceforth call the structure that follows the preposition the preposition's complement. This complement can be either a noun, a pronoun or a noun phrase. A few examples will make this clear.

Examples

(Noun Complement:) ***with*** *Jack*$_{N}$*,* ***for*** *dogs*$_{N}$*,* ***in*** *Russia*$_{N}$
(Pronoun Complement:) ***beside*** *them*$_{Pron}$*,* ***above*** *everybody*$_{Pron}$
In a prepositional phrase with a noun phrase complement, the noun phrase may have any one of the five patterns which we described on pages 116–117:
(Complement with Pattern 1 NP:) ***except*** *[this very fat man]*$_{NP}$
(Complement with Pattern 2 NP:) ***inside*** *[the stone jug]*$_{NP}$
(Complement with Pattern 3 NP:) ***behind*** *[the man with the beard]*$_{NP}$
(Complement with Pattern 4 NP:) ***against*** *[people unable to swim]*$_{NP}$
(Complement with Pattern 5 NP:) ***over*** *[the fence that Jim built]*$_{NP}$

Complexity

In the examples above we have omitted the internal structure of each noun phrase pattern so that each prepositional phrase can be easily seen. If we look in detail at the example with the Pattern 3 noun phrase, however, we see how extraordinarily complex such a simple sounding phrase can be. The following version of this prepositional phrase shows each constituent surrounded by a labelled pair of square brackets:

*[**behind**$_{Prep}$ [the **man**$_{N}$ [**with**$_{Prep}$ [the **beard**$_{N}$]$_{NP}$]$_{Prep\ P}$]$_{NP}$]$_{Prep\ P}$*

Here we see that the prepositional phrase *behind the man with the beard,* has the preposition *behind* as its head and the noun phrase *the man with the* beard as its complement. If we look deep into this structure we find the noun phrase *the beard,* which is embedded within the prepositional phrase ***with*** *the beard.* This prepositional phrase is in turn embedded within the noun phrase *the **man** with the **beard*** and, as we saw at the beginning, this noun phrase is embedded within our original prepositional phrase as the complement of the preposition *behind.*

General Remarks

We shall use the term *verb phrase* (VP) to refer to any of the structures in which a **main verb (= lexical verb)** is **preceded by one or more auxiliary verbs**, e.g.

[has$_{Aux}$ *been*$_{Aux}$ ***reading***$_{Main\ Verb}$*]*$_{VP}$

It should be pointed out that the term *verb phrase* is used in a much broader sense in generative grammar and in some other grammatical models to refer to the predicate of a sentence, i.e. the constituent (usually the verb plus its objects, etc.) which combines with the subject to form a sentence, e.g. *[Julian]*$_{Subject}$ *[has given the book to his brother]*$_{Verb\ Phrase}$

Characteristics

As is the case with all other types of phrases in traditional grammar, a verb phrase contains a head word which gives its name to the type of phrase. Thus the head word here is a verb. Whatever other words may optionally accompany the verb, a verb phrase always continues to function as if it were a single verb. In the following sentences the head verb is shown in bold type and the verb phrase is underlined .

Examples

*(Alice) [<u>is **reading**</u>]*$_{VP}$ *(a magazine)*
*(James) [<u>has been **digging**</u>]*$_{VP}$ *(the garden)*
*(The dog) [<u>must have been **snoring**</u>]*$_{VP}$ *(in its kennel)*

In normal English, the head verb can be preceded by up to three auxiliary verbs, as our examples show. In modern conversational style, it is possible to hear sentences of the following type where four auxiliary verbs precede, although not all speakers find *be(en) being* acceptable:

*(The machine) [<u>might have been being **repaired**</u>]*$_{VP}$ *(at the time of the explosion)*

Phrasal Verbs

When the head verb is a phrasal verb (see page 98), it is usually more convenient to include the adverbial particle in the verb phrase when the particle immediately follows the verb, as in the following examples (where the adverbial particle is underlined).

*(The forester) [has **cut** <u>down</u>]*$_{VP}$ *(all the trees in the wood)*
*(The shop-keepers [have **paid** <u>back</u>]*$_{VP}$ *(all their debts)*

If the particle is separated from the verb, it may be treated as a separate adverbial phrase or, more logically, the verb phrase can be treated as **discontinuous**, i.e. interrupted by another constituent of the sentence. These two possibilities are illustrated in the following examples, where all the phrases (including those consisting of only one word) are labelled:

a. *[They]*$_{NP}$ *[will **send**]*$_{VP}$ *[all the letters]*$_{NP}$ *[<u>off</u>]*$_{AdvP}$ *[tomorrow]*$_{AdvP}$
b. *[The robbers]*$_{NP}$ *[have **handed**] [all the money]*$_{NP}$ *[<u>back</u>]*
 |__________VP__________|

Note that discontinuous verb phrases are not at all uncommon. They often occur when an adverbial phase interrupts the sequence of auxiliary verbs before the head verb. Thus, in the following example, the adverb *never* (here, like *off* in (a), analysed on the phrase level as a one-word adverb phrase) breaks the verb phrase *would have said* into two:

*[Hillary]$_{NP}$ [would] [never]$_{AdvP}$ [have **said**] [such a thing]$_{NP}$*

________VP________

2 Final Remarks on Phrases

1 Form and Function

Before we leave the phrase level, it is necessary to point out that what was said about form and function in the introductory remarks to the section on adverbial phrases is true of most other kinds of phrases. In our discussion of the five different kinds of phrase we have considered them all only with regard to their form. When we come later to sentence level analysis, we shall see that phrases (as well as clauses) have an important functional role to play which often has no connection with their grammatical form. We have already mentioned that prepositional phrases can function as adverbial constituents. For example, in the sentence *The friends were sitting on the lawn*, the prepositional phrase *on the lawn* functions as an adverbial constituent, telling us where the friends were sitting, and is thus comparable to the adverb of place *there*. Similarly, in the sentence *Alice arrived the day before yesterday,* the noun phrase *the day before yesterday* also functions as an adverbial constituent, in this case telling us when Alice arrived. The noun phrase here could thus be replaced by the adverb of time *then.* We have also seen that even on the phrase level some prepositional phrases can function as adjectives, e.g. in the noun phrase *the woman in the telephone box*, the prepositional phrase *in the telephone box* functions as if it were an adjective postmodifying the head noun *woman.* Furthermore, noun phrases themselves can function as adjectives, as is the case with the noun phrase *stainless steel* when it premodifies the head noun *saucepans* in the noun phrase *stainless steel saucepans.*

2 Structural Complexity

What was said above in connection with prepositional phrases about the astonishing complexity of some simple sounding structures can be repeated here for most other types of phrases. Since adjectives can be modified in various ways and since such adjectives can themselves modify nouns, any structure which contains a noun can have an adjective phrase embedded within the noun phrase. Furthermore, these nouns phrases with embedded adjective phrases can themselves be embedded either within a prepositional phrase as the complement (= object) of the preposition or within another noun phrase as part of the premodification or the postmodification of the head noun. It is therefore not surprising that through all these embeddings of one type of phrase within another, considerable complexity can be achieved. We have seen that even clauses, i.e. units from a higher level, can sometimes be embedded within phrases: e.g. a relative clause can post-modify the head noun in a Pattern 5 noun phrase (page 117), and a noun clause introduced by *that* or *whether* can post-modify an adjective in Pattern 8 adjective phrases (page 120).

4 CHAPTER Clauses

1 Introduction

1 General Remarks

Definition

A clause is a grammatical construction which is either a whole simple sentence (Mary coughed) or part of a sentence *(Mother looked worried when Mary coughed)*. A clause normally consists of a **subject** and a **predicate**. In the clause (sentence) *The porter returns the case to its owner every morning*, the subject (the person or thing performing the action) is *the porter*, and the rest of the clause, i.e. *returned the case to its owner last night*, is the predicate, i.e. what is said about the subject. The predicate usually consists of a **finite verb**, i.e. one which shows differences for the person of the subject and for tense. For example, in our clause above, we have the verb *returns* which carries a final *s* for the third person singular and is present tense, but we could also have had *returned* which is past tense).With certain verbs, the predicate may also contain **different kinds of object** (direct object, indirect, etc.). In our clause above, *the book* is the direct object of *return* (what the porter returned), and *to its owner* is the indirect object (the person to whom the porter returned something). The predicate may also contain other constituents such as an **adverbial**, e.g. in our example clause, *every morning* is an adverbial constituent telling us when the subject performed the action. We shall examine all these constituents more carefully in Chapter 5 when we deal with sentences.

2 Types of Clause

1 Classification

General Remarks

Clauses can be classified in three different ways. The **traditional** classification is concerned with their importance in a sentence; another classification considers their **functional** role in the sentence; and the third classifies them according to whether the verb they contain is **finite** or **non-finite**.

Hierarchy

The traditional classification of clauses into **main clauses**, **subordinate clauses** and **co-ordinate clauses** is based on their hierarchical importance in the structure of a sentence.

Main Clause

A main clause is either the only clause in a sentence (as in <u>*The train arrived*</u>) or else it is the hierarchically most important one (as in <u>*The train arrived*</u> *while all the passengers were asleep*). The hierarchical status of the main clause can be looked at in two different ways: either we consider the main clause as the topmost clause into which another clause may be embedded or as the most important clause on which another clause depends. In the first analysis, where one clause contains another clause embedded within it, the topmost clause is sometimes referred to as the matrix clause. Note that in this kind of analysis, the term *main clause* is used to refer to a matrix clause together with its embedded clauses. Thus in the sentence *When the train arrived at the platform, the passengers thought that it would stop*, the main clause is not only *the passengers thought*, but all the rest of the sentence too. The other kind of analysis limits the main clause to just *the passengers thought* and considers *when the train arrived at the platform* and *that it would stop* as two clauses which are separate from the main clause but which are dependent on it.

Subordinate Clause

Whether we think of the main clause as including clauses embedded within it or as excluding clauses that are dependent on it, these lower-ranking clauses are traditionally called **subordinate clauses**. Thus, in our example above, the clauses *when the train arrived at the platform* and *that it would stop* are subordinate clauses. Since it saves space, we shall use the second analysis and say that these two subordinate clauses are dependent on the main clause *the passengers thought*. Note that it is possible for a subordinate clause to depend on another subordinate clause, which itself is dependent on a higher-ranking clause. For example, *They say that they sold the house when we were in America*. The subordinate clause *when we were in America* is dependent on the higher-ranking clause *that they sold the house* but this too is a subordinate clause dependent on the main clause *They say*.

Co-ordinate Clause

A co-ordinate clause is one of two (or more) clauses which are linked together by one of the co-ordinating conjunctions *and* or *but*. Whereas main clauses are by nature higher-ranking and subordinate clauses lower-ranking, co-ordinate clauses are of equal rank. Thus we find co-ordinate main clauses, as in the sentence <u>*The train stopped*</u> *and* <u>*the passengers alighted*</u>, and also co-ordinate subordinate clauses, as in *When the train stopped and the passen-*

gers alighted, the police appeared on the platform, where the same two clauses (now introduced by the conjunction *when*) are dependent on the main clause *the police arrived on the platform.*

3 Classification according to Grammatical Function

Substitution

Another rather different kind of classification of clauses looks at the word class of the words for which the clause can be substituted, and labels them according to this class. In fact, clauses can be substituted for only three classes of word: nouns, adjectives and adverbs. In this kind of classification we therefore find **nominal (= noun) clauses**, **adjectival (= relative) clauses**, and **adverbial clauses**. Strictly speaking, clauses which function like a noun, adjective or adverb should only be referred to as nomin<u>al</u>, adjectiv<u>al</u>, or adverbi<u>al</u>, the suffix *-al* indicating that they do not have a noun, adjective or adverb as their head word. However, nominal clauses are often referred to as noun clauses in the literature, and occasionally relative clauses are also called adjective clauses.

Nominal Clauses

Just as a noun or a noun phrase can function as the **subject** or **object of a verb**, so too can a nominal clause.

As Object

Nominal clauses are most frequent as indirect statements (introduced by *that*) or indirect questions (introduced by *whether/if* or by an interrogative adverb), i.e. as the **objects** of **verbs of saying** or of **verbs of asking, wondering, knowing**, etc. For example, in *Ellen told them that she had sold her house,* the clause *that she had sold her house* is the direct object of the verb *told* (i.e. it is what Ellen told them), and we can see that it is a nominal clause as we can replace it by the noun *lies* or the noun phrase *the truth* (*Ellen told them lies* or *Ellen told them the truth*). Similarly in the sentence *Everybody asked themselves why John had married Jane*, the clause *why John had married Jane* is the direct object of the verb *ask* (what everybody asked), and it is clear that it is a nominal clause since it can be replaced by the noun *questions* or by the noun phrase *this question* (*Everybody asked themselves questions* or *Everybody asked themselves this question*). For nominal clauses as prepositional objects which have lost their preposition, see pages 157–158.

As Subject

Rather less frequently a nominal clause can be found as the subject of a sentence. In this case it usually occurs **before a copular** (= linking) verb (such as *be* or *seem*) and takes the form of an indirect statement or an indirect question. For example, in the sentence *That Sarah had passed the examination with flying colours was no surprise*, the subject of the verb *was* is the nominal clause *That Sarah had passed the examination with flying colours.* The clause has the form of a statement introduced by the conjunction *that*. We can prove its noun-like status by replacing it with the noun phrase *this fact* (*This fact was no surprise*). Similarly, in the sentence *Why Frank had left the party seemed to be a mystery*, the subject of the copular verb *seemed* is the nominal clause *Why Frank had left the party*. In this case it has the form of an indirect question. We can prove that it has nominal function as we can fill the slot which it occupies in the sentence by a noun phrase such as *Frank's disappearance* (*Frank's disappearance seemed to be a mystery*).

Adjectival or Relative Clauses

Relative clauses are clauses which function like adjectives. They modify a noun or a noun-like structure, which is usually called the **antecedent**. In grammatical terminology, relative clauses are said to **refer** to this antecedent rather than to modify it. Depending on the type of antecedent, relative clauses can be classified as **adnominal**, i.e. those which have a noun or noun phrase as their antecedent, and **sentential**, i.e. those which have a sentence or part of a sentence as their antecedent. There is also a third kind, the **nominal relative clause**, which does not function like an adjective but like a noun. This is because its antecedent is included in the relative pronoun introducing the clause. Since all three kinds of relative clauses were amply illustrated when we dealt in Chapter 2 with relative pronouns (pages 60–62), sentence relative pronouns (page 62) and nominal relative pronouns (page 62), we shall give only one example of each here to refresh the reader's memory. In the first two examples, the antecedent is printed in bold type and the relative clause referring to it is underlined. The sentence in brackets after each example shows the antecedent or its equivalent in the position it would take if the relative clause were a main clause.

Examples

(Adnominal) *We enjoyed the* ***holidays*** *<u>which we spent in Spain</u>*. (*We spent holidays in Spain*)
(Sentential) ***He coughed loudly***, *<u>which surprised everyone</u>*. (*His loud coughing* (or *That he coughed loudly*) *surprised everyone*)
The third example shows a nominal relative clause. Here only the relative clause can be underlined as the relative pronoun introducing it is fused with the antecedent into one word. In the sentence in brackets following the example, the hidden antecedent has been taken out of the nominal relative and is shown in bold type followed by a normal adnominal relative clause:
(Nominal) *She stared at <u>whoever passed by</u>*. (*She stared at* ***everybody*** *<u>who passed by</u>*)

Restrictive & Non-Restrictive

Relative clauses which have a noun as their antecedent can be sub-classified as **restrictive** (also called **defining**) or **non-restrictive** (also called **non-defining**), depending on whether the information which they provide is **necessary for the identification of**

the antecedent or whether it is **unnecessary**, i.e. merely additional and could be left out with no harm to the sense. For example, if I want to tell you about a particular group of three boys on a playing field full of other boys and girls, I can say *The **three boys** who are playing football are brothers.* The relative clause identifies which particular group of three boys I am referring to. It is a **restrictive** relative clause because it says 'this group of three boys and no other.' On the other hand, if there are only three boys on the field and we have already talked about them and furthermore if they are all wearing very clean shorts, I could say *The **three boys**, who were all wearing very clean shorts, looked like an advertisement for washing powder.* This relative clause does not identify the group of three boys I am referring to. You already know which boys I mean, as there are no others and we have already mentioned them. The relative clause here is a **non-restrictive** one, giving additional information, which could easily be omitted. A good example of a noun clause which under normal circumstances could only take a non-restrictive relative clause is *my mother*. As I have only one mother, the adnominal relative clause in the sentence ***My mother**, who is an excellent cellist, is performing in tonight's concert* does not tell us which mother is performing tonight and must therefore be non-restrictive. Notice however, that the situation is quite different when the antecedent is the noun phrase *my uncle*. If I have several uncles and if it is not clear to the listener which uncle I am referring to, then the relative clause in the sentence ***My uncle** who works at Ford's would know* identifies this uncle as 'the uncle who works at Ford's and no other' and is therefore restrictive. However, if I have only one uncle or if the listener already knows to which uncle I am referring, the same relative clause could then be non-restrictive and would be separated from the rest of the sentence by commas: ***My uncle**, who works at Ford's, would know.*

Commas

Notice that in English, a **non-restrictive** relative clause **must have a comma in front of it**, whereas **no comma is placed in front of a restrictive** one. (If the non-restrictive relative clause is not at the end of the sentence, it will also need a comma **after** it too, as we see in the example at the end of the preceding paragraph.) In reading aloud and in conversation the comma before (and after) the non-restrictive relative clause is often indicated by a pause. Restrictive relative clauses, on the other hand cannot be separated by a pause from the rest of the sentence.

Relative Clause with Zero Pronoun

In one kind of **restrictive** relative clause in non-formal English it is possible to have a relative clause with **no relative pronoun** introducing it. This can occur when the antecedent of the relative clause is referred to by a relative pronoun which is the **direct** or **indirect object** of the verb in the relative clause. Consider for a moment the sentence *Harry sent the letter to his friend*, where we have a direct object (*a letter*), and an indirect object (*to his friend*). Related to this sentence, we can form the following two sentences containing relative clauses: (a) *I saw the* ***letter*** *(which) Harry sent to his friend* and (b) *I am the* ***friend*** *(who) Harry sent the letter to*. As the verb *sent* in (a) has the relative pronoun *which* as its direct object, and as the same verb in (b) has the relative pronoun *who* as its the indirect object, both pronouns can optionally be omitted. The relative pronoun can also be left out if it is the **object of a prepositional verb**, e.g. in (c) *This is the* ***book*** *(which) Wendy was looking at*, where *which* is the prepositional object of the verb *looking at*. Note that in relative clauses of this kind the preposition can be placed in front of the relative pronoun in more formal style (*the book at which Wendy was looking*) but it must always follow the verb when the pronoun is omitted (*the book Wendy was looking at*, and not **the book at Wendy was looking*). In some grammatical analyses this omitted relative pronoun is considered to be present in the sentence as a **zero relative pronoun**. In other words, the slot in the sentence where the relative pronoun would normally be found is said to be marked by a zero pronoun which cannot be heard or seen but which makes itself felt grammatically: it tells us that what follows the slot is a relative clause.

Relative Clause with Relative Adverb

Another type of restrictive relative clause is one in which the antecedent can be referred to either by a relative pronoun with a preposition in front of it or by one of the relative adverbs *where, when* or *why*. The adverb *where* always refers to an antecedent of place, the adverb *when* to one of time, and the adverb *why* almost always refers to the noun *reason*. In the following examples, the antecedent is in bold type, the relative pronoun underlined, and the alternative relative clause with the preposition + relative pronoun placed in brackets at the end:

That was the ***month/year*** *when he broke his leg. (= in which he broke his leg.)*

Do you remember the ***house*** *where you first met him? (= at which you first met him?)*

That was the ***reason*** *why I wrote to them.*

Note that in colloquial style the relative adverbs *when* and *why* (but not *where*) can usually be omitted with no change in meaning: e.g. *That was the* ***month*** *he broke his leg. That was the* ***reason*** *I wrote to them.*

Adverbial Clauses

Just as adjectival clauses function like adjectives, so adverbial clauses function like adverbs. As there are many kinds of adverb clauses corresponding to the many kinds of adverb, we shall not have enough space to talk about them all. Among the ten most important ones are adverbial clauses of **time, place, manner, rea-**

son, condition, concession, purpose, comment, result and **comparison**. Below we shall show for each kind the commonest conjunctions introducing the clause and provide a few illustrative examples. Explanatory comments will be added where necessary.

Time

Some of the conjunctions introducing adverbial clauses of time are: *when, after, as, as long as, as soon as, before, by the time (that), directly, immediately, now (that), since, until/till, whenever, while.* In the following examples the conjunction is in bold type and the adverbial clause underlined:

*<u>**Directly**</u>* (or *<u>**Immediately**</u>* or *<u>**As soon as**) I mentioned it</u>, he turned red.*

*<u>**Now (that)** she has come</u>, you might as well ask her in.*

*We have not seen them, <u>**since** they moved to Edinburgh</u>.*

Note that adverbial clauses of time answer the question 'When?' and can be placed both in front of and after the main clause.

Place

The number of conjunctions which can introduce place adverbial clauses is restricted: *where, wherever, anywhere, everywhere.*

*Put the book <u>**where** I can reach it</u>.*

*You can play the instruments <u>**wherever** you want to</u>.*

*<u>**Everywhere** you go today</u>, you find trouble.*

Place adverbial clauses answer the question 'Where?' They are not always free with regard to position. Whereas the clause with *everywhere* in the last example could also come after the main clause, those with *where* and *wherever* in the first two examples can only follow the main clause.

Manner

Manner adverbial clauses are introduced by the conjunctions *as, as if, as though,* and colloquially by the conjunction equivalents *just how, just the way.*

*The fish is not cooked <u>**as** I like it</u>.*

*She walked <u>**as if** she suffered from arthritis</u>.*

*They welcomed him <u>**just how**</u>* (or *<u>**just the way**) they welcomed everybody</u>.*

Adverbial clauses of manner answer the question 'How?' or 'In what way?' They are only found following the main clause.

Reason

The usual conjunctions introducing an adverbial clause of reason are *as, because, since*. They answer the question 'Why?' or 'For what reason?' and can be placed both before and after the main clause.

*<u>**As** Barbara had no money</u>, they did not charge her for it.*

*She accepted their offer <u>**because** she felt rather lonely</u>.*

*<u>**Since** they had no other plans</u> they preferred to stay at home.*

The position of the adverbial clause depends on the information the speaker wishes to convey. Since the final position in a sentence with a normal stress pattern is the most important, the speaker of the first sentence above (with *as* introducing the reason adverbial clause) wants to draw our attention to the fact that Barbara did not have to pay. If he puts the adverbial clause **after** the main clause, it is now the reason for Barbara's not paying that is more important, i.e. the fact that she had no money.

Condition

Adverbial clauses of condition answer the question 'If what?' or 'On what condition?'. The typical conjunctions found at the beginning of them are *if, if ... not, unless.* Conditional clauses are traditionally divided into those with **realistic conditions**, i.e. conditions which can be or have already been fulfilled, and those with **hypothetical conditions**, i.e. conditions which cannot (or can only theoretically) be fulfilled or have not been and can no longer be fulfilled. German speakers should note that in British English (though not always in American) the modal auxiliary *would* is normally found **only in the main clause** of sentences with hypothetical conditional clauses (i.e. there is usually **no** *would* in the conditional clause). In the examples below, the first three contain realistic conditions and those following contain hypothetical conditions.

*<u>**Unless** the weather is very bad</u>, we'll go to the zoo tomorrow.*
*<u>**If** you look on the top shelf</u>, the book is there.*
*I always get a headache, <u>**if** I read too long at night</u>.*
*<u>**If** Janet lived nearer</u>, we would visit her more often.*
*We would have informed the police, <u>**if** we had seen the accident</u>.*
*<u>**If** the boy had **not** lied</u>, he would not have been punished.*

Note that *unless* cannot replace *if ... not* in the last sentence, as *unless* is not normally found introducing hypothetical conditional clauses. Compare the first sentence above where the condition is realistic. Here *if ... not* and *unless* are interchangeable (*<u>**If** the weather is **not** very bad</u>, ...* or *<u>**Unless** the weather is very bad</u>, ...*). Note also that in hypothetical conditional sentences where the main clause contains *would have* the conjunction *if* can be omitted in formal style provided the subject is placed after *had* in the conditional clause, e.g.

<u>Had the boy not lied</u>, he would not have been punished.

Realistic and hypothetical conditional clauses can be found both before and after the main clause.

Concession

Adverbial clauses of concession answer the questions 'Although what?' and 'Despite the fact that what?' They can be introduced by the following conjunctions or conjunction equivalents: *although, though, even though, considering (that), while, however* (+ Adverb/Adjective), *no matter how* (+ Adverb/Adjective). With the exception of clauses with concessive *while*, which always precede, clauses of concession can be placed both before and after the main clause, as we see in the following examples.

*<u>**Although** they knew him</u>, they didn't say hello.*
*They were never invited, <u>**even though** they were friends of the family</u>.*

Considering (that) they earn so little, they have a very luxurious house.
While I admit that the problem is difficult, I do not agree that it cannot be solved.
***However** (or **No matter how**) carefully I write, my mother can never read my letters.* (= ***Although** I write carefully ...*)

*They persistently ignore us, **however** (or **no matter how**) polite we are to them.*

Note also that a clause with an initial preposed adjective or adverb followed by *as* also has concessive function:

*Powerful **as** you are, you will not succeed.*
(= ***Although** you are powerful ...*)
*Much **as** I like them, I cannot invite them to the wedding.*
(= ***Although** I like them a lot ...*)

In the last example, the preposed adverb *much* must be changed to *a lot* in the regular concessive clause with *although*, as *much* cannot normally be used in affirmative contexts. In the concessive clause beginning with *much as*, the use of *much* in a non-negative context is idiomatic; one cannot say **A lot as I like them ...* .

Purpose

Adverbial clauses of purpose answer the questions 'For what purpose?' and 'To what end?' They are commonly introduced by the conjunctions *so (that), in order that* and in formal English by *lest.*

*We always keep the food covered **so (that)** the flies cannot get at it.*
***In order that** they could entertain guests, they had another bedroom built onto their house.*
*They fortified the city **lest** the enemy should break into it unawares.*
(= ***in order that** the enemy should **not** break into it unawares*)

Purpose clauses are found both preceding and following the main clause.

Result

Adverbial clauses of result answer the question 'With what result?' and are often introduced by the conjunction equivalent *with the result that.* They always follow the main clause.

*Jane missed the bus **with the result that** she was late for work.*
(= *and this meant that she was late for work*)

Result clauses like purpose clauses can also be introduced by the conjunction *so that*. There is usually no confusion as they answer different diagnostic questions. Only purpose clauses can precede the main verb and they usually require different tenses. Compare the following two sentences:

a. *They put the glasses on the table very carefully **so that** the contents **did not** spill over. (= and this meant that the contents did not spill over)* [Result]
b. *They put the glasses on the table very carefully **so that** the contents **would not** spill over.* [Purpose]

__So that__ the contents __would not__ spill over they put the glasses on the table very carefully. [Purpose]

Notice that the difference in tense in the two kinds of clauses produces different presuppositions. The sentence with the result clause presupposes that the contents did not spill over, whereas in the sentence with the purpose clause we cannot be sure: maybe they did or maybe they did not.

Comment

The type of adverbial clause which is called a **comment clause** differs from all the other adverbial clauses in being only loosely related to the rest of the sentence in which it is found. It behaves as if it were in parentheses and, as its name suggests, comments on the sentence or clause it goes with. Comment clauses are typically introduced by the conjunction *as*, sometimes by *so*, and frequently have no conjunction at all. They can be found at the beginning, in the middle, and at the end of a sentence.

__As__ you know, the firm is now bankrupt.
The new hospital is now open, __so__ we hear.
Your brother's car, I believe, was involved in an accident.
The deputy manager has been given the job, __as__ is often done when the manger retires.

Note that the subject *it* is always omitted in comment clauses when they contain one of the following constructions: a passive verb (as in the last example above), a modal plus a passive verb, the simple tense of a verb like *happen, occur, transpire*, or else *be* plus a noun phrase or *be* plus an adjective, e.g.

*The house has been burgled, __as__ (*it) can be seen from the chaos inside.*
*Our pond has frozen over, __as__ (*it) often happens in winter.*
*She took the food without saying a word, __as__ (*it) was the custom among these people.*
*The Queen spoke on television this afternoon, __as__ (*it) is usual on Christmas Day.*

Part of Another Sentence Constituent

All the adverbial clauses which we have described above were adverbial constituents of a sentence, i.e. they function in an adverbial relationship to the main clause or to the verb in the main clause. There are some adverbial clauses, however, which do not always or never have this function and are then part of another sentence constituent. For example, some **result** clauses are part of an adverb phrase of manner which functions as the adverbial constituent of a sentence; others are part of a noun phrase which functions as a direct object. The former are introduced by *that* following *so* plus an adverb; the latter by *that* following *so* plus a quantifying determiner or pronoun:

The man on the stage spoke [so fast$_{Adv}$ [__that__ nobody could understand him]$_{Advl\ Cl\ Result}$]$_{AdvP\ Manner\ =\ Advl}$

*They wasted [so much$_{Det}$ time [**that** they arrived too late for the concert]$_{Advl\ Cl\ Result}$]$_{NP = dO}$*
*When the presents were handed out, the child was given [so few$_{Pron}$ [**that** the mother felt ashamed]$_{Advl\ Cl\ Result}$]$_{NP = dO}$*

Comparison

Adverbial clauses of comparison are particularly complicated. To be dealt with thoroughly they need more space than we have in this little book. We have already seen some examples of them on page 121 above, when we discussed the postmodification of adverbs in adverb phrases. Clauses of comparison always form part of another structure within the sentence and can never stand alone as a sentence constituent. One kind is introduced by the conjunction *than* following a structure with *more*. This structure may be a noun phrase, an adverb phrase (of manner) or an adjective phrase, depending on the word class of *more* in each case. Some examples will make this clear.

Examples

If *more* is a pronoun or a determiner, the comparative clause is part of a noun phrase, which in the following two examples functions as the direct object (dO) of a sentence (see direct objets, pages 152–154) :

*He owned [more$_{Pron}$ **than** anybody else did]$_{NP = dO}$*
*Sandra sees [more$_{Det}$ films **than** the whole family does]$_{NP = dO}$*

When *more* is an adverb, it can itself be the head of an adverb phrase containing a comparative clause or it can premodify another adverb with the same function. In each case the adverb phrase functions as an adverbial constituent in the sentence:

*We laughed at Jean [more$_{Adv}$ **than** we laughed at Bill]$_{AdvP = Advl}$*
*The group of elephants moved [more slowly$_{Adv}$ **than** the hippos did]$_{AdvP = Advl}$*

As an adverb, *more* can also modify a predicative or attributive adjective and thus be part of an adjective phrase:

*The book was [more entertaining$_{Adj}$ **than** we had expected it would be]$_{AdjP = sC}$*
*It was [a [more boring] film [**than** I thought it would be]]$_{NP = sC}$*
____AdjP____

In the first example above, the adjective phrase functions as the subject complement constituent of the sentence (see page 160). In the second example the adjective phrase is part of a noun phrase with this same function. Note that the adjective phrase in the last example is discontinuous, i.e. interrupted by the noun *film*. Note too that clauses of comparison, like comment clauses, obligatorily lose their subject *it* when they consist of a finite form of the verb *be* followed by either an adjective phrase or a noun phrase, e.g.

*They ate [more meat **than** (*it) was usual for Africans]$_{NP}$*
*They spoke [more slowly **than**(*it) was the custom in France]$_{AdvP}$*

Unequal and Equal Comparison

Before we leave adverbial clauses of comparison, it must be observed that two kinds are often distinguished in the grammar books: clauses of unequal comparison and clauses of equal comparison. Those which we have dealt with so far (containing *more .... than*) show **unequal comparison**. Others of the same type are introduced by the conjunction *than* after comparative items such as *less, better, worse* or an adjective or adverb with the comparative suffix *-er*. Examples:

*Agatha's father was [**less** fierce$_{Adj}$ [**than** any of us had expected]$_{Adv\ Cl}$]$_{AdjP\ =\ sC}$*
*He spoke French [**better**$_{Adv}$ [**than** his mother had ever spoken English]$_{Adv\ Cl}$]$_{AdvP\ =\ Advl}$*
*The house was [big**ger**$_{Adj}$ [**than** they needed]$_{Adv\ Cl}$]$_{AdjP\ =\ sC}$*

Clauses of **equal comparison** (also called **comparative clauses of equality**) are introduced by *as* after an adjective or adverb preceded by another *as.*

*The children's clothes did not look [**as** expensive$_{Adj}$ [**as** they actually were]$_{Advl\ Cl\ Comparison}$]$_{AdjP}$*
*The children ran [**as** fast$_{Adv}$ [**as** their tiny legs could carry them]$_{Adv\ Cl\ Comparison}$]$_{AdvP}$*

Both types of comparative clause are characterized by often having the same auxiliary verb as in the main clause or by replacing a simple tense main verb by the corresponding tense of *do*. Furthermore both kinds are often elliptical.

*Cedric **could** eat more **than** any of his brothers (**could**)*
*Stella **learnt** more quickly **than** her schoolmates (**did**)*
*Arnold **was** as pompous **as** (he) always (**was**)*
*Tracy **smokes** as many cigarettes **as** Jake (**does**)*

4 Classification as Finite or Non-Finite Clause

General Remarks

The third big general classification of clauses is into finite and non-finite clauses. A **finite clause** normally contains an **explicit subject** and a **finite verb**, which may have various other constituents (objects, complements, adverbials) dependent on it. In many languages the finite forms of the verb have different suffixes for different persons and different tenses. In English, special forms for the different persons of the verb can only be seen in the present tense singular of the very irregular verb *be*. Regular verbs have only one special suffix indicating person (for the third person singular of the present tense), the forms for other persons being unmarked. As there are only three non-finite forms of the English verb, it is easier to list them and to declare all other forms as finite. The **three non-finite forms** are the **present participle**, the **past participle** and the **infinitive**. Clauses which contain one of these non-finite forms of the verb and which have an implicit or explicit subject can be called **non-finite clauses**.

Finite Clauses

We do not need to spend much time on finite clauses, as all those which we have described so far (under the traditional classification and under the classification according to grammatical function) were of this kind. The reader is reminded that some finite clauses may **not always contain an explicit subject**. Among the subordinate clauses, we saw this to be the case with some comment and comparative clauses. In main clauses it is also usually the case with commands: the imperative form of the verb is finite, and therefore an imperative main clause is a finite clause, even if the subject is omitted. Notice that in commands the subject can always be restored: *(You) go home! Don't (you) speak to me like that!*

Non-Finite Clauses

In addition to the **present participle, past participle** and **infinitive** clauses which were mentioned above, we can also look at the **verbless non-finite clauses** which arise when the verb with its subject is omitted from a clause which should contain a linking verb followed by a predicative adjective. Each of these types will be dealt with separately below.

Present Participle Clauses

Non-finite clauses with a present participle usually have adverbial function in a sentence, e.g. similar to an adverbial clause of time (*when he saw the policeman)* in the first example below, or to an adverbial clause of reason (*because she had lost her key*) in the second:

Seeing *the policeman, Derek ran away.*

Having *lost her key, Phyllis couldn't get into the flat.*

Although *seeing* is a non-finite form it clearly has an implicit subject (*Derek*) as well as an explicit object (*the policeman*). In the second example, we shall consider *having lost* as a present participle construction as it begins with the present participle of the auxiliary verb *have*. When *having* is followed by the past participle of a lexical verb, the combination (here *having lost*) is often referred to as the perfect participle of that verb, although strictly speaking it is two participles. In the second example above, the participle clause clearly has an implicit subject (*Phyllis*) as well as an explicit object (*her key*). Sometimes the adverbial function of a present participle clause is made clear by the addition of an appropriate conjunction:

Although not ***believing*** *a word he said, she listened patiently.*

Here the non-finite clause is the equivalent of a finite adverbial clause of concession (*Although she did not believe a word he said*).

Past Participle Clauses

Past participle clauses usually have the same function in a sentence as an adverbial clause of reason, but by the addition of a conjunction they can be given other functions, e.g. as the equivalent of an adverbial clause of time (in the second example below) or of condition (in the third):

Suffocated *by the smoke, they rushed out of the burning building.*
(= Because they were suffocated by the smoke)
When ***rescued*** *from the blaze, they were too exhausted to speak.*
(=When they were rescued)
Unless clearly ***marked****, the path through the woods will not be found.*
(= Unless it is clearly marked)

In the finite clause in brackets after each example the explicit subject of the verb makes clear the implicit subject of each past participle clause.

Infinitive Clauses

Infinitive clauses differ from participle clauses in that they **often have** an **explicit subject** (underlined in the examples below), usually in the form of a prepositional phrase introduced by *for*, but sometimes lacking the preposition. Infinitive clauses are almost always introduced by *to*, though sometimes only the bare infinitive is found. They mostly function as **nominal** or **adverbial** phrases or as the **complements of adjectives or nouns**. Consider the following pairs:

Inf Cl = NP

1a *[For them to open a shop]$_{Inf\ Cl = NP}$ would be financial suicide.*
1b *[To open a shop]$_{Inf\ Cl = NP}$ would be financial suicide.*

The logical subject of the verb *open* in 1a is *they*, as we can see from the following paraphrase of the whole sentence: *If they open a shop it would be financial suicide.* The logical subject is included in the infinitive clause in the form of the prepositional phrase *for them*. In 1b, on the other hand, where there is no explicit subject in the form of a prepositional phrase with *for*, the logical subject must be supplied from the context. It could be *you* (the person or persons we are talking to), or *he, she* or *they* (some other person or persons we know) or even *somebody* (if we are talking in general). In both 1a and 1b the infinitive clause functions like a noun (i.e. as a nominal phrase) and is the subject of the main verb (*would be*). In 2a and 2b the infinitive clause also functions as a nominal phrase but is this time the direct object of the main verb:

2a *I want [John to sing at the concert]$_{Inf\ Cl = NP}$*
2b *I want [to sing at the concert]$_{Inf\ Cl = NP}$*

In 2a we see an infinitive clause whose verb (*sing*) has an explicit subject (*John*) without the preposition *for*. The verb *want* is one of the few verbs like *prefer, like, desire* which require no preposition before the subject of the infinitive that follows them. Example 2b illustrates a different situation, found with all verbs that can take an infinitive clause as their complementation: if the subject of the infinitive is the same as that of the verb on which it depends, it is omitted. With some verbs this is the only possible non-finite construction, e.g. ***I*** *hope [to finish the work tomorrow] =* ***I*** *will finish.* ***They*** *refuse [to stay at the inn] =* ***They*** *will not stay.* ***She*** *determined [to offer them the job] =* ***She*** *offered them a job.*

Inf Cl = Adv Cl

The infinitive clause can also have adverbial function, as we see in the following example:

[To be frank]$_{\textit{Inf Cl = Advl}}$*, the property is worthless.*

Here the infinitive clause is the equivalent of the sentential adverb *frankly* (see page 106) or of the adverbial clause of condition *if I may be frank with you*, and thus functions as the adverbial constituent in the sentence. The **implicit** subject of the infinitive is *I*, the speaker of the sentence. In the following example the infinitive clause is the equivalent of an adverbial clause of purpose and has an **explicit** subject (in bold type):

The merchant distributed food [(in order) ***for the poorest of the people*** *to feed their children]*$_{\textit{Inf Cl = Adv Cl}}$

Another example where the infinitive clause is equal to an adverbial clause of purpose but this time with an **implicit** subject (the same as that of the main verb) is:

Jack played [to win]$_{\textit{Inf Cl = Adv Cl}}$

Here too, as in the preceding example, the infinitive clause functions as the adverbial constituent of its sentence.

Inf Cl in Adj P

We saw some examples of infinitive clauses as the complements of adjectives when we discussed the postmodification of adjectives on page 120 (Pattern 7). Some adjectives admit an explicit subject, again in the form of a prepositional phrase with *for*, e.g.

*Sally will be [****happy***$_{\textit{Adj}}$ *[for you to come]*$_{\textit{Inf Cl}}$ *]*$_{\textit{Adj P}}$

*This book is [****easy***$_{\textit{Adj}}$ *[for them to read]*$_{\textit{Inf Cl}}$ *]*$_{\textit{Adj P}}$

When the infinitive clause contains a bare infinitive the implicit subject may be identical with that of the main verb, as in

*Sally will be [****happy*** *[to come]*$_{\textit{Inf Cl}}$ *]*$_{\textit{Adj P}}$ (= *Sally will come*)

but sometimes (e.g. when it would be illogical for the implicit subject of the infinitive to be identical with the explicit subject of the main verb) the listener can supply a subject from the context, as in

*This book is [****easy*** *[to read]*$_{\textit{Inf Cl}}$ *]*$_{\textit{Adj P}}$

Here the listener may feel that this is a general statement and supply a general subject for the infinitive such as *anybody (This book is easy for anybody to read)*. On the other hand, if the speaker offers the book to a listener for the listener herself to read, we understand *you* (i.e. *for you*) as the subject of the infinitive, whereas if the listener has asked for a book for her son, we would then understand *he* (i.e. *for him*) as the subject.

Inf Cl in NP

A certain number of nouns can take the same infinitive clause complement as the adjective from which they are derived. In the resulting noun phrase the infinitive clause can be given an explicit subject with the usual prepositional phrase introduced by *for*, e.g.

We did not understand [his ***unwillingness***$_{\textit{N}}$ *[for them to appear in public]*$_{\textit{Inf Cl}}$ *]*$_{\textit{NP}}$

Notice that if the prepositional phrase indicating the subject is left out, as in

We did not understand [his ***unwillingness***$_{N}$ *[to appear in public]*$_{Inf\ Cl}$*]*$_{NP}$

the implicit subject can be determined by using the head noun in the nominal phrase to form an equivalent sentence with the related adjective; e.g. ***he*** *was* ***unwilling*** *to appear in public.* This answers the question 'Who (in the example sentence) would not appear?' and tells us that the subject of the infinitive clause is *he* and not *we* (the subject of the main verb *did not understand*). Another pair of examples of this kind is given below. Compare the sentence

[Donald's ***eagerness*** *[<u>for all his sons</u> to attend the football match]*$_{Inf\ Cl}$*]*$_{NP}$ *rather surprised his wife*

where the explicit subject has been underlined, with

[Donald's ***eagerness*** *[to attend the football match]*$_{Inf\ Cl}$*]*$_{NP}$ *rather surprised his wife*

As the infinitive clause in the latter sentence has no overt subject, we can ask the question 'Who (in the example sentence) would attend the football match?' and then determine the implicit subject (*Donald*) by constructing the sentence with the corresponding adjective: ***Donald*** *was* ***eager*** *to attend the football match*, which ultimately reduces to ***Donald*** *would attend the football match.*

Verbless Non-Finite Clauses

To complete our brief survey of non-finite clauses, we must examine one kind which can be loosely called non-finite as it contains no verb at all. Both the subject and the verb can sometimes be omitted from a clause which should contain a form of the **copula (linking verb)** *be* followed by a **predicative adjective** (or **adjective phrase**). For example, in place of

Sidney ***was***$_{Cop}$ ***suspicious***$_{Adj}$ *of the man's intentions and followed him into the car park*

we can construct the following sentence, which begins with a non-finite verbless clause (underlined):

<u>***Suspicious*** *of the man's intentions*</u>*, Sidney followed him into the car park.*

Similarly, from the sentence

Since it ***was***$_{Cop}$ *[as* ***light***$_{Adj}$ *as a feather]*$_{Adj\ P}$*, the note fluttered out of the window*

we can form the sentence

<u>*(As)* ***Light*** *as a feather*</u>*, the note fluttered out of the window.*

As the conjunction *since* introduces an adverbial clause of reason in the original sentence, it is clear that the verbless non-finite clause containing the adjective or adjective phrase must have the same function in the second sentence. If we compare the examples above with the following

*Although always **drunk**$_{Adj}$, the man made an honest living*

we see yet another proof that verbless clauses characteristically behave like adverbial clauses. The conjunction *though* normally introduces a finite adverbial clause of concession. So the non-finite verbless clause which it here introduces must have this same adverbial function. This example also illustrates another general characteristic of verbless clauses, namely that their implicit subject is always identical with the explicit subject of the main verb. If we ask here 'Who was always drunk?', the answer is 'the man (who made an honest living)'.

Final Remarks

In our examination of clauses in this chapter, we have seen that, like phrases and words, they may be analysed not only with respect to their grammatical structure but also with respect to their grammatical function. As we have progressed in this book from the word level to the phrase level and then on to the clause level, we have seen many times that units from a higher level can be used at any of the lower levels and that they then assume the function of the unit they replace. For example, the noun *Tomorrow* in the sentence *Tomorrow will not be convenient* can be replaced not only by the prepositional phrase *After eight o'clock,* which then has the function of a noun, but also by the non-finite clause *For you to come after eight o'clock,* which also functions as a noun here. In addition to structure and function, in this chapter we have had to introduce another dimension of analysis, namely that of the **constituents of the clause**, those elements such as subject, object, complement, etc. which play important roles in the organisation of the clause. Thus in order to prove that a structure is a non-finite clause, we had to show that it has a subject and that this subject is either implicit or contained as an explicit subject in a *for*-phrase. It was also necessary to show that although verbless clauses have no visible subject, their implicit subject must be the same as that of the main clause on which they depend. In the next chapter, we shall meet these same clause constituents (subjects, objects, complements, adverbials) again, but now as constituents of the sentence. In this chapter we have only been able to refer to them briefly or to deal with them fleetingly, as the detailed description of their roles and functions is the main subject of sentence level analysis, with which we shall be occupied in most of Chapter 5.

5 CHAPTER Sentences

Introduction

Much of what was said about clause structure in the last chapter can also be said about sentences, for a sentence is really a special kind of clause: an independent main clause. Or considered in another way, a clause is really a kind of dependent sentence. However, whereas most clauses need to be introduced by a conjunction, a sentence stands on its own and does not need an introductory conjunction. Furthermore, a sentence is the higher structure containing the elements on which most clauses depend. In this chapter it will be our main task to look more closely at all these elements and to determine their roles (functions) in the sentence. We have seen in previous chapters that these constituents of the sentence may be clauses or phrases or just single words.

1 Sentence Constituents

1 General Remarks

Roles

A sentence consists of a number of grammatical units which some grammarians call **constituents**, others **components** or **elements**. With the exception of a few kinds of adverbial constituents (which behave like linking adverbs in joining sentences together or like sentential adverbs in announcing the speaker's field of reference or showing the speaker's attitude to what he says), the role of most sentence constituents is defined in relation to the **verbal constituent**, i.e. to the main verb in the sentence or to what at the phrase level we called the verb phrase. Some grammarians refer to the verbal constituent merely as the verb. This relationship of dependency on the verbal constituent is especially true of the **subject** and the various kinds of **object**. However, the constituents which are referred to as **complements** are defined directly in relation to subjects and objects, but also indirectly with regard to the kind of verb which they accompany (copular verbs). Finally, most **adverbial constituents** have a direct relation with the verbal constituent since they qualify it in a variety of ways. In the sections below, in which this relationship to the verbal constituent will become clear, we shall deal with the sentence constituents in the following order: **verbal constituent, subject, direct object, indirect object, prepositional object, subject complement, object complement**, and **adverbial**. Remember that these same constituents can also be found within clauses, since clauses, as we mentioned above, are structurally similar to sentences.

2 Verbal Constituent

Definition

The verbal constituent of a sentence is the central constituent upon which all other constituents (with a few exceptions) depend. It consists either of the lexical main verb alone or of this verb preceded by one or more auxiliary verbs. Thus in the following examples the verbal constituent (underlined) is either a single word (a lexical verb) or a verb phrase: *Pamela <u>plays</u> the harpsichord. He <u>is eating</u> an apple. Shirley <u>may have been watching</u> TV then.* If the main verb is a phrasal verb, i.e. a verb which takes an adverbial particle to complete its meaning, the adverbial particle must be considered as part of the verbal constituent, as we see in the following examples: *Philip <u>has given up</u>. The dog <u>ran away</u>. <u>Do come in</u>!* In the case of prepositional verbs, i.e. verbs which require a special preposition after them, we shall see below (in our discussion of prepositional objects) that the preposition may sometimes be included in the verbal constituent and sometimes in the prepositional object. For reasons of space, it will often be more convenient in the rest of this chapter to label the verbal constituent with the abbreviation **Vbl** and sometimes to refer to it merely as **the verbal**.

Verbless Sentence

Although almost all English sentences have a verbal constituent, there are a few fixed sentence types which contain no verb. Thus we find

(a) exclamations of the kind:
Up with the Socialists! Down with the Fascists!
Out with the whole band of them!

(b) proposals in the form of a question beginning with *What about:*
What about another cup of tea?
What about playing another game of cards?

(c) elliptical sayings of the kind:
The more (we, you, they are), the merrier (we, you, they will be).

As these verbless types of sentence are all idiomatic, we can exclude them from our analysis.

3 Subject

Definition

The subject of a sentence is the person or thing which answers the question 'Who?' or 'What?' when this interrogative pronoun is placed in front of the verbal constituent. The subject of the sentence *Alec is wearing a smart suit* can thus be determined as *Alec* if we ask the simple question ***Who** is wearing a smart suit?* The role of the subject in a sentence (or clause) depends upon whether the lexical verb in the verbal constituent is a dynamic or a stative verb (see pages 78, 85). If the verb is a **dynamic verb**, the **subject** is the **performer of the action** which the verb expresses. It will be remembered that dynamic verbs are verbs of 'doing' and only these can be used in the expanded tenses with *-ing*. Thus in regard to the sentence *Simon is smoking a pipe*, we can ask 'Who is performing the action of smoking?' and the answer to this more complicated question (*Simon*) also gives us the subject of the verbal constituent (*is smoking*). On the other hand, if the verb in the verbal constituent is a **stative verb**, the **subject** is the **person** or **thing** which is **in the state expressed by the verb**. In contrast to dynamic verbs, stative verbs do not normally occur in the expanded tenses with *-ing*. Thus in regard to the sentence *The poor man believes he is Napoleon*, it would be illogical to ask 'Who is performing the action of believing?' It does, however, makes sense to ask 'Who is in the state of believing that he is Napoleon?' The answer to the latter question (*The poor man*) again provides us with the subject of the verbal constituent (*thinks*).

No Overt Subj

An overt subject is necessary in most types of sentences, but it is often missing in imperatives, e.g. *Go home! Don't stay here!* We can see that these sentences have a hidden (or implicit) subject *you*, as this can be inserted if the command needs to be less insistent, e.g. ***You** go home! Don't **you** stay here!* Furthermore, the direct object of an imperative reflexive verb must be *yourself* or *yourselves* confirming that the implicit subject of the verb must be second person singular or plural, e.g. *Don't blame yourself! Introduce yourselves!* The subject is obligatorily omitted in a few types of clauses, e.g. in comment clauses (*she rose at 11 a.m., as (*it) was her custom on Sundays*), and in comparative clauses (*They spent more time at the fair than (*it) was expected*). See page 135 for comment clauses, and page 136 for clauses of comparison.

Subj = N, Pron or NP

Normally the subject is either a **noun**, **pronoun** or a **noun phrase**, as we saw in the examples in the foregoing paragraphs. Sometimes, however, it can be a unit from a higher level, which then has the same function as a noun or noun phrase. In the following examples we see a **nominal clause** (underlined) in subject position: <u>*What you need*</u> *is a nice cup of tea.* <u>*That we have no money*</u> *makes no difference to her plans.* The subject can also be an **infinitive** (with *to*) or a **gerund** (the noun-like *-ing* form of a verb, which must not be confused with the present participle): <u>*To make frequent objections*</u> *does not really help.* <u>*Breaking down the door*</u> *does not appeal to him as a sensible solution to the problem.*

Agreement between Subj & Vbl

Wherever this is possible, there must be agreement between the subject and the first auxiliary verb (usually called the **operator**) in a multi-word verbal constituent or between the subject and the lexical verb in a **one**-word verbal constituent, e.g.

[Our dog]$_{Subj}$ **has** (not **have*) *been gnawing the leg of the chair.*
[I]$_{subj}$ *am* (not **is, *are*) *very happy.*
[Anna)$_{Subj}$ *swims* (not **swim*) *like a fish.*

When the subject is not a noun, pronoun or noun phrase, but an infinitive with *to*, a gerund, or a nominal clause, then singular agreement is found (see the examples in the preceding paragraph). However, if the subject is a nominal relative clause with plural marking, the verb in the verbal constituent will also be plural, e.g.

[What at the time were small bushes]$_{Subj}$ *have now grown into tall trees.*

In Chapter 1, when we discussed grammatical number in nouns (pages 22–27), we saw several cases of unusual agreement where a noun which appears to be singular may take a plural verb and vice versa. To these we may add here those plural nouns which are used as names, quotations, or titles of books, plays, films, etc. When these are the subject of a sentence the verb in the verbal constituent takes singular agreement:

['War and Peace']$_{Subj}$ *is Tolstoy's best novel.*
['The Four Feathers']$_{Subj}$ *opens on 1st March and is certain to be a great hit.*
['Senior citizens']$_{Subj}$ *means, in common parlance, people over sixty.*

Position of Subj

In a normal affirmative **declarative** sentence (statement), the **subject** always comes **in front** of the **verbal constituent** (as in all the examples in the last paragraph), but in **questions** and in **some negative commands** it is found **immediately after the operator** (the first auxiliary verb) in a complex verbal constituent:

Would$_{Op}$*[you]*$_{Subj}$ *like me to take them?*
└_____ *Verbal* _____┘
Could$_{Op}$ *[the professor]*$_{Subj}$ *have been joking?*
└__________ *Verbal* __________┘
Don't$_{Op}$ *[you]*$_{Subj}$ *mow the lawn, that's John's job!*
└_____ *Verbal* _____┘

In the last example where the negative adverb *not* is reduced to the clitic form *-n't*, which cannot stand alone but must be attached to the word preceding it, we have chosen to underline it as part of the operator (see also page 168 for analysis of *-n't* as part of verbal constituent).

If the lexical verb in the verbal constituent of a declarative sentence has no auxiliary in front of it, e.g. because it is in the simple present or simple past tense, then in the corresponding interrogative sentence ***do*-support** is necessary, i.e. the present or past tense of the auxiliary verb *do* must be inserted, so that the subject here too can come after an operator. For example, instead of the ungrammatical sentence **Goes she very often?* (compare German *geht sie sehr oft?*) we must have

<u>Does</u>$_{Op}$ [she]$_{Subj}$ <u>go</u> very often?

  /____Verbal____/

Notice that in this question, as in the two others above, the verbal constituent is discontinuous, i.e. interrupted by the subject.

Subj -Vbl Inversion

There are one or two exceptions to the rule for the position of the subject. For example, where the subject of the sentence is the most important piece of information in the speaker's message, it may be placed **after the whole verbal constituent** and is then usually last in the sentence. This kind of inversion is sometimes referred to as **total** or **full inversion** and is typically found in the following environments:

(a) It is obligatory with the subject of ***come* and *go*** when these are **used with the locative adverbs *here* and *there*** preceding them in sentences of the kind:

*Here **comes** [the bus]$_{Subj}$*

*There **goes** [my last penny]$_{Subj}$*

A similar type of sentence is also found with *lie*, but only on gravestones:

*Here **lies** [Thomas Smith]$_{Subj}$*

Note that if the subject is a pronoun, there is no inversion as pronouns do not present new or important information:

Here it comes! There she goes! Here he lies!

(b) Inversion of the subject after the whole verbal constituent is not uncommon **in narratives** and occurs in such sentences as

*There beneath the trees **stood** [a woodcutter's hut]$_{Subj}$*

where the final position of the subject makes it easy for the narrator to continue talking about it with a relative clause or a new sentence.

(c) Total inversion is sometimes found **with phrasal verbs**, again for rhetorical effect, as it brings the subject into final position in a clause or sentence, the position normally reserved for the most important piece of information. It is, however, restricted to **phrasal verbs expressing movement**, where the adverbial particle (underlined in the example below) has a meaning associated with place and not a metaphorical meaning. In this kind of inversion the particle is placed before the verb and often comes first in the sentence or clause. In this respect, the construction resembles that in (a) above:

*<u>In</u> **went** [the sun]$_{Subj}$ and <u>down</u> **came** [the rain]$_{Subj}$*

*<u>Up</u> **jumped** [a young sailor, who till now had been silent]$_{Subj}$*

Notice that we cannot say **Out died all the dinosaurs*, as the verb *die* is not a verb of motion and the particle *out* does not have a locative meaning.

(d) One common case of total inversion can be observed in written English where direct speech is quoted. The verbs of saying, used outside the quotation marks to show who has spoken, often precede their subject:

'Grab his arm!' ***said*** *[one man]$_{Subj}$. 'And don't let him get away!'* ***shouted*** *[another]$_{Subj}$.*

The reason for the inversion here is the same as in all the cases above. The speaker or writer feels that the subject is the more important item of information and therefore puts it after the verb in the stressed position at the end of the sentence (or clause). It is more important to know **who** said something rather than to know that it was **said**.

(e) Finally, there are a few **idiomatic expressions** in which total inversion occurs:

Suffice *[it]$_{Subj}$ to say that the party was a success.*
Long ***live*** *[the Queen]$_{Subj}$!*

Subject – Operator Inversion

Another set of exceptions to the rule for the normal position of the subject in front of the verb involves placing the **subject after the operator** and not after the whole verbal constituent. This is sometimes referred to as **partial inversion**. Some of the cases where this type of inversion occurs are described in (a - c) below:

(a) When a **negative** constituent would otherwise appear immediately **before the subject**, the subject and the operator must be inverted. If no operator is present, then *do* in the corresponding tense must be inserted as an operator (*do*-support). Thus instead of the ungrammatical sentence:

Under no circumstances they$_{Subj}$* ***allow* *visitors*
we must say:
Under no circumstances ***do***$_{Op}$ *[they]$_{Subj}$* ***allow*** *visitors.*
Examples which already have an operator are:
Never ***have***$_{Op}$ *[I]$_{Subj}$* ***seen*** *such chaos.*
Nowhere in the world ***can****Op [you]$_{Subj}$* ***find*** *better plums.*

This rule also applies to broad negative (also called negative-feel) adverbs such as *seldom, scarcely, rarely, hardly, barely* and *only* (see Chapter 3, page 104). When one of these precedes the subject, inversion of subject and operator must take place:

Seldom ***have***$_{Op}$ *[I]$_{Subj}$* ***read*** *such nonsense!*
Scarcely ***had***$_{Op}$ *[she]$_{Subj}$* ***given*** *the youth the money when he rushed away on his motorcycle.*
Rarely ***had***$_{Op}$ *[the old man]$_{Subj}$* ***felt*** *so moved.*
Hardly ever ***does***$_{Op}$ *[she]$_{subj}$* ***go*** *to bed before midnight.*
Barely ***was***$_{Op}$ *[the picture]$_{Subj}$* ***framed*** *before the owner appeared.*
Only on Mondays ***do***$_{Op}$ *[the museums]$_{Subj}$* ***close****.*

In all the examples above the discontinuous verbal constituent has been printed in boldface type. Note that sentences of this kind with partial inversion are stylistically more formal. If the initial negative adverbial constituent is given its usual word order, there is no longer any inversion of subject and operator:

*[The museums]$_{Subj}$ **close** only on Mondays.*

(b) Inversion of subject and operator is also found, again for rhetorical effect, when another type of adverbial constituent, namely ***so*** **+ an adverb of manner**, would otherwise immediately **precede the subject:**

*So slowly **had**$_{Op}$ [the lecturer]$_{Subj}$ **been talking** that the students had fallen asleep.*

*So skilfully **did**$_{Op}$ [the dressmaker]$_{Subj}$ **repair** the hole that it could no longer be seen.*

Inversion also occurs in a similar construction with *so* preceding an adjective in front of the verb *be*. Here *be* behaves like an auxiliary although it is in fact a lexical (full) verb. Compare the following:

*So delicious **was** [the pudding]$_{Subj}$ that she ate three helpings.*

*So softly **was** [the choir]$_{Subj}$ **singing** that we could barely hear it.*

The second sentence is clearly like the others above, since *was* is the operator in the verbal constituent *was singing*. In the first sentence, however, *was* is not an auxiliary verb going with the present participle of a lexical verb: it is itself the lexical verb and stands alone as the verbal constituent. Thus in this latter case we have full inversion instead of partial inversion.

(c) One final case of partial inversion is seen in the **idiomatic** construction *well may you* + verb:

*Well **may**$_{Op}$ [you]$_{Subj}$ **ask** why he did not return.*

*Well **may**$_{Op}$ [you]$_{Subj}$ **be alarmed** by his behaviour.*

Double Inversion

An interesting case of double inversion is sometimes found in written English, especially in newspapers. This involves full inversion of the subject and verbal constituent as well as the inversion of the operator with the rest of the verbal constituent. The following examples should make this clear:

***Playing** the violin at the concert **was**$_{Op}$ [the famous musician Frank Peter Zimmermann]$_{Subj}$*

***Helping** with the children **is**$_{Op}$ [Brian's mother]$_{Subj}$*

Notice that double inversion only occurs when the sentence contains the simple present or past tense of the auxiliary verb *be* together with the *-ing* form of a lexical verb, i.e. the expanded (continuous) present or expanded (continuous) past tense of that verb. Other tenses do not permit this kind of inversion: thus we cannot have

Helped* the children **has Brian's mother.*

This meaning must be rendered by one of the following sentences with the subject in its normal position in front of the verbal constituent:

*[The children]$_{Subj}$ **have been helped** by Brian's mother.*

*[Brian's mother]$_{Subj}$ **has helped** the children.*

Unrelated to the examples of double inversion described above is the **idiomatic** expression *come what may (= whatever may happen)* in sentences like:

***Come** [what]$_{Subj}$ **may**, we still leave for China tomorrow.*

Grammatical versus Logical Subj

Above we defined the subject of a dynamic verb as the performer of the action denoted by that verb. It is now time for us to observe that in some kinds of sentences the **performer** of the action is **not necessarily** the **grammatical subject**, i.e. the noun, pronoun or noun phrase preceding the main verb and with which the main verb agrees in number. For example, in passive sentences such as

*[The tables]$_{Subj}$ **were**$_{Op}$ **repaired** by the carpenter.*

The grammatical subject is clearly *the tables*, since the operator in the verbal constituent agrees with it in number (plural *were*). However, it is also clear that *the carpenter* is the performer of the action of repairing. We can refer to this noun phrase as the **logical subject**, although it is embedded in a prepositional phrase, whose role in the sentence is that of an adverbial constituent. This *by*-phrase is roughly equal to an adverb of manner telling us how the tables were repaired.

Dummy Subj

Sometimes it is not possible to assign a logical subject to certain dynamic verbs in English, for example those denoting **meteorological phenomena** (*rain, drizzle, hail, snow, sleet*). Whereas in many languages no overt subject is required for such verbs (e.g. Italian *piove*, Spanish *llueve, está llovendo*), English does not permit a finite verb without a subject. We cannot say **Is raining* or **Rains*. The slot in the sentence reserved for the subject must be filled here by the dummy (i.e. meaningless) pronoun *it*, e.g. *it is raining, it has been drizzling, it was hailing, it will snow, it is sleeting.* Other languages solve the problem by using the equivalent of 'the rain is raining', 'the snow is snowing' or even 'the sky is raining', 'the sky is snowing', etc. Another set of verbs requiring dummy *it* in English are time expressions such as *It is six o'clock* or *It is five minutes past four.* We could argue that the subject *it* in these sentences and other related time expressions refers to the word *time*, especially as this word can replace the dummy *it* here, e.g. *The time is six o'clock.* However, most native speakers do not feel that the pronoun *it* is equivalent to *the time* in such sentences. Thus we must consider the *it* in a time expression to be just another dummy subject like the one in *It is dark now* or *It is cold here,* where it makes no sense to ask *What is dark now?* or *What is cold here?*

Double Subj

In the cases we have just described, the dummy subject *it* is the only subject of the verb. Sometimes, however, it is used to fill the subject slot in a sentence where the real subject has been removed to the end of the sentence, a process often referred to as **extrapo-**

sition. In formal English we can have sentences with an infinitive clause or a *that*-clause as subject, e.g.

[To think of him eating all that cream]$_{Subj}$ *makes me feel sick.*

[That he has not replied]$_{Subj}$ *is very peculiar.*

In normal spoken English, however, such sentences have the subject extraposed to the end of the sentence, with the slot which the subject has left empty now filled by the dummy subject *it*, e.g.

It makes me feel sick [to think of him eating all that cream].

It is very peculiar [that he has not replied].

In this kind of sentence we now have two subjects. The position-filling subject *it* is the **grammatical** subject, whereas the extraposed subject *to think of him eating all that cream* is the **logical** subject. Although the use of the dummy subject *it* with extraposition of the logical subject is optional in most cases, there are a few verbs for which it is **obligatory**:

It$_{Subj}$ ***seems/ appears/ happened/ chanced*** *[that we were together in the same room]*$_{Subj}$

Existential *there*

In sentences which assert the existence of something, we find a parallel to the double subject sentences of the foregoing paragraph. Existential sentences begin with the word *there* followed by some form of the verb *be*, which in turn is followed by the logical subject. The normal subject slot in front of the verb is filled by *there*, which in this position is unstressed, has no locative meaning at all and functionally must be classified as a pronoun. Consider the following examples:

There ***is*** *[a hair]*$_{Subj}$ *in my soup.*

There ***are*** *[some birds]*$_{Subj}$ *sitting on the roof.*

Although *there* is in the subject position in these two sentences, notice the peculiarity that in careful style it does not determine the number agreement of the verb as a normal grammatical subject would do: it is the logical subject *a hair* which produces the singular *is* in the first sentence, and the logical subject *some birds* which produces the plural *are* in the second. In colloquial speech existential *there* may, however, behave like a normal subject and take singular agreement as in:

*There****'s*** *some birds sitting on the roof.*

In other respects there is nothing irregular about *there* as a pronominal subject. It inverts with the verb (*be*) in normal questions and in the tag of tag questions:

Are *there*$_{Subj}$ *any more biscuits?*

There is nobody at the door, ***is*** *there*$_{Subj}$*?*

and it can be the subject in an infinitive clause or in a gerundial construction (*-ing* clause):

We wouldn't like [there$_{Subj}$ *to be any bad feelings between them]*$_{Inf\,Cl}$.

They were very disgruntled about [there$_{Subj}$ *not being enough tickets for the concert]*$_{Gerundial\,Cl}$

(We shall see below that as a sentence level constituent the infinitive clause in the first of these last two examples is a direct object, and the gerundial *(-ing)* clause in the second is either a part of the subject complement or else it is a prepositional object if *were very disgruntled* is treated as a verbal constituent.)

4 Direct Object

Note on Objects

Semantically, the object plays an important part as the 'goal' or 'receiver' of the action of a dynamic verb. Traditionally, three kinds of grammatical object are distinguished: **direct object** (dO), **indirect object** (iO) and **prepositional object** (pO). Each of these will be dealt with in detail below.

Determination of dO

The sentence constituent which we call the direct object can be determined by placing the interrogative pronoun '*who(m)?*' or '*what?*' immediately after the verbal constituent. Thus with regard to the sentence

[The dog]$_{Subj}$ [has eaten]$_{Vbl}$ ***[all the food in the dish]$_{dO}$***

if we ask the question *The dog has eaten what?*, the answer *all the food in the dish* identifies this as the direct object constituent. These words are the direct object of the verb 'has eaten'. Similarly, in the case of the sentence

[The mother]$_{Subj}$ [sent]$_{Vbl}$ ***[her daughter]$_{dO}$*** *[to the market]$_{Advl}$*

we can see that *the daughter* is the direct object of the verb *sent* as these words are the answer to the question *The mother sent who(m)?* It will be remembered that verbs which admit a direct object are referred to as **transitive** verbs. Sometimes, sentences or clauses that contain a verb with a direct object are also referred to as being transitive.

dO = N, Pron or NP

Usually the direct object is a noun, pronoun or noun phrase. In the examples in the foregoing paragraph we saw only noun phrases with this function. The following sentences give examples with the object as a noun or a pronoun:

*[The policeman]$_{Subj}$ [accompanied]$_{Vbl}$ [**Jane**$_N$]$_{dO}$ [to the post office]$_{Advl}$*

*[Her boyfriend]$_{Subj}$ [could have met]$_{Vbl}$ [**her**$_{Pron}$]$_{dO}$ [somewhere else]$_{Advl}$*

dO = Finite Clause

Direct objects may, however, consist of more complicated structures such as finite or non-finite clauses, provided these have the function of nouns. For example, after many verbs of 'saying, knowing, hoping, etc.', i.e. in indirect statements, we find a finite clause as the direct object. This clause may begin with *that* but the conjunction is often omitted:

[The manager]$_{Subj}$ [knew]$_{Vbl}$ ***[(that) his staff were underpaid]***$_{dO}$
[We]$_{Subj}$ [hope]$_{Vbl}$ ***[(that) you can come tomorrow]***$_{dO}$

Similarly, in indirect questions, after verbs of 'asking, knowing, etc.' the direct object may be a finite clause introduced by a *wh*-word:

[They]$_{Subj}$ [asked]$_{Vbl}$ ***[why the bus was late]***$_{dO}$
[We all]$_{Subj}$ [realized]$_{Vbl}$ ***[what had happened]***$_{dO}$
[The porter]$_{Subj}$ [didn't know]$_{Vbl}$ ***[whether the guest had arrived]***$_{dO}$

Notice too that the words, clauses or sentences uttered in direct speech which are placed in inverted commas before (or after) a verb of saying are also the direct object of that verb:

['I think they have arrived,']$_{dO}$ *[said]$_{Vbl}$ [Melanie]$_{Subj}$*
['What do you want?']$_{dO}$ *[inquired]$_{Vbl}$ [the shopkeeper]$_{Subj}$*
[Then]$_{Advl}$ [Oliver]$_{Subj}$ [shouted,]$_{Vbl}$ ***['Yes, I can!']***$_{dO}$

dO = Non-Finite Clause

After verbs like *want, prefer* the direct object is often a non-finite *to*-infinitive clause:

[My father]$_{Subj}$ [wanted]$_{Vbl}$ ***[me to study law]***$_{dO}$
[Olivia]$_{Subj}$ [would prefer]$_{Vbl}$ ***[to live in Paris]***$_{dO}$

Other verbs such as *dislike, enjoy* take a non-finite gerund clause:

[She]$_{Subj}$ [dislikes]$_{Vbl}$ ***[talking about her troubles]***$_{dO}$
[Some of them]$_{Subj}$ [are enjoying]$_{Vbl}$ ***[watching a film]***$_{dO}$

Position of dO

Here we shall look at two positions for the direct object: (a) the **normal position** in the sentence when the verb is modified by an adverbial constituent, and (b) **initial position** in certain emphatic sentences. A third position with respect to the indirect object will be discussed when we come to that constituent below.

Normal Position

The normal position for the direct object is immediately after the verbal constituent. This position is obligatory if the direct object is a pronoun, e.g.

[The children]$_{Subj}$ [liked]$_{Vbl}$ ***[him]***$_{dO}$ *[immensely]$_{Advl}$*

The direct object cannot be separated from the verbal constituent by an adverbial constituent, i.e. English does not allow:

[The children]$_{Subj}$ [liked]$_{Vbl}$ [immensely]$_{Advl}$* *[him]***$_{dO}$

On the other hand when the direct object is a noun phrase, it may be separated from the verbal constituent by an adverbial if the noun phrase is long or the final position of the adverbial might lead to ambiguity. Thus instead of

The children posted all the letters that they had written to their uncle yesterday

which can be analysed in two ways: either

[The children]$_{Subj}$ [posted]$_{Vbl}$ ***[all the letters that they had written]***$_{dO}$ *[yesterday]$_{Advl}$*

(i.e. they posted the letters yesterday), or

[The children]$_{Subj}$ ***[posted]***$_{Vbl}$ ***[all the letters that they had written yesterday]***$_{dO}$

(i.e. they wrote the letter yesterday), we can bring out the meaning of the first analysis by changing the word order to

[The children]$_{Subj}$ [posted]$_{Vbl}$ [yesterday]$_{Advl}$ ***[all the letters that they had written]**$_{dO}$*

Initial Position

If the direct object needs to be emphasized it can be fronted, i.e. placed at the beginning of the sentence. The subject then remains in its normal position before the verbal constituent, as we see in the following examples:

***[That kind of book]**$_{dO}$ [you]$_{Subj}$ [can buy]$_{Vbl}$ [anywhere]$_{Advl}$*

***[The best bottles of wine]**$_{dO}$ [my aunt Jane]$_{Subj}$ [always]$_{Advl}$ [kept]$_{Vbl}$ [until Christmas]$_{Advl}$*

In more formal English, fronting can also take place when the direct object is a clause:

***[That he was very handsome]**$_{dO}$ [nobody]$_{Subj}$ [denied]$_{Subj}$*

***[Where they had gone]**$_{dO}$ [she]$_{Subj}$ [never]$_{Advl}$ [discovered]$_{Vbl}$*

***[Whatever he needed]**$_{dO}$ [Paul]$_{Subj}$ [took]$_{Vbl}$ [from the case]$_{Advl}$*

Note that when a *that*-clause is fronted, the conjunction *that* cannot be omitted: thus we cannot say **He was very handsome nobody denied.* Notice also that when the fronted clause is an indirect statement or an indirect question (as in the first two examples), the main clause is usually negative, i.e. has a negative subject (e.g. *nobody*) or contains a negative adverb (e.g. *never*). When the fronted clause is a nominal relative (see pages 62–63), as in the third example, the main clause does not have to be negative.

5 Indirect Object

Characteristics

Indirect objects usually accompany direct objects. Whereas the direct object is often a thing, the indirect object is the person who receives that thing or who benefits or suffers from it. The indirect object can be preceded by one of the prepositions *to* or *for* and then follows the direct object. It is then customary for the preposition to be treated as part of the indirect object, as in

[The manager]$_{Subj}$ [brought]$_{Vbl}$ [some wine]$_{dO}$ ***[to the waiting French guests]**$_{iO}$*

[Muriel]$_{Subj}$ [has given]$_{Vbl}$ [the tickets]$_{dO}$ ***[to her brother]**$_{iO}$*

[William]$_{Subj}$ [had made]$_{Vbl}$ [a kite]$_{dO}$ ***[for his children]**$_{iO}$*

This is the normal word order when the **indirect** object is the more important piece of new information, e.g. in answer to the questions: *Who did the manager bring some wine to? Who has Muriel given the tickets to? Who had William made a kite for?* However, it is more common for the **direct** object to contain the more important new information. In this case the indirect object loses its preposition and is placed immediately in front of the direct object. Thus in answer to the question *What did the manager bring (to) the waiting French guests?* one response could be:

[The manager]$_{Subj}$ *[brought]*$_{Vbl}$ ***[the waiting French guests]***$_{iO}$ *[some wine]*$_{dO}$

The other two examples above can be similarly reworded:

[Muriel]$_{Subj}$ *[has given]*$_{Vbl}$ ***[her brother]***$_{iO}$ *[the tickets]*$_{dO}$
[William]$_{Subj}$ *[had made]*$_{Vbl}$ ***[his children]***$_{iO}$ *[a kite]*$_{dO}$

Pronoun Objects

When both objects are pronouns, both of the 'cross-over' patterns just described can be used without any difference in meaning, provided that no emphatic stress is put on either of the objects:

[The teacher]$_{Subj}$ *[has lent]*$_{Vbl}$ *[one]*$_{dO}$ *[to them]*$_{iO}$
[The teacher]$_{Subj}$ *[has lent]*$_{Vbl}$ *[them]*$_{iO}$ *[one]*$_{dO}$

When both objects are **personal** pronouns, the preposition in front of the pronoun in the indirect object is occasionally omitted by some speakers. This pattern is, however, not very common. Thus alongside the normal sentences *The teacher has lent it to them* and *The teacher has lent them it*, we may sometimes hear *The teacher has lent it them*. Notice that the latter pattern is not possible with a non-personal pronoun like *one* as direct object: **The teacher has lent one them*.

Ditransitive Verbs

Whereas verbs which take a direct object are called transitive verbs, those which can take two objects (e.g. a direct and an indirect object) are often referred to as **ditransitive**. Most of them permit the 'cross-over' pattern described in the preceding paragraph, i.e. they can be used with their objects in both of the following orders:

V + dO + to/for + iO
V + iO + dO

Some of the commonest 'cross-over' ditransitive verbs with an indirect object that can be introduced by *to* are: *bring, feed, grant, hand, lend, mail, offer, owe, pass, pay, post, quote, read, sell, send, teach, tell.* Others with an indirect object introduced by *for* are: *build, buy, cook, design, fetch, find, get, keep, order, prepare, save, win.* A few 'cross-over' ditransitive verbs can take indirect objects with both *to* and *for* (with slight changes in meaning): *bring, leave, play, sing, take, write.*

iO versus Advl

Not all constituents which appear in the indirect object position and which begin with the preposition *to* are indirect objects. Consider the following two sentences:

1. *[The postman]*$_{Subj}$ *[brought]*$_{Vbl}$ *[the letters]*$_{dO}$ ***[to the old widow]***$_{iO}$
2. *[The postman]*$_{Subj}$ *[brought]*$_{Vbl}$ *[the letters]*$_{dO}$ ***[to the railway station]***

Apart from the fact that the noun phrase in the constituent *to the railway station* does not refer to a person, the second sentence does not allow the cross-over pattern of direct and indirect object:

The postman brought **the railway station the letters*
whereas the first sentence does:
*The postman brought **the old widow** the letters*
Clearly the old widow in the second sentence is the receiver of the letters, the person who benefits from the bringing of the letters. The railway station, however, neither receives nor benefits: it is the place to which the letters are brought. Thus the constituent *to the railway station* must be an adverbial constituent (with the function of an adverb of place).

iO = N, Pron, NP or Clause

As we have seen in the examples above, the indirect object, like all verbal objects, is normally a noun, pronoun or noun phrase. Since the indirect object is usually a person, the number of more complicated structures which can take the place of a noun, pronoun or noun phrase with this function is severely restricted. Almost the only one is a clause introduced by a nominal relative pronoun (see pages 62–63). Thus in formal English we find such sentences as:

*[You]$_{Subj}$ [can give]$_{Vbl}$ [your money]$_{dO}$ **[to whoever needs it]**$_{iO}$*
*[They]$_{Subj}$ [sent]$_{Vbl}$ **[whoever had applied]**$_{iO}$ [a detailed account of the job they were offering]$_{dO}$*

6 Prepositional Object

Definition

We must be careful to distinguish between the prepositional object, which is a constituent of the sentence in sentence level analysis, and the object of a preposition, which is a constituent of the phrase in phrase level analysis. When we looked at phrases (in Chapter 3) we saw that a prepositional phrase consists of a preposition followed by a noun, pronoun or noun phrase, and for convenience of reference we called this noun, pronoun or noun phrase the object of the preposition. At the sentence level, we use the term **prepositional object** (pO) to refer to the sentence constituent which is the **object of a prepositional verb in the verbal constituent**. Since a prepositional verb can sometimes be separated from its preposition, it will be convenient to assign this preposition sometimes to the prepositional object and sometimes to the verbal constituent in order to avoid a discontinuous constituent. Thus, in the following sentence it makes no difference whether we assign the preposition *at* to the prepositional object or to the verbal constituent. Both analyses can be justified:

*[The doctor]$_{Subj}$ [looked]$_{Vbl}$ **[at the patient]**$_{pO}$*
*[The doctor]$_{Subj}$ [looked at]$_{Vbl}$ **[the patient]**$_{pO}$*

In the second example we are saying that the verbal constituent of the sentence consists of the prepositional verb *look at* which takes an object *the patient*. As this object is dependent on the preposition in the verbal constituent, we must call it a prepositional object rather than a direct object. The first analysis with the preposition included in the prepositional object makes it clearer why this constituent is given this name, although it separates the verb from it characteristic preposition. If we consider the two analyses of the example shown below, it is clearly more elegant and convenient to include the preposition in the verbal constituent here:

*[**What newspaper**]$_{pO}$ [is] [the doctor]$_{Subj}$ [looking **<u>at</u>**]*

Vbl

rather than to analyse the sentence as:

*[**What newspaper**] [is] [the doctor]$_{Subj}$ [looking][**<u>at</u>**]*

Vbl

pO

since we are now forced to have two discontinuous constituents instead of only one. On the other hand, when the verb in the verbal constituent is ditransitive, i.e. takes an indirect object followed by a prepositional object, it is more convenient to assign the preposition to the prepositional object, as the following example shows:

*[The firm]$_{Subj}$ [informed]$_{Vbl}$ [its clients]$_{dO}$ [**<u>of</u> its new name**]$_{pO}$*

If we analyse this sentence with the preposition as part of the verbal constituent, the result is an awkward discontinuous verbal constituent:

*[The firm]$_{Subj}$ [informed] [its clients]$_{dO}$ [**<u>of</u>**] [**its new name**]$_{pO}$*

Vbl

When the assignment of the preposition is not a matter of convenience, we shall follow the practice of including the preposition in the prepositional object constituent.

pO = N, Pron or NP

Prepositional objects are just like direct objects and indirect objects in that they normally consist of a noun, a pronoun, or a noun phrase. In the examples above we have only seen noun phrases (*the doctor, what newspaper, its new name*), but we can also have examples with a single noun or a pronoun as in:

*[The ship]$_{Subj}$ [ran]$_{Vbl}$ [**into trouble**]$_{pO}$*

*[My mother]$_{Subj}$ [is looking]$_{Vbl}$ [**after her**]$_{pO}$*

pO = *that*-Clause

One peculiarity of prepositional objects needs special attention. When they begin with the conjunction *that*, the preposition which normally precedes them is dropped. For example, although we must use the preposition when the prepositional object includes a noun phrase, e.g.

*[They]$_{Subj}$ [informed]$_{Vbl}$ [his parents]$_{dO}$ [**of** the accident]$_{pO}$*

the same preposition **must** be omitted when the prepositional object consists of a *that*-clause, e.g.

[They]$_{Subj}$ [informed]$_{Vbl}$ [his parents]$_{dO}$ [that he had had an accident]$_{pO}$

It is ungrammatical to say: *They informed his parents [****of** that he had had an accident].*

Note that this analysis can be applied to sentences containing predicative adjectives which take a *that*-clause complement, provided that we now treat the verbal constituent as complex, i.e. consisting of the verb *be* plus the adjective. Compare the following:

[The child]$_{Subj}$ [is annoyed]$_{Vbl}$ [that it has no milk]$_{pO}$

*[The child]$_{Subj}$ [is annoyed]$_{Vbl}$ [**about** the missing milk]$_{pO}$*

We shall see below (under Subject Complements, page 160) that *be* + Adj +Adj Complement can be given an alternative analysis:

[The child]$_{Subj}$ [is]$_{Vbl}$ [annoyed that it has no milk]$_{sC}$

pO = *Wh*-Clause

When the prepositional object of a ditransitive verb consists of a clause introduced by a *wh*-word, the preposition **cannot usually** be omitted:

*[They]$_{Subj}$ [informed]$_{Vbl}$ [his parents]$_{dO}$ [**of** what had happened]$_{pO}$*

However, it can be optionally dropped when a verb does not take two objects but only a prepositional object in the form of a *wh*-clause. The following two sentences show the optional preposition in parentheses:

*[We]$_{Subj}$ [inquired]$_{Vbl}$ [(**about**) whether the museum was open]$_{pO}$*

*[Jim]$_{Subj}$ [hasn't decided]$_{Vbl}$ [(**on**) which boat he'll use]$_{pO}$*

pO = Non-Finite Clause

Since the prepositional object always consists of a noun or a structure which functions as a noun, the only possible **non-finite** clause which can be the prepositional object of a verb is a **gerund structure** (i.e. one containing the nominal *ing*-form of the verb). An infinitive clause is ruled out as it already begins with the preposition *to*. In the following examples the gerund in the gerund clause is shown in boldface type:

*[They]$_{Subj}$ [count]$_{Vbl}$ [on **winning** some money in the lottery]$_{pO}$*

*[We]$_{Subj}$ [are planning]$_{Vbl}$ [on **building** a new house]$_{pO}$*

[He]$_{Subj}$ [laughed]$_{Vbl}$ [at our (or *at us*) ***wanting** to pay him]$_{pO}$*

[They]$_{Subj}$ [disapproved]$_{Vbl}$ [of his (or *of him*) ***leaving** home]$_{pO}$*

Phrasal-Prepositional Verbs

In sentences whose verbal constituent consists of a phrasal-prepositional verb, i.e. a verb which requires both an adverbial particle and a special preposition, it is usually easier to consider the preposition as part of the prepositional object, as in:

*[They]$_{Subj}$ [put up]$_{Vbl}$ [**with** a great deal of noise]$_{pO}$*

*[Most students]$_{Subj}$ [have gone in]$_{Vbl}$ [**for** jogging daily]$_{pO}$*

*[We]$_{Subj}$ [get on]$_{Vbl}$ [very well]$_{Advl}$ [**with** our neighbours]$_{pO}$*

The last sentence shows us the advantage of analysing the prepositional object as containing the preposition. If we had included the preposition in the verbal constituent, the latter would have become discontinuous, i.e. interrupted by an adverbial constituent (*very well*). In the first two sentences both analyses are possible, but for the sake of consistency we have analysed all three sentences in the same way. Note, however, that all three sentences are statements. If we convert them into questions, then the analysis with the preposition **inside** the verbal constituent is more convenient:

*[What]$_{pO}$ [did] [they]$_{Subj}$ [put up **with**?]*
/ Vbl /

*[What]$_{pO}$ [have] [most students]$_{Subj}$ [gone in **for**?]*
/ Vbl /

*[Who]$_{pO}$ [do] [our neighbours]$_{Subj}$ [get on **with**] [very well?]$_{Advl}$*
/ Vbl /

This solution is more elegant as it enables us to have only **one** discontinuous constituent, namely the verbal. The alternative (with the preposition assigned to the prepositional object) necessitates **two** discontinuous constituents: in addition to the discontinuous verbal constituent we then have a discontinuous prepositional object, as the interrogative pronoun is at the beginning of the sentence and the preposition at the end. For example, the last sentence must then be analysed:

*[Who] [do] [our neighbours]$_{Subj}$ [get on] [**with**] [very well?]$_{Advl}$*
/ Vbl /
/ pO /

Note that the alternative version of the above question with the preposition after the adverbial constituent is best analysed with a three-part verbal constituent:

*[Who]$_{pO}$ [do][our neighbours]$_{Subj}$ [get on][very well]$_{Advl}$ [**with**?]*
/ / /
Vbl

Although the verbal constituent is interrupted twice here (once by the subject and once by the adverbial), this analysis still contains only **one** discontinuous constituent, which is preferable to the alternative with two:

*[Who] [do] [our neighbours]$_{Subj}$ [get on] [very well]$_{Advl}$ [**with**?]*
/ Vbl /
/ pO /

7 Subject Complement

Note on Complements

At the beginning of this chapter it was pointed out that whereas most other constituents are defined in relation to the main verb in a sentence, complements are defined in relation to the subject or the object. We can refer to this relation as a copular relation as it is found only in connection with copular verbs for the **subject complement** (sC) or in connection with certain transitive verbs which allow a copular relation between the direct object and the

object complement (oC). This will become clear when we deal with each kind of complement below. Suffice it to say here that, although the verb does not play a primary role in the definition of complements, it is nevertheless indirectly of considerable importance.

Definition of sC

The subject complement consists either of an adjective or adjective phrase or else of a noun, pronoun or noun phrase. It is the constituent which immediately follows the verbal constituent when this is a copular (linking) verb, such as *be, become, grow.* The function of the subject complement is to inform us of some characteristic of the subject.

sC = Adj/Adj P

Let us look first at some examples with adjectival subject complements:

[The scenery]$_{Subj}$ *[is]*$_{Vbl}$ ***[magnificent]***$_{sC}$
[The children]$_{Subj}$ *[grew]*$_{Vbl}$ ***[very weary]***$_{sC}$
[The apple]$_{Subj}$ *[was]*$_{Vbl}$ ***[full of maggots]***$_{sC}$
[Bill's behaviour]$_{Subj}$ *[became]*$_{Vbl}$ ***[even more aggressive than usual]***$_{sC}$
[The child]$_{Subj}$ *[is]*$_{Vbl}$ ***[annoyed that it has no milk]***$_{sC}$

In each of these sentences the adjective or adjective phrase in the subject complement is used predicatively and clearly refers to the subject. Corresponding to the first two examples we can construct the noun phrases *the magnificent scenery* and *the very weary children*, where the same adjective or adjective phrase is used attributively and now **premodifies** the noun of the subject. Corresponding to the third example we can construct the noun phrase *an apple full of maggots*, where the same adjective phrase as in the subject complement now **postmodifies** the subject noun. In the case of the fourth and fifth examples, we cannot construct a comparable noun phrase from subject and subject complement because the latter contains a clause in each case. However if we leave this clause out, we can still use most of the adjective phrase attributively and construct the noun phrases *Bill's even more aggressive behaviour* and *the annoyed child.* This conversion of the predicative adjective or adjective phrase into a corresponding attributive structure may be considered as a diagnostic test for an **adjectival** subject complement. (For another analysis of the fifth example, see page 158 and also page 120.)

sC = N/NP

The test described in the last paragraph will, of course, not work if the subject complement is a noun or a noun phrase. Consider the following examples:

[Those men]$_{Subj}$ *[are]*$_{Vbl}$ ***[soldiers]***$_{sC}$
[My sister]$_{Subj}$ *[has become]*$_{Vbl}$ ***[a famous lawyer]***$_{sC}$
[Most of the books]$_{Subj}$ *[were]*$_{Vbl}$ ***[novels that nobody read]***$_{sC}$

At first sight we might feel tempted to analyse the bold face noun or noun phrase in these examples as a direct object, since we can ask *what?* after the verbal constituent, as we can for direct objects (*Those men are what?* Answer: *soldiers*.) However, a closer look shows us that these sentences are really equational sentences. In place of the verbal constituent we can easily write an equals sign without any great change in meaning:

Those men = soldiers
My sister = a famous lawyer
Most of the books = novels nobody reads

This cannot be done with a direct object. For example, the sentence

[Tim]$_{Subj}$ [broke]$_{Vbl}$ [his arm]$_{dO}$

is not equivalent in meaning to the equation

**Tim = his arm*

Thus the equal sign test can be considered as a reliable method of diagnosing a **nominal** subject complement.

sC after Verbs with Copular Function

In our definition of the subject complement above we said that it is the adjectival or nominal constituent which follows a copular verb such as *be, become, grow*, and we have limited the examples so far to sentences with these three verbs. However, subject complements also occur after verbs which contain more lexical information than the three 'pure' copular verbs but which also have a copular function. One special group of such verbs are those referring to particular senses: the verbs of sensory perception (underlined in the following examples).

*[This cloth]$_{Subj}$ [<u>feels</u>]$_{Vbl}$ [**very soft**]$_{sC}$*
*[The soup]$_{Subj}$ [<u>tasted</u>]$_{Vbl}$ [**rather salty**]$_{sC}$*
*[Your piano]$_{Subj}$ [<u>sounds</u>]$_{Vbl}$ [**slightly flat**]$_{sC}$*
*[The roast pork]$_{Subj}$ [<u>smells</u>]$_{Vbl}$ [**most delicious**]$_{sC}$*
*[The poor beggar]$_{Subj}$ [<u>looked</u>]$_{Vbl}$ [**extremely dejected**]$_{sC}$*

Although each of the verbs *feel, taste, sound, smell, look* contributes a different element to the meaning of these examples, it nevertheless behaves like a copula, for it can be replaced by *is* or *was* and the resulting sentence still remains semantically roughly equivalent to the original. Furthermore, the conversion test from predicative to attributive adjective shows that the constituent following these verbs is a subject complement. If the cloth feels very soft, then we have *some very soft cloth*; if the soup tasted rather salty, we must have had a plate of *rather salty soup*; if your piano sounds slightly flat, then you possess *a slightly flat piano*. Similarly, corresponding to the last two examples we can construct the noun phrases *some most delicious roast pork* and *an extremely dejected poor beggar*.

Further Examples

Other lexical verbs with copular function may take a subject complement which is a noun or noun phrase. One of these is *turn*, as in

[The whole class]$_{Subj}$ [turned]$_{Vbl}$ ***[informer]$_{sC}$*** *(and [betrayed]$_{Vbl}$ [him]$_{dO}$).*

Another is the verb *make* in a sentence of the following kind:

[Her son]$_{Subj}$ [will make]$_{Vbl}$ ***[a good teacher]$_{sC}$***

where the sense of the verb is 'has the necessary qualities to become'. Certain passive verbs also take a subject complement:

[Her daughter]$_{Subj}$ [was appointed]$_{Vbl}$ ***[headmistress]$_{sC}$***

[Bill Clinton]$_{Subj}$ [has been elected]$_{Vbl}$ ***[President of the USA]$_{sC}$***

[Mary Smith]$_{Subj}$ [was nominated]$_{Vbl}$ ***[chairman of the board]$_{sC}$***

Like *turn* and *make* in the first example, the underlined verbs in these last three sentences all correspond in at least part of their meaning to the copular verb *become*, which can be substituted for them. Note that the subject complement of these passive verbs can be optionally introduced by the preposition *as*: *as headmistress, as President of the USA, as chairman of the board.* With other kinds of passive verbs the preposition is sometimes obligatory:

[What I said]$_{Subj}$ [was meant]$_{Vbl}$ ***[as a joke]$_{sC}$***

Restricted sC

Whereas some verbs (e.g. *appear* and *seem*, which are synonymous with *look*, one of the sensory perception verbs mentioned above), can take a whole variety of adjectives as subject complement, others may be severely restricted. In the following examples, only the adjective or adjectives shown in the subject complement can occur with each particular verb:

*[Their excuse]$_{Subj}$ [doesn't ring]$_{Vbl}$***[true]$_{sC}$** */[rings]$_{Vbl}$* ***[false]$_{sC}$***

[The prisoner]$_{Subj}$ [fell]$_{Vbl}$ ***[silent]$_{sC}$***

[The river]$_{Subj}$ [has run]$_{Vbl}$ ***[dry]$_{sC}$***

[The collar of his shirt]$_{Subj}$ [was wearing]$_{Vbl}$ ***[thin]$_{sC}$***

Restricted combinations of this kind are usually referred to as **idioms**.

sC = Pron

Unlike the various kinds of object constituent of the sentence, complements rarely consist of a pronoun. Personal pronouns seem only to be possible with the copula *be*, as in equational sentences of the kind

[It]$_{Subj}$ [is]$_{Vbl}$ ***[me]$_{sC}$***

[The person in the photo]$_{Subj}$ [is]$_{Vbl}$ ***[you]$_{sC}$***

[It]$_{Subj}$ [must be]$_{Vbl}$ ***[him]$_{sC}$***

The oblique case personal pronouns (*me*, *him*) which we see in the first and last examples can be replaced in formal English by the subject case pronouns (*I*, *he*), the latter being normal in careful English when the pronoun is postmodified by a relative clause:

[It]$_{Subj}$ [is]$_{Vbl}$ ***[I who am complaining]$_{sC}$***

[It]$_{Subj}$ [was]$_{Vbl}$ ***[he who made the decision]$_{sC}$***

The use of the subject case pronoun in the complement shows clearly the equational character of these sentences, as they then have a nominative pronoun on either side of the copula.
Other pronouns can sometimes be found with *be* and with other verbs that have copular function:

[This]$_{Subj}$ [is]$_{Vbl}$ ***[all you need]$_{sC}$***
[Later]$_{Advl}$ [she]$_{Subj}$ [became]$_{Vbl}$ ***[somebody we all admired]$_{sC}$***
[The job]$_{Subj}$ [was considered]$_{Vbl}$ ***[nothing special]$_{sC}$***

8 Object Complement

Charac-teristics

Object complements bear the same copular relationship to direct objects as subject complements bear to subjects. They too consist of either an adjective or an adjective phrase or else of a noun or a noun phrase, each of which refers to some characteristic describing the direct object. Consider the following examples, where the direct object is underlined and the object complement is in boldface type:

[Their reply]$_{Subj}$ [made]$_{Vbl}$ [me]$_{dO}$ ***[very angry]$_{oC}$***
[They]$_{Subj}$ [painted]$_{Vbl}$ [the main door]$_{dO}$ ***[bright red]$_{oC}$***
[The children]$_{Subj}$ [have got]$_{Vbl}$ [their clothes]$_{dO}$ ***[rather dirty]$_{oC}$***

The verbs in these three sentences are all causative, i.e. they cause something to be or become something. For example, the result of the first sentence is that *I was very angry*. In this new sentence we recognize the same copular relationship between the subject (*I*) and the complement (*very angry*) as between the object (*me*) and complement (*very angry*) in the original example. We can thus test for an object complement by constructing a subject complement sentence from the direct object in the original sentence and the constituent following it. So from the second example we can construct the new sentence *the main door was bright red*, and from the third the new sentence *their clothes were rather dirty*, thus proving that the suspected constituent in each of the original examples is indeed an object complement.

Further Examples

Among other verbs which take a direct object followed by an object complement are **verbs of appointing**, such as *make, elect, appoint, nominate*, whose passive forms we saw above taking a subject complement (page 162). With the exception of *make*, the complement of these verbs can usually be introduced optionally by *as*. Two further groups of verbs found with an object complement are **verbs of naming**, such as *call, name, christen, declare*, and **verbs expressing an opinion**, such as *consider, think, find, regard*. The following examples show some of these with a **noun/noun phrase** as object complement:

[They]Subj [have made]Vbl [him]dO ***[Mayor of London]****oC*
[The Governor]Subj [appointed]Vbl [her]dO ***[his personal secretary]****oC*
[We all]Subj [called]Vbl [the wretched man]dO ***[a traitor]****oC*
[My neighbours]Subj [have named]Vbl [their cat]dO ***[Humphrey]****oC*
[Most people]Subj [considered]Vbl [the musician]dO ***[a genius]****oC*

The following sentences illustrate some of these verbs with an **adjective/adjective phrase** as object complement:

[The mayor]Subj [declared]Vbl [the bazaar]dO ***[open]****oC*
[We]Subj [found]Vbl [most of the exhibits]dO ***[rather boring]****oC*
[The other actors]subj [regarded]Vbl [him]dO ***[as very foolish]****oC*

Prepositional oC

Note that the preposition *as* is obligatory with the verb *regard* and also with *accept, acknowledge, define, describe, treat*. It is a little strange to have a preposition governing an adjective or adjective phrase, but we can see that *as* must be a preposition here, since the same verbs can take an object complement consisting of *as* followed by a noun or noun phrase, and this complement often has the same function and meaning as an object complement with *as* followed by an adjective or adjective phrase. This becomes clear if we compare the following sentence with the last example in the preceding paragraph:

[The other actors]Subj [regarded]Vbl [him]dO ***[as a fool]****oC*

Another pair showing this same relationship are the sentences:

[They]Subj [accepted]Vbl [this]dO ***[as true]****oC*
[They]Subj [accepted]Vbl [this]dO ***[as the truth]****oC*

The reader will recognize the verb in each of these examples as a kind of prepositional verb. In the same way as we have called the second object of a ditransitive verb the **prepositional** object, because it has a preposition in front of it, so we can call the object complement of these verbs for the same reason a **prepositional** object complement.

With Extraposed dO

The group of verbs expressing an opinion which were mentioned on the previous page are sometimes found with the direct object extraposed from its normal position after the verbal constituent and placed after the object complement. This occurs when the direct object is a clause beginning with the conjunction *that*. Instead of the stylistically rather awkward and formal sentence:

[They]Subj [found]Vbl [that he had already gone]dO ***[very upsetting]****oC*

it is usual in non-formal English to remove the direct object to the end of the sentence and to mark its original position by inserting there the pronoun *it*. This means that the sentence now contains two direct objects (the substitute or prop pronoun and the extraposed *that*-clause):

[They]Subj [found]Vbl [it]dO ***[very upsetting]****oC [that he had already gone]dO*

Further examples are:

[She]$_{Subj}$ [thought]$_{Vbl}$ [it]$_{dO}$ ***[strange]**$_{oC}$* *[that the light was on]$_{dO}$*

[I]$_{Subj}$ [consider]$_{Vbl}$ [it]$_{dO}$ ***[a disgrace]**$_{oC}$* *[that he was invited]$_{dO}$*

The same construction with extraposition can also be found when the direct object is an infinitive clause or a gerund:

[We]$_{Subj}$ [considered]$_{Vbl}$ [it]$_{dO}$ ***[an honour]**$_{oC}$* *[to be there]$_{dO}$*

[They]$_{Subj}$ [found]$_{Vbl}$ [it]$_{dO}$ ***[uncomfortable]**$_{oC}$* *[having to wear a hat indoors]$_{dO}$*

9 Adverbial

General Remarks

Having seen in Ch.2 that adverbs as a word class are very heterogeneous, we shall not be surprised to find that the adverbial constituents of the sentence are equally varied in structure and role. In an earlier chapter we classified adverbs semantically into eight broad classes: **manner, place, time, degree, focussing, interrogative, linking and sentential** adverbs. **All of these can be found as adverbial constituents** of a sentence, though some like the focussing adverbs are most common as part of another constituent. It should be noted that there can often be **more than one adverbial constituent in a sentence**, a characteristic which other sentence constituents do not possess. With regard to their role in the sentence, these eight constituents can be subdivided into **three classes**: (a) those which in some way modify the verb in the verbal constituent, (b) those which primarily modify some other element in the sentence but which can refer to the main verb, and (c) those which play a role above the sentence either by linking sentences together or by showing the speaker's attitude to what is said in the sentence. Before we can illustrate each of these types of adverbial, it will be necessary to look at some of the many different kinds of grammatical structures by which the adverbial constituent can be realized.

Realizations

In the simple sentence below, the adverbial constituent (underlined) is shown first with a single adverb, which is then replaced successively by different and more complicated grammatical structures. For convenience of reference the structures have been labelled and given a number.

Edward came in | *yesterday*. Adverb (1)
| *very early*. Adverb Phrase (2)
| *at noon*. Prepositional Phrase (3)
| *dejected*. Adjective (4)
| *weary from the long journey*. Adjective Phrase (5)
| *when the shops closed*. Finite Clause (6)
| *whenever possible*. Verbless Clause (7)

| *while preparing for his exams*. Non-Finite Clause (8)
| *expecting to meet her*. Present Participle (9)
| *to collect his money*. Infinitive Clause (10)

Class (a) Advls

All the adverbial constituents shown after the vertical stroke in the last paragraph are class (a) adverbials, i.e. adverbial constituents which modify the verb in the verbal constituent (here the phrasal verb *came in*). The adverbial constituents 1, 2, 3, 6, 8 tell us **when** Edward came in and are therefore adverbials of **time**, whereas the verbless clause 7 is an adverbial of **frequency**. The adjective 4 and the adjective phrase 5 are adverbials of **manner**, informing us **how** Edward came in. Also the present participle structure 9 functions as an adverbial constituent telling us the **manner** (or **state**) in which he came in, whereas the infinitive clause 10 indicates the **purpose** of his coming in. Notice that although the two adverbial constituents 4 and 5 consist of an adjective and an adjective phrase which clearly refer to the subject of the sentence, we should not be tempted to think that they are subject complements. **Subject complements** must come after a copular verb or a verb with copular function and cannot be omitted from the sentence without it becoming ungrammatical or semantically deviant. This is not the case with adverbial constituents: these can be omitted with no severe grammatical or semantic consequence. Thus in place of 4 and 5 we can easily write: *Edward came in*, where the verb has the same meaning as in the original sentence. However, from a copular sentence such as

[Edward]$_{Subj}$ [looked]$_{Vbl}$ [weary from the long journey]$_{sC}$

we do not obtain a semantically equivalent sentence when the final constituent is omitted: **Edward looked.*

Advl versus oC

Care must also be taken with **object complements**, which can sometimes be confused with class (a) adverbials. The former sometimes occur in structures which seem to be identical with others containing a class (a) adverbial. Compare the following:

*[The owner]$_{Subj}$ [left]$_{Vbl}$ [the house]$_{dO}$ [**empty**]$_{oC}$*

*[The owner]$_{Subj}$ [left]$_{Vbl}$ [the house]$_{dO}$ [**drunk**]$_{Advl}$*

Structurally, the two sentences are identical, but semantically it is the house which is empty in the first sentence, whereas in the second it is the owner who is drunk. Hence the difference in the grammatical analysis: *empty* is an adjective referring to *the house* and thus functions as an object complement in the first example, whereas *drunk* though an adjective tells us how or in what state the owner left the house and thus functions as an adverbial constituent.

Class (b) Advls

Unlike the class (a) adverbial constituents, the class (b) ones usually modify an element in another sentence constituent. They can, however, sometimes focus on the verbal. It is this latter role that we are interested in here, since as modifiers of elements in other sentence constituents they are then not discrete sentence constituents themselves but parts of other constituents. Consider the role of the focussing adverb *only* in the following sentences:

[Maureen]$_{Subj}$ *[was]* *[**only**]*$_{Advl}$ *[guessing]*
/______ *Vbl* ______/

There is no verb 'to only guess'; the adverb *only* is clearly a separate element modifying the verb *guess* and thus a separate adverbial constituent of the sentence. This is, however, not the case in the following sentences:

[Judy]$_{Subj}$ *[visited]*$_{Vbl}$ *[them]*$_{dO}$ *[**only** in the autumn]*$_{Advl}$
[Judy]$_{Subj}$ *[visited]*$_{Vbl}$ *[**only** them]*$_{dO}$ *[in the autumn]*
*[**Only** Judy]*$_{Subj}$ *[visited]*$_{Vbl}$ *[them]*$_{dO}$ *[in the autumn]*$_{Advl}$

In each of the three cases above *only* is best analysed as belonging to the constituent which follows it. In the colloquial version of these sentences, where *only* has a fixed position in front of the verb and the element it focusses upon (underlined in the examples below) is separated from it and given emphatic stress, it is also preferable to analyse the adverb together with this latter constituent. The combination is then discontinuous:

[Judy]$_{Subj}$ *[**only**]* *[visited]*$_{Vbl}$ *[them]*$_{dO}$ *[in the autumn]*
/______________ *Advl* ______________/
[Judy]$_{Subj}$ *[**only**]* *[visited]*$_{Vbl}$ *[them]* *[in the autumn]*$_{Advl}$
/________ *dO* ________/

Another Analysis

An alternative analysis for these last two sentences would be to treat the focussing adverb as a separate adverbial, as we did in the very first example above where it modified the verbal constituent. This would mean that there are now two adverbial constituents in the sentence, but this is not uncommon. This analysis may be more attractive with some of the other focussing adverbs, which do not seem to be so naturally a part of the constituent they are focussing upon:

[He]$_{Subj}$ *[was][**simply**]*$_{Advl}$ *[talking]* *[nonsense]*$_{dO}$ *[yesterday]*$_{Advl}$
/______ *Vbl* ______/
[She]$_{Subj}$ *[**merely**]*$_{Advl}$ *[forgot]*$_{Vbl}$ *[to make the beds]*$_{dO}$
[We]$_{Subj}$ *[**especially**]*$_{Advl}$ *[objected]*$_{Vbl}$ *[to their tone of voice]*$_{pO}$
[They]$_{Subj}$ *[now]*$_{Advl}$ *[support]*$_{Vbl}$ *[**particularly**]*$_{Advl}$ *[their own team]*$_{dO}$

Negative Advl *not*

The negative adverb *not* at the sentence level behaves more like a class (b) adverbial constituent, as it can modify not only the main verb but also other constituents. However, when it modifies the verb it is unique in having an optional enclitic form *-n't*, which forms part of the verb preceding it. This suggests that when it appears in this form we should analyse it as part of the verbal constituent. We followed this practice on page 146 above when, in the discussion of the position of the subject, we chose to include *-n't* as part of the operator (*Don't*$_{Op}$). We also used this analysis of *-n't*, namely as part of the verbal constituent, in the final example illustrating the use of a finite clause as a direct object in indirect questions on page 153, and again in one of the examples illustrating the use of a finite (*wh-*) clause as a prepositional object on page 158. For convenience these are repeated here:

[The porter]$_{Subj}$ *[did**n't** know]*$_{Vbl}$ *[whether the guest had arrived]*$_{dO}$
[Jim]$_{Subj}$ *[has**n't** decided]*$_{Vbl}$ *[on which boat he'll use]*$_{pO}$

When the negative adverb is not enclitic but written as a separate full word, it is more logical to analyse it as a separate adverbial constituent, as in

[Jim]$_{Subj}$ *[has] [**not**]*$_{Advl}$ *[decided] [on which boat he'll use]*$_{pO}$
______ *Vbl* ______

This analysis is, however, less convenient as it makes the verbal constituent discontinuous and some grammarians may therefore prefer to treat the full negative adverb in the same way as the enclitic *-n't* and assign it to the verbal constituent. Note that *not* will usually be analysed as part of another constituent when it does not modify the main verb, e.g.

*[**Not** a single person]*$_{Subj}$ *[has voted]*$_{Vbl}$ *[for him]*$_{pO}$
[The problem]$_{Subj}$ *[was]*$_{Vbl}$ *[**not** important]*$_{sC}$

We can justify the treatment of *not* in this way by arguing that *not a single person* is equivalent to *nobody* and that we can replace *not important* by the single word *unimportant*. However, in the second example the alternative with *not* analysed as a separate adverbial sentence constituent is also admissible:

[The problem]$_{Subj}$ *[was]*$_{Vbl}$ *[**not**]*$_{Advl}$ *[important]*$_{sC}$

Class (c) Advls

The adverbials belonging to class (c) do not in any way modify the verbal constituent, but have two other important functions. Some of **them link sentences logically together** (e.g. *hence, therefore, thus, so, moreover, however*), as in

[He]$_{Subj}$ *[was]*$_{Vbl}$ *[an inveterate gambler]*$_{sC}$. *[**Hence**]*$_{Advl}$, *[most people]*$_{Subj}$ *[avoided]*$_{Vbl}$ *[him]*$_{dO}$.
[The office door]$_{Subj}$ *[has been locked]*$_{Vbl}$ *[for a long time]*$_{Advl}$.
[We]$_{Subj}$ *[must] [**therefore**]*$_{Advl}$ *[get in][via the cellar]*$_{Advl}$.
______ *Vbl* ______
[They]$_{Subj}$ *[wore]*$_{Vbl}$ *[stolen clothes]*$_{dO}$. *[**So**]*$_{Advl}$ *[we]*$_{Subj}$ *[considered]*$_{Vbl}$ *[them]*$_{dO}$ *[criminals]*$_{oC}$.

Others show the **attitude or field of reference of the speaker** (e.g. *surprisingly, fortunately, maybe; chemically, stylistically, artistically*), as in

*[**Surprisingly**]Advl [she]Subj [offered]Vbl [no resistance]dO.*
*[**Maybe**]Advl [you]Subj [can give]Vbl [us]iO [a clue]dO.*
*[**Chemically**]Advl [this reaction]Subj [should be]Vbl [impossible]sC.*
*[**Artistically**]Advl [the performance]Subj [was]Vbl [a failure]sC.*

Other examples can be found under adverbs in the chapter on word classes (pages 106–107).

2 Simple, Complex, Compound

1 General Remarks

Constituents versus Types

In the first part of this chapter we looked at the syntax of the sentence only from the point of view of the different kinds of constituents of which the sentence is composed. In traditional grammar, sentences are often classified in two other ways: according to their **clause structure** and according to the **syntactic form typically used for the kind of message which they convey**. In the former case they are divided into three main types: **simple, complex** and **compound**; in the latter into **declarative, interrogative, imperative** and **exclamatory** sentences. Let us look briefly at each of these below.

2 Classification according to Clause Structure

Simple Sentence

A simple sentence consists of a **main clause with no subordinate clauses** dependent on it, as in:

[Last night]Advl [the woman in the corner house]Subj [left]Vbl [at eight o'clock]Advl
[Fred]Subj [opened]Vbl [the letter]dO [with his uncle's silver knife]Advl
[Vicky]Subj [was]Vbl [very distressed about the news from Africa]sC
[With his rough speech to the woman]Advl [the sailor]Subj [had made]Vbl [the captain]dO [very angry]oC

All of these sentences are syntactically fairly elaborate and contain some complex constituents, but none of them has a subordinate clause as a constituent or as part of a constituent.

Complex Sentence

A complex sentence contains at least one constituent which is a subordinate clause or which contains a subordinate clause. For example:

*[**When the piano arrived**]Advl [the men]Subj [couldn't get]Vbl [it]dO [through the door]pO*
*[**Though the men had already left**]Advl [nobody]Subj [knew]Vbl [**what they had wanted**]dO*
*[The person **who made the phone call**]Subj [had given]Vbl [them]iO [more information **than they had expected**]dO*

The first sentence contains an adverbial clause of time as an adverbial constituent; the second sentence has an initial adverbial clause of concession as an adverbial constituent and a noun clause as the direct object; the third sentence has no constituent that is a subordinate clause but contains a relative clause as part of the subject and an adverbial clause of comparison as part of the direct object.

Compound Sentence

A compound sentence consists of two or more main clauses, usually joined together by a co-ordinating conjunction, though this may sometimes be omitted. In the following examples the main clauses are shown between angle brackets <.....>:

*<[**Frank**]$_{Subj}$ [**cleaned**]$_{Vbl}$ [**the windows**]$_{dO}$> and <[**Mary**]$_{Subj}$ [**washed**]$_{Vbl}$ [**the floor**]$_{dO}$>*

*<[**The house**]$_{Subj}$ [**wasn't**]$_{Vbl}$ [**empty**]$_{sC}$> but <[**most of the inhabitants**]$_{Subj}$ [**had fled**]$_{Vbl}$>*

Note that co-ordinated main clauses may often show ellipsis in order to avoid the repetition of elements from the first main clause. In the examples below these omissible elements are shown between parentheses:

*<[**Some**]$_{Subj}$ [**wanted**]$_{Vbl}$ [**happiness**]$_{dO}$>, <[**others**]$_{Subj}$ (wanted) [**prosperity**]$_{dO}$> but <[**most of them**]$_{Subj}$ (wanted) [**freedom**]$_{dO}$>*

*<[**Duncan**]$_{Subj}$ [**has lived**]$_{Vbl}$ [**in London**]$_{Advl}$> but <[**Lilian**]$_{Subj}$ [**hasn't**]$_{Vbl}$ (lived in London)>.*

As we see in the last example, the ellipsis may overlap from one constituent to a neighbouring constituent. Thus *lived in London* consists of part of the verbal constituent and the whole of the adverbial constituent following it.

Extended Definition

Some grammarians extend the definition of a compound sentence to include those sentences containing co-ordinated subordinate clauses, as in

*[They]$_{Subj}$ [protested]$_{Vbl}$ [loudly]$_{Advl}$ <[**when the landlord arrived**]$_{Advl}$> and <[(when he) **wanted to evict them**]$_{Advl}$>*

Other grammarians define compound sentences as including those sentences which show co-ordinated elements inside their constituents. This analysis could be made of the following example which shows two co-ordinated noun phrases in the subject. However, it seems more logical to analyse this type of sentence as a simple sentence, e.g.

[The cat and the dog]$_{Subj}$ [were]$_{Vbl}$ [bitter enemies]$_{sC}$

since the plural form of the verb in the verbal constituent and of the noun phrase in the subject complement clearly show agreement in number with the whole of the co-ordinated subject. The analysis of the example as a compound sentence would suggest that it is equivalent semantically to *The cat was a bitter enemy and the dog was a bitter enemy*, but this expanded compound sentence seems to mean that both animals were the enemy of a third animal, whereas our example sentence means that they were enemies of each other.

3 Classification according to Syntactic Form of Message

Declarative

A declarative sentence typically has the grammatical form of a statement, i.e. it consists of a subject followed by a predicate which tells us something about the subject. The predicate may be just a single verb or a verb accompanied by an object or a complement and/or by one or more adverbial constituents. In the following examples the predicate is underlined:

All the people applauded loudly.
The sailor was carrying a cage with a parrot in it.
The theatre was exceptionally full yesterday.

We must be careful to use the term *declarative* only for the grammatical **form** of a sentence and **not** for **the message** it contains. For example, both of the sentences below are declarative in form (i.e. they look like statements) but the first functions as a command whereas the second functions as a question:

You will leave at six o'clock!
You are not going to lend him the money?

Interrogative

An interrogative sentence has the grammatical form of a typical question, i.e. it shows inversion of subject and operator (occasionally of subject and verb) in yes/no questions, and in *wh*-questions it begins with a question word such as *why* (interrogative adverb), *which* (interrogative determiner), or *who* (interrogative pronoun).

Can you help me?
Why did you leave them there?
Which book did he read first?
Who made this delicious apple pie?

Sentences with interrogative form function almost invariably as questions, but they may sometimes be used as threats, e.g.

Are you questioning my authority!
Do you dare to say that openly to my face!

Imperative

An imperative sentence has the grammatical form of a typical command. When affirmative, it usually has no overt subject and consists of the bare verb root either alone or accompanied by an object or a complement and/or one or more adverbial constituents. e.g.

Stop! Hurry up! Take care! Be nice to them!
Stop laughing so raucously! Wash the dishes carefully today!

Notice that when an imperative sentence does contain a subject, it is then identical in form with a declarative sentence, but can normally be recognized by its intonation or by the context.

You just sit down and drink a cup of tea!

When negative, an imperative sentence typically has no subject and has the form of an affirmative imperative sentence preceded by *don't* or *do not*, e.g.

Don't stop now! Do not open the door until the train stops!

If the subject is included, the negative imperative resembles a negative interrogative in form but has falling intonation instead of the rising intonation of a question:

Don't you tell him that I was here!

Exclamatory

Semantically, exclamatory sentences express the feelings of the speaker. In form, they typically begin with *how* or *what*, are characterized by having no inversion of the subject and operator (nor of subject and verb) and are often elliptical:

How clever you are! How delightful (that is)!

What an intelligent dog you have! What a pity (it is)! What a shame (it is that they had to leave so early)!

Note that interrogative sentences can sometimes function as exclamations. If one has caused another person great distress, one can exclaim: *What on earth have I done?* The utterance looks like a question, but clearly does not require an answer.

4 Conclusion

Final Notes

With the classification of sentences we have completed our survey of the grammatical levels of the English sentence. The reader should now be equipped with sufficient knowledge to undertake the detailed analysis of most types of sentence at all the levels we have studied.

Word Level

In Chapter 2 we began on the lowest level with the word and discussed the various word classes which make up a sentence. This enables us to analyse each word in a sentence such as:

When$_{Conj}$ *the*$_{Det}$ *long*$_{Adj}$ *train*$_{Noun}$ *had*$_{Verb}$ *arrived*$_{Verb}$ *the*$_{Det}$ *man*$_{Noun}$ *whom*$_{Pron}$ *Inspector*$_{Noun}$ *Smith*$_{Noun}$ *was*$_{Verb}$ *observing*$_{Verb}$ *waited*$_{Verb}$ *with*$_{Prep}$ *obvious*$_{Adj}$ *impatience*$_{Noun}$ *for*$_{Prep}$ *the*$_{Det}$ *porter*$_{Noun}$ *to*$_{Prep}$ *fetch*$_{Verb}$ *his*$_{Det}$ *case*$_{Noun}$

Phrase Level

In Chapter 3 we moved to the next level and examined the various kinds of phrases which make up a sentence. The sentence above can now be analysed as follows:

When [the long train]$_{NP}$ *[had arrived]*$_{Verb\ P}$ *[the man whom Inspector Smith was observing]*$_{NP}$ *[waited]*$_{Verb\ P}$ *[with obvious impatience]*$_{Prep\ P}$ *[for [the porter to fetch his case]*]*$_{Prep\ P}$

Note that *When the long train had arrived* is a finite clause (an element from a higher level) which has here the function of an adverb phrase. The noun phrase *the man whom Inspector Smith was observing* itself consists of the noun phrase *the man*, postmodified by a finite (relative) clause *whom Inspector Smith was observing*, which functions here as an adjective phrase. This finite clause consists of a noun phrase *Inspector Smith* and a verb phrase *was observing*. Note that the last prepositional phrase in the sentence is also quite complex. The starred element inside it is an embedded infinitive clause (again an element from a higher level, here functioning as a noun phrase after the preposition *for*). The embedded infinitive clause itself consists of a noun phrase (*the porter*) and a non-finite verb phrase (*to fetch*) followed by a noun phrase (*his case*).

Clause Level

In Chapter 4 we turned our attention to the clause level and examined the principal kinds of clauses. With this knowledge, we can now re-analyse our sentence at this level as follows:

[When the long train had arrived]$_{Advl\ Cl}$ the man [whom Inspector Smith was observing]$_{Rel\ Cl}$ waited with obvious impatience for [the porter to fetch his case]$_{Inf\ Cl}$

For simplicity of representation we have labelled only the subordinate clauses and not the main clause *the man waited with obvious impatience for (the porter to fetch his case)*. The latter consists of a subject *the man*, a verbal constituent *waited*, an adverbial *with obvious impatience*, and a prepositional object *for the porter to fetch his case*. The subordinate clause beginning with the conjunction *when* is clearly an adverbial clause of time. It modifies the verb *waited* in the main clause and has a subject *the long train* and a verbal constituent *had arrived*. The relative clause is an adjectival clause postmodifying the subject of the main clause *the man*. It has a subject *Inspector Smith*, a verbal constituent *was observing*, and a direct object the relative pronoun *whom*. The infinitive clause depends on the prepositional verb (*waited for*) in the main clause and has an overt subject *the porter*, a non-finite verbal constituent *to fetch* and a direct object *his case*.

Sentence Level

In Chapter 5 we reached the highest level of our analysis, the sentence level. Here we looked in detail at the constituents of the sentence, and saw that these are also those of the clause since the simplest kind of sentence consists just of a main clause. Finally, we looked at two classifications of sentence types. At this level the constituent analysis of our sentence is as follows:

[When the long train had arrived]$_{Advl}$ [the man whom Inspector Smith was observing]$_{Subj}$ [waited]$_{Vbl}$ [with obvious impatience]$_{Advl}$ [for the porter to fetch his case]$_{pO}$

With regard to its clause structure, this sentence is a complex sentence, and with regard to its syntactic form it is a declarative sentence.

Text Level

At the level above the sentence, the text level, sentences are combined in different ways to produce various kinds of texts, and various grammatical mechanisms are used for this purpose. Unfortunately, the limited space available in this little book will not allow us to look at the rules of text analysis which we glimpsed at in Chapter 1 (pages 14–15). The interested reader is recommended to consult the next section for further reading on this topic.

5 Further Reading

General Introduction

An easily readable general introduction to the study of grammar can be found in Wardhaugh 1995. Some useful books introducing the reader to the grammar of English are Bache & Davidsen-Nielsen 1997, Downing and Locke 1992, Huddlestone 1984, Huddlestone 1988.

Grammars

For readers who wish to follow up some of the aspects of grammar we have discussed throughout this book or who wish to widen their knowledge, one of the best of the **shorter modern reference grammars** is Sinclair 1990, which is very clearly set out and contains useful lists of words with similar grammatical behaviour. Other comparable shorter grammars are Greenbaum & Quirk 1990, Eastwood 1994, Alexander 1988. Two older grammars containing useful information are Leech & Svartvik 1975, which concentrates on the communicative aspects of written and spoken language, and Close 1975, which provides valuable insights into grammar for foreign learners of English. For readers who require detailed information on a particular point the **largest modern reference grammar** is Quirk, Greenbaum, Leech & Svartvik 1985, which deals with both British and American English and contains a very full index. (A shorter, earlier version of this book, Quirk, Greenbaum, Leech & Svartvik 1972 is easier to use but not so up to date.) The latest large grammar (over 1200 pages!) is Biber etc. 1999, which is based entirely on large corpora of American and British English and contains valuable insights into the differences between the grammar of conversational English and of academic (written) English.

Syntax

For readers who are especially interested in syntax a useful introduction is provided by Thomas 1993. Also valuable is Burton-Roberts 1986. Aarts 1997 gives an interesting introduction to grammatical argumentation in syntax, while Cowper 1992 introduces syntax from a transformational generative point of view.

Berk 1999 deals with syntax on all levels from the word up to discourse.

Transformational Grammar

Two good introductions to transformational generative grammar and syntax are Radford 1988 and Baker 1978. A more modern treatment concentrating on government and binding is to be found in Haegeman 1991, and a concise account of generative syntax again with emphasis on government and binding is given by Cowper 1992. Cook 1988 discusses universal grammar within a transformational framework, providing an account of those grammatical and syntactic phenomena which frequently reappear in many different languages.

Text Analysis, Discourse Analysis

Books on text analysis and discourse analysis usually go beyond the grammar and syntax of units above the sentence level, and additionally examine various kinds of texts and conversations with a view to their **pragmatic** and **sociolinguistic** features. Brinker 1988 gives a useful account of the analysis of German texts, whereas Werlich 1983 does the same for English texts. Different approaches to discourse analysis are dealt with competently in Brown & Yule 1983, while the relationship between discourse and grammar is the topic treated in Erdmann 1991.

Functional Grammar

A valuable account of functional grammar is given by the initiator of this approach in Halliday 1985, which in Part I deals with functional aspects of the clause in texts and speech and in Part II with functional aspects above, below and beyond the clause. Later work along functional lines can be seen in Givon 1993 in his two-volume introduction to English grammar.

Reference Books

Many useful pieces of information on English grammar can be collected from reference books other than grammars. Among the most useful reference works are: Chalker & Weiner 1998, Crystal 1991, McArthur 1992, Sinclair 1992 and Trask 1993. The best English learners' dictionaries such as CIDE, LDCE and OALD also provide a great deal of valuable grammatical information. A useful learners' grammar in dictionary form (i.e. with alphabetical entries) is Leech 1989.

Bibliography

General

AARTS, Bas: *English Syntax and Argumentation*. Basingstoke & London: Macmillan 1997.

AITCHISON, James: *Cassell Dictionary of English Grammar.* London: Cassell 1997.

ALEXANDER, Louis: *Longman English Grammar.* London & New York: Longman 1988.

BACHE, Carl & N. Davidsen-Nielsen: *Mastering English Grammar.* Berlin & New York: Mouton de Gruyter 1997.

BAKER, Carl: *Introduction to Generative Transformational Grammar.* Englewood Cliffs, N.J.: Prentice Hall 1978.

BERK, Lynn: *English Syntax: From Word to Discourse.* Oxford: Oxford University Press 1999.

BIBER, Douglas, S. Johansson, G. Leech, S. Conrad & E. Finegan: *Longman Grammar of Spoken and Written English.* Harlow: Longman 1999.

BRINKER, Klaus: *Linguistische Textanalyse. 2. Auflage.* Berlin: Schmidt 1988.

BROWN, Gillian & G. Yule: *Discourse Analysis.* Cambridge: Cambridge University Press 1983.

BURTON-ROBERTS, Noel: *Analysing Sentences: An Introduction to English Syntax.* London: Longman 1986.

CHALKER, Sylvia & E. Weiner (Editors): *Oxford Dictionary of English Grammar.* Oxford: Oxford University Press 1988.

CLOSE, Reginald: *A Reference Grammar for Students of English.* London: Longman 1975.

COOK, Vivian: *Chomsky's Universal Grammar: An Introduction.* Oxford: Basil Blackwell 1988.

COWPER, Elizabeth: *A Concise Introduction to Syntactic Theory: The Government-Binding Approach.* Chicago, Ill.: University of Chicago Press 1992.

CRYSTAL, David: *A Dictionary of Linguistics and Phonetics. Third Edition. Oxford: Basil* Blackwell 1991.

DOWNING, Angela & P. Locke: *A University Course in English Grammar.* New York & London: Prentice Hall 1992.

EASTWOOD, John: *Oxford Guide to English Grammar.* Oxford: Oxford University Press 1994.

ERDMANN, Peter: *Discourse and Grammar.* Tübingen: Niemeyer 1991.

GIVON, Talmy: *English Grammar: A Function-Based Introduction. Volumes I & II.* Amsterdam: John Benjamins 1993.

GREENBAUM, Sidney & R. Quirk: *A Student's Grammar of the English Language.* London: Longman 1990.

HAEGEMAN, Liliane: *Introduction to Government and Binding Theory.* Oxford: Basil Blackwell 1991.

HALLIDAY, Michael: *An Introduction to Functional Grammar.* London: Edward Arnold 1985.

HUDDLESTONE, Rodney: *Introduction to the Grammar of English.* Cambridge. Cambridge University Press 1984.

HUDDLESTONE, Rodney: *English Grammar: An Outline.* Cambridge: Cambridge University Press 1988.

LEECH, Geoffrey: *An A-Z of English Grammar and Usage.* London: Edward Arnold 1989.

LEECH, Geoffrey & J. Svartvik: *A Communicative Grammar of English.* London: Longman 1975.

MCARTHUR, Tom: *The Oxford Companion to the English Language.* Oxford: Oxford University Press 1992.

QUIRK, Randolph, S. Greembaum, G. Leech & J. Svartvik: *A Grammar of Contemporary English.* London: Longman 1972.

QUIRK, Randolph, S. Greenbaum, G. Leech & J. Svartvik: *A Comprehensive Grammar of the English Language.* London & New York: Longman 1985.

RADFORD, Andrew: *Transformational Grammar:* A First Course. Cambridge: Cambridge University Press 1988.

SINCLAIR, John (Editor): *Collins COBUILD English Grammar.* London: Collins 1990.

SINCLAIR, John (Editor): *Collins COBUILD English Usage.* London: Harper Collins 1992.

THOMAS, Linda: *Beginning Syntax.* Oxford: Basil Blackwell 1993.

TRASK, Robert: *A Dictionary of Grammatical Terms in Linguistics.* London & New York: Routledge 1993.

WARDHAUGH, Ronald: *Understanding English Grammar.* Oxford: Basil Blackwell 1995.

WERLICH, Egon: *A Text Grammar of English.* Heidelberg: Quelle & Meyer 1983.

Learner's Dictionaries

[CIDE] *Cambridge International Dictionary of English.* Edited by Paul Proctor. Cambridge: Cambridge University Press 1995.

[LDCE] *Longman Dictionary of Contemporary English. Third Edition.* Edited by Della Summers. Harlow: Longman 1990.

[OALD] *Oxford Advanced Learner's Dictionary of Current English. Fifth Edition.* Edited by Jonathan Crowther. Oxford: Oxford University Press 1995.